Robin Levett

The Girls

HUDSON

HAWTHORN

Hudson Publishing

The publishing division of
N. S. Hudson Publishing Services P/L
6 Muir Street, Hawthorn, Victoria 3122

First published 1997

Typeset by the publishers

Printed by Currency Productions, Melbourne

National Library of Australia cataloguing-in-publication data:

Levett, Robin, 1925–
The girls.

ISBN 0 949873 65 9

1. Levett, Robin, 1925–. 2. Australia. Royal Australian Navy. Women's Royal Australian Naval Service – Biography. 3. Great Britain. Army Women's Auxiliary Service (Burma) – Biography. 4. World War, 1939-1945 – Personal narratives, Australia. 5. World War, 1939-1945 – Great Britain – Participation, Female. I. Title.

940.548194

Contents

PART ONE

1

Sorrento

IT WOULD BE EASY ENOUGH to imagine that our Sorrento, the one on the edge of Port Phillip Bay in Victoria, was given its name by some romantic, homesick Italian. There are times when the Bay is every bit as blue as the Mediterranean and the summer climate just as balmy, but there the likeness stops. Or rather that's where the likeness stopped in the old days, before Melbourne made Sorrento fashionable.

In fact the village was named after a property in Ireland owned by the family of a long dead Premier, Sir Charles Gavan Duffy, and heaven knows what imaginative, ancestral Duffy could have produced an Irish Sorrento. Sir Charles, having emigrated to Australia, fell in love with the place, named it and shrewdly invested in land with beach frontage. This was in the late 1800s, when Sorrento's citizens made their living by the burning and quarrying of lime. They built their cottages of limestone too, small and white, square as dice and simple as a child's drawing.

When we first went to live at Sorrento it was self-sufficient, gossipy, insular and as much like its Italian namesake as a broody hen is like a peacock, The village looked more Irish than Latin, with its white houses plumped around a curve of Port Phillip Bay, only a few miles from Point Nepean where the land narrows into a crab's-claw tip and disappears into Bass Strait. The villagers felt rather special because Melbourne was hours away and Tasmania just a name to them; to all intents and purposes they were the guardians of Land's End.

Our house, The Haven, was built of white limestone like all the rest, plain and solid as a country Church, and it challenged the Bay from the middle of two acres of open land. It stood between Sorrento and Portsea where the sea had scalloped out little scoops of beach with rocky points at either end, and anyone who lived above one of these beaches regarded it as their own. This may not have been legally correct, but everyone with a beach built their own jetties and swimming baths, and strangers on their sand were trespassers, to be savaged and sent slinking away. A mile or so south at Point King there were large, imposing houses with rich owners, but the Point King beach was public property, and we pitied them.

When you were out on the Bay in a boat and looked back at the cliff The Haven stood out, although it was the smallest cliff-house between Sorrento and Portsea. The other houses hid from the wind and sea behind pine trees and hedges while The Haven stood stripped to the waist like a boxer, ready for any punches that came its way. It was at the end of a short lane called Lentil Avenue, but Avenue was too grand and it was known as the Lane. It had tall, ragged pine trees down one side and on the other a thick, lethal boxthorn hedge. The Lane was death on cars because pine roots criss-crossed its sand, sticking out like old bones, and the boxthorns punctured tyres like icepicks. Depending on the strength of the wind the pines sighed or roared day and night, and the sea murmured or bellowed so that you stopped hearing either sound consciously, except as a background for gulls' and children's voices. It was only when you were away, somewhere like Melbourne where all the noises were mechanical or man-made, that there was an emptiness inside you as though something vital was missing.

You walked out of The Haven's front door across thirty feet of bull-ant infested buffalo grass, through a small wooden gate and down a steep dirt path to the beach. It was a shallow, tiny cove of sand, shells and rock pools, rich with curiosities at low tide, creatures who moved in on one tide and out on the next, and in between they hid in the rock pools waiting for us to find them. There were sea-horses and jellyfish and starfish and crabs, and a constant variety of small, nameless fish, sometimes spiked and horned, sometimes fantastically coloured and marked. The seaweed that waved under the surface of the water looked edible as lettuce, and whereas on fine days fat baby waves danced onto our sand like a chorus of cupids, the sea that slammed against the cliff in a storm was the colour and consistency of minestrone, carrying bits of rubbish from Melbourne at the top of the Bay.

Our jetty was a disgrace to the foreshore; nothing was ever done to it, bar the odd, essential replacement of a rotting upright. All the other jetties were painted and smooth, but ours was raw, splintery wood, with gaps between the planks. The boats moored round the other jetties were smart and elaborate as Hyde Park prams while we had only The Jack, a grubby 12-foot wooden dinghy, infinitely seaworthy and perfect for fishing. There was a tiny boatshed at one end of the jetty, with a door that always jammed, and at the other end was the baths, a rough, wooden structure designed to let the sea in and keep the sharks out. We scorned swimming there; it was dull and claustrophobic compared with the open sea, and although there were plenty of sharks in the Bay then there were also a lot more fish for them to eat, and they didn't seem to fancy humans. The relative shabbiness of our beach didn't worry us; we knew it to be the result of honest poverty rather than shiftlessness, and neither The Girls nor I ever felt poor.

Sorrento was a proper village then, not the up-market suburb it has become. The only tarred road was the one which ran through Sorrento and ended in the sand at Portsea pier. The inland side of the road was thick scrub, and almost the only houses along it were the ones along the cliff. Sorrento's main shop was Stringer's Store which had wooden floors and everything else a village shop should have, including tiny cable-cars which zinged up and down wires from the cash booth near the ceiling, carrying change. There were bolts of material and axes and patent medicine, corsets and cookware and hammers and nails, flour and sugar and canned foods, all in a muddle that only old Mr Stringer understood.

Apart from Stringers, there was the butcher and the baker, a flea-pit for the movies, an ice-cream shop, a chemist with coloured jars in the window, and Mr Johnson the fisherman who sold fresh fish down near the beach. There was the Sorrento Hotel where people one knew could stay if they weren't too fussy, and the ordinary pub for drinking, where nobody one knew ever went. The wide main street ran east and narrowed down to a sand-track leading to the Back Beach and the ocean, and along it were the small cottages where the real Sorrento people lived; they had geranium and hollyhock gardens bordered with white stones and haunted by garden gnomes. We knew most of the locals and loved them, and I think they liked us but they couldn't rightly place us. We had Pommie voices and we acted like Poms, like the people who came down to their cliff houses for the summer holidays and vanished again, whereas we stayed all the year round. We acted queer in a lot of ways but we paid our bills and gave them something to talk about, so they put up with us.

Day trippers came in summer, thrashing down the Bay in two paint-bright old paddle steamers, the *Weeroona* and the *Hygeia*, and they spilled out all over the village, loaded with picnic baskets and wailing children and bunnioned grandparents. The younger ones, in mating pairs, would wander off along the cliff, looking for somewhere to be alone. There was a right-of-way along the front of our land leading to Point King, and sometimes they'd duck through the little gate down to the beach, arms entwined, to do a spot of quiet necking. They were always known as The Neckers because physical contact below neck-level was so unthinkable then that it was better to pretend it never happened. My sisters, The Girls, kept a hose on a tap near the cliff edge, and when a pair of Neckers was nicely settled on the beach they'd aim the hose over the cliff directly above them, and turn the tap full on.

Our parents bought The Haven in the late 1920s. The Haven wasn't their sort of name for a house, but they realised that even if they changed it the locals wouldn't; they were shamefaced about the name, but it stayed. In fact it was a perfect name, because of our situation and because of the personality of the house itself.

Disaster had overtaken the financial affairs of my mother's family, and Pa had been summoned from India by his in-laws to take over the management of a number of huge Queensland grazing properties which were floundering in a morass of drought and debt. He knew nothing of sheep or cattle, there was no money left to pay him for his efforts, and his Indian Army pension clearly wouldn't maintain a wife and three daughters in Melbourne. I don't know how or why some benevolent chance led him to Sorrento to look for a haven, but he quite literally found one.

There our family spent its uncomplicated days, before it fell apart like a moth-eaten ball of wool, all fragments and loose ends. There The Girls and I were trained to accept the values and to respect the taboos that our parents held dear. Black Holes existed in our knowledge of the world outside, but they were voids that Mama worked hard to preserve, and we weren't even conscious of them until after we left The Haven.

Now the little limestone house has been used again for a story about three sisters. When I saw the film 'Hotel Sorrento' I recognised it at once, though it was heavily disguised by a false facade. Everything looked so much smaller than I remembered, but the sweep of Bay beyond the cliff was clear as a desert seen from a hilltop, and the little living-room-cum-dining-room where I put the possum up Pa's pants was there, almost exactly as we left it. The Girls were there, hidden somewhere beyond the cinema screen and Trixie, our labrador bitch, and so much else. I wished, watching it, that my father hadn't taught me not to cry.

2

Whitings

WHEN THE WALKERS arrived in Australia from India in 1925, travelling en famille with all their worldly goods in the hold, there were only four of them. There was Pa, Geoffrey Beresford Walker, Mama who was born Aileen Whiting, and their daughters Betty and Jenny, collectively known as The Girls. I travelled *in utero*, and appeared as the fifth member of the family shortly after they landed in Melbourne.

I was a girl too, but Betty had been around for ten years and Jenny for seven, and I began as a mistake. Mama must have been horrified by her pregnancy, but she consoled herself by taking it for granted that I'd be a boy because she and Pa were forty years old and this was their last chance for a son. When the baby turned out to be a girl they could scarcely believe it and avoided giving me a name for a whole year, hoping that the mistake might miraculously be rectified. During the year of hope they called me It, then grudgingly gave me a name that would fit either sex. Pa went on hoping for a long time and insisted that I learn to ride Sandhurst fashion, without reins or stirrups, and to fish and shoot; tears were forbidden and dolls were banned from the house. Mama made the best of the disaster feeling, perhaps, that it was partly her fault, and I don't think she really lost hope until I reached puberty.

All through my childhood I was jealous of The Girls because they'd been born in India. India had glamour, our parents talked of it as second only to England in the order of Promised Lands, and being born in Melbourne made me feel that I belonged to some inferior subculture. Mama had been born in Melbourne but she never seemed or sounded Australian, and when she and Pa talked of England they always called it Home with an unmistakable capital 'H'. If Pa had stayed in India we would have been brought up in England by his relations, because it was believed to be impossible to bring up white children in India. We were taught subtly to feel that by coming to Australia we'd been deprived of something precious, and that constant vigilance was necessary to prevent us becoming identifiably Australian.

Mama's parents, Robert and Rose Whiting, were both born in Australia, and until the 1920s they were in what the Irish call 'a good way of going'. They had money and they spent it, apparently on the principle of the Cut-and-Come-Again-Pudding. The origins of grandfather Whiting's money was a subject his family avoided. He was a big man with a walrus moustache, and the kind of figure, fashionable at that time, that warns of heart attacks in later life. Prosperous, tall men of his kind were shaped rather like ice-cream cones, all the weight at the top when they were young, but slipping unbecomingly down their middles with age. He was a lawyer, and rumour has it that when Melbourne planned its first tram lines, the routes being a closely guarded State secret, grandfather had mysteriously and at little cost bought many prime corner sites along their way. He sold the sites at great profit to people who had the foresight to build pubs close to tram stops.

He then went into partnership with a friend of his who also liked the good things in life, and who was Australia's only hereditary Baronet. Together, for about a shilling an acre, they bought themselves vast tracts of sheep and cattle country across Queensland. The properties were stocked, managers installed, and for a number of years money rolled southwards as if from a giant cornucopia, the partners and their families living like kings in what must have seemed the most stable of all possible worlds.

Queensland is hard country, giving and unforgiving in unpredictable cycles. The revelation that a mixture of over-stocking, over-spending and absentee management combined with drought can spell disaster came too late. The partners were old; it was beyond them to go to Queensland themselves, to inspire the managers with hope or to sack them as the case might be, and unless someone could take control of the situation both families were ruined. The banks were beating on the door, and no one except 'that husband of Aileen's in India', was old enough or capable enough to be of use.

Pa responded to the cries for help without argument, abandoned everything he'd lived for until then, took on the impossible and in the fullness of time achieved it. It's hard to believe that he left India without regret but he never spoke of being sorry. Australia suited him; it was a new battlefield, and all his training had been for battles.

Mama's parents lived well during their palmy days, and when the Victorian era expanded into the more permissive lifestyle of the Edwardian era Robert took to it like a duck to water. Clubs, racecourses and mistresses occupied a lot of his time and that of his friends, but Rose, whose horizons were more limited, remained a perfect specimen of Victorian womanhood to her dying day.

Rose was tiny , only 4ft 9ins in her stockinged feet, fashioned and coloured like a piece of Dresden china. She came from a Danish-Jewish family named Cohn, worthy, cultured people with immaculate manners and conservative values. She bore four children, but firmly denied any knowledge or experience of the sexual act essential to child-bearing. Proudly laying claim to what amounted to four immaculate conceptions, she lived happily in the intellectual vacuum thought proper for Victorian wives. Her favourite advice, given repeatedly to Mama, and to us as children, was: 'Never contradict a man,' followed by, 'A man is always right!' She obeyed these principles herself until she was little more than an acquiescent murmur in the presence of her husband, or indeed of any other man.

The Whiting children, were Harry, Claire, Aileen and Dorothy. Harry, being a son, was given a proper education while the girls, being intended only for the marriage market, were not. They graduated from nannies to governesses who taught them to read and write, but the educational emphasis was on the social graces and accomplishments which might lead to a good match. Claire and Aileen co-operated but Dorothy the youngest girl, was so diabolical that no governess would stay with her, and she alone was sent to school. There she behaved abominably, ran way and was expelled. She was to marry a charming, docile and distinguished Italian, have three daughters, and to become more Italian than anyone else in Italy, demonstrating her Latin temperament by language and behaviour which would have shocked the most virulent Neapolitan fishwife.

Claire and Aileen were nice, normal girls, quite free of the rattlesnake venom that flawed their sister. They were attractive rather than pretty, with thick-flowing pre-Raphaelite manes of hair. In the formal photos which survive from their girlhood the hair is larded with flowers, the eyes demurely downcast, and frequently one girlish hand clutches a lily. The lynch-pin of their upbringing, driven home by Rose, the governess, and every other member of their adult world, was the constant care needed to preserve that most precious jewel on which marriage would depend. It became Mama's creed, and as we grew up she reminded us repeatedly: *'If you're not a Virgin, no decent man will ever marry you!'*

Claire wasn't nearly as impressionable as Mama; she was by far the tougher and more sophisticated of the two, and had a nice, dirty sense of humour. She proved her toughness by surviving a long marriage to Herbert, one of the least likeable men ever to wear a Royal Navy uniform.

Mama was far less worldly than Claire. She never smoked, and alcohol tasted nasty to her, so she never drank it. The life that Claire lived in the moderately fast lane of Knightsbridge would have killed Mama, yet in her own way she was talented and amusing. She drew, producing silhouettes and woodcuts, wrote witty verse and was brilliant at after-dinner charades. It was only when confronted with Claire's rather chic friends or with the man-eating Memsahibs of India that she felt inadequate. It's strange that Pa chose her as his wife because outside his marriage he showed a strong preference for sophisticated women, bordering on the Fast.

There were times when his liking for such women caused Mama pain; Pa would be absent at times and she'd be tense and pale, but always he came back to her. He'd be nicer to her than ever and she'd glow again, and Pa would turn on us children, as though we'd done something wrong, and say, 'Your mother is a Saint!' It was a long time before I realised that in spite of these little aberrations she manipulated him subtly, and that end results of importance were always the ones that Mama wanted. She was far cleverer in her choice of husband than Claire. If Pa strayed it was like the flight of a well-thrown boomerang, and he always landed back at her feet. If Herbert was faithful to Claire it was because no on else would have put up with him, and besides that he was too uniquely devoted to Herbert to be interested in anyone else.

When Claire and Aileen were growing up, the Whiting family's year was divided into three stages, and one wonders how Robert Whiting found time to conduct a law practice. Part of the year, including Melbourne Cup week, was spent in town, the winters were devoted to a lengthy visit to England and the summers were spent at Hascombe, a rambling old house with a famous garden about forty miles from Melbourne at Mt Macedon. At Hascombe there were house parties and picnics, and the girls had their ponies and tennis, and relative freedom. Rose was preoccupied with entertaining and with the garden; it was her cherished and widely declared fantasy that the huge, overstaffed garden was all the work of her own hands.

The annual Grand Tour was important, in Robert's and Rose's view, to the future of their daughters. It was organised on almost military lines, involving mountains of luggage, endless planning and a five week sea journey at either end. It was also appallingly expensive, but how else were one's daughters to meet the right people and, above all, the kind of men one hoped they would marry? They were dragged through London Seasons as debutantes, presented at Court and generally displayed like fish on a slab in the hope that they'd make a truly brilliant marriage.

Claire succumbed to the questionable charms of Herbert

Hammond Chambers, and there was general rejoicing until her parents got to know him, but Mama stayed stubbornly single. She and my father finally met on board a ship between India and England in 1914, Pa going Home on Leave and Mama at the start of the annual Grand Tour. She was twenty-eight by then, and in Rose's view irrevocably on the shelf. To Rose's great relief our parents were married in Hove, Sussex in 1916, when Pa was leave from the war in Mesopotamia. Mama once confessed that her ignorance of sex was so great that the day she named for her wedding was the day on which she got her period. She was always a quick learner and Betty was born on the 16 December of that year, nine months and fifteen days after their wedding, when Pa had gone back to his war.

Herbert Hammond-Chambers, the first matrimonial trophy, was a prime example of the risks involved in husband-hunting on the other side of the world. It was a mystery what Claire could ever have seen in him, but, as he continually reminded everyone he was very well related and in marrying a Colonial he had actually married beneath him, thereby giving her a social status she'd never have known otherwise. It didn't escape notice that he'd believed her to be a very rich Colonial at the time when he proposed to her

Even as a young man Herbert was unattractive. Photos of him taken then show a thin, down-turned mouth, limp hair parted in the middle and drooping eyes, cold as oysters. As he grew older he walked with his head poked forward, his collar a size too large, and he looked increasingly like an ancient, ill-tempered tortoise. His voice owed a lot to his youth when he twice rounded the Horn under sail as midshipman and had to make himself heard from the top of the mast in a blizzard. When he raised his voice, which was usually in anger, it was formidable. His laugh was a rare phenomenon, so rusty that it sounded like the shunting of an old steam engine.

Claire and Herbert came to Australia quite often after the Second World War. Claire, of course, was one of the beneficiaries of the Queensland estate which by then, thanks to Pa's efforts, was paying dividends. Herbert, who felt he'd been badly cheated when the family finances collapsed, now feared that he was being deprived of some of the money which should have come to him through his wife, and this forced him to make repeated, costly journeys to a country which he despised. He and Claire still lived in Knightsbridge, but annually leased the top salmon beat on the River Ness for the northern summer. Their style of fishing involved all the conventional trappings; ghillies, boats, heavy two-handed rods and rush baskets for the fish, and Herbert was convinced that he was among the world's most skilled salmon fishermen

During one of their post-war visits I ran into Herbert by accident on a crowded pavement in Collins Street in the heart of Melbourne. He saw me first or I would have been gone, and he grabbed my shoulder with a skinny hand, like a reincarnation of the Ancient Mariner. He had been looking for an audience as usual, for he said without preamble: 'Robin, did I ever tell you what old Angus the ghillie said to me last summer?'

'No,' I said dismally. 'I don't think so, Uncle Herbert.'

Herbert made a string of his shunting noises, indicating that he had a joke to tell, and raised his voice several decibels. Passers-by eyed him nervously, and made a detour.

'Well, I was casting my fly… shunt, shunt, shunt… and Angus said… shunt, shunt, shunt… Captain Hammond Chambers, Sir, you cast a fly so bloody light… shunt, shunt, shunt… the *BLOODY MOSQUITOS COME DOWN AND FUCK IT… shunt, shunt, shunt."*

Two old ladies sat down abruptly on the steps of a nearby bank, and fanned themselves, a well-dressed man who had caught the full blast of the punch-line muttered something about the police, and I departed in haste without saying goodbye. It was still long before the time when the 'F' word was permissible in public. Herbert shuffled off happily along the pavement, shunting to himself as he went, and clearing a path by repeating in ringing tones: 'Come down and *FUCK* it, eh? Come down and *FUCK* it!'

Herbert and Pa didn't know each other well, but well enough to dislike each other cordially. Pa thought that Herbert was ill-mannered and offensive beyond all civilised bounds, and Herbert considered the Army, except for the Guards, an inferior, second-rate service, officered by nobodies. In addition Pa was Irish, and Herbert despised the Irish, unless they had a title. Their dislike for each other had created a cooling-off between Mama and Claire, and luckily the two men seldom came together.

3

Walkers

PA CAME OF AN ANGLO-IRISH FAMILY which bred and trained its sons for India as one breeds and trains a gun-dog for shooting. His parents spent most of their lives there, grandfather ultimately as the first British Financial Advisor to the Nizam of Hyderabad, then the richest man in the world. The men in both his and my Grandmother's families were drawn to India as the moon draws the tide, and uncles, brothers and cousins studded the subcontinent like raisins in a pudding. Pa arrived there by way of Sandhurst, graduated with a King's Commission, served in the Indian Army and was seconded to the Political Service as a Major.

Even in those twilight days of the Raj the Political Service was considered something of a career pinnacle, being a small, elite body of men who dealt exclusively with the rulers of the Indian Princely States. Pa was relatively young when he became a Political, and it must have torn the very fibres of his heart to leave the Service so soon. He could tell wonderful stories about India, strange and funny stories about legendary people, and about the ghosts he'd met in old palaces and who were as real to him as his friends. His stories were never quite the same twice because he was far too Irish to spoil things for want of embroidery, but they were always fascinating. When we lived at Sorrento and India was still fresh in his mind Pa was in Queensland most of the time, or we would have heard more of them. I would kill now to have him back again and to cram his stories into a tape recorder, the magic of the Indian Princes and their palaces, of hunting and deserts and tribal uprisings, and all the fading colour of the sunset India of the Raj.

He was Black Irish, as the Protestant Irish were called, but he had the red Irish hair, and the temper and the charm to match. His temper, when it hit you, was like running into a hidden electric fence, and after the shock was over you wondered where it could have come from. He never lost his temper with Mama or Betty but I, and to a lesser extent Jenny, used to trigger it with awful regularity. The charm overrode the temper. Turned full-on it caused strong women to weaken at the knees, and it worked wonders with everyone else as well, from antagonistic Queensland stockmen and bank managers down to children and animals. Besides his charm he was over six feet tall, he held himself like a soldier, and he was good to look at.

There was a bit of both his parents in Pa. George Casson Walker, his father, was good-looking, diplomatic, and so rigidly honourable that people mistakenly thought him cold. His children were always slightly in awe of him but in fact he had both humour and tenderness, and the children only knew him as a remote, God-like figure when they were growing up. They were sent Home, like all British children in India, to be raised by relations and educated at an English school. Once or twice, at the end of the 1939-45 war, I met ancient survivors of grandfather's time in Hyderabad and they spoke of him with reverence and love, and simply because I was his granddaughter they treated me as though I was someone special.

If grandfather was loved then Fanny, his wife, was adored. The old men I met laughed with remembered pleasure when they spoke of her. She was a big, tall woman, with a mouth that turned up at the corners so that she was always smiling, never sad or sour. She came from Cork, and she had a crashing brogue tucked away under her ordinary voice; she would produce it at the least suitable moments, turning from Lady Walker to a Cork strumpet for the sheer joy of upsetting the self-important. She was brave and wicked and intelligent and kind, and she was awarded a medal called the *Kaiseri Hind*, the Star of India, for her work in famines and cholera epidemics. It was a medal normally given only to men because those were the days when Memsahibs were expected simply to sit beside punkahs in shaded rooms, pressing a handkerchief to their nose against the smells of India and the risk of contagion. Fanny learned several Indian languages, worked with Indian women to help them break down the barriers of purdah, and when grandfather's enemies, the Hyderabadi nobles whose corruption he had been sent to stop tried to kill him, she sat beside his bed every night with a gun, trusting nobody else to defend him. She was a friend of Queen Mary's; they both had the backbone that goes with ramrods and bugles and troops rallying to the charge, and the old Queen, I'm told, could be just as much of a devil as Fanny could when she chose.

Hyderabad was an independent State when the Walkers were sent there. Because it had never been officially conquered by Britain the British Government viewed it with concern, but were unable to interfere with its administration. The State even had its own currency, distinct from that of the rest of India. Grandfather's instructions were to straighten out, as tactfully as possible, a Court whose dishonesty, nepotism and skulduggery had become notorious, and if necessary to bring the currency into line with that of the rest of India. To save the Nizam's face he was given the ambiguous title of Financial Adviser.

The Nizam, like many other Indian rulers, was surrounded by relations, courtiers and hangers-on whose sole aim was to acquire for themselves as much money and power as possible, and to this end they were prepared, in fact eager, to lie, cheat, rob or murder whoever stood in their way. Such practices had been honoured for centuries in most Eastern and many European courts but the Hyderabadis had developed it into an art form, and considered it perfectly legitimate. They were outraged when a strange Englishman appeared, escorted by two Companies of infantry, and set about changing things. They were even more horrified when he turned out to be unbribeable, for no one else they knew had such strange inhibitions. To round off their dismay the Nizam, who had formerly viewed the most bizarre villainies of his court with a detached tolerance, said that the Englishman must be obeyed.

I have included an extract from a letter written by H. Emon Chubb of the family which made Chubb locks and safes. He stayed with the Walkers in Hyderabad in 1905, and his letter describes the Court as it was then.

He had kept up his friendship with George and Fanny Walker. Grandfather had persuaded the British Government to let Hyderabad keep its currency, cleaned up the Court, and at the Nizam's request stayed on there after he was due for retirement, for he and the Nizam had become friends. He was made a Knight Commander of the Star of India, and he and Fanny finally came back to England and settled in Sussex. Mr Chubb had stayed with them there in the house they shared with another old friend, Rudyard Kipling. The letter was written from the Connemara Hotel in Madras, in 1905.

> To start with Mr and Mrs Cassan Walker are two of the very best people I've met; he slow, solid and humorous, she sharp, intelligent, bright, girlish, largely built, with a kind face and an enormous Irish brogue. She's the only lady I've ever felt I should like to say to, "Are there any more at home like you?" for if there were I'd write and ask them on the spot. I had a simply topping time with them, and felt I was living on the fringe of a medieval court or else during the Arabian Nights.
>
> Hyderabad is the most Native of Native States, never conquered by the British it is quite independent though we have a Resident there, but being Native its corruption is very great. And a great government said, "let us see if we cannot put their finances in a better state," and so Casson Walker was sent there to see what could be done. He found that there were hordes of wasters living on life pensions for no apparent reason, that the Nizam's Govt. were losing hundreds of thousands of pounds through slackness and corruption. So he began by wiping out many pensions, and on arrival at the office he found thousands of files of lawsuits, some thirty years old, against the Nizam and the Govt. for recovery or appropriation of money. He has wiped out many of these and is nearly up to date. Naturally the Nobles hate him, and there is little doubt he has been poisoned twice; the first time nearly killed him, and now a Native detective lives in the house and the servants are very strictly watched, and Mrs Walker promised to pay double the

amount on the nail to any servant who gives proof that he has been offered money to use poison. The cook is highly paid, and brings all the food into the dining-room himself. Walker never speaks of this, but Mrs Walker told me all about it. Some of the stories are most amusing. Jacobs, an Armenian Jew, sold a diamond to the Nizam for, I think, 80,000 pounds, several times its value, and the Nizam paid part and had it valued, and found he had paid too much already and refused to pay the balance, so Jacobs now lives in Hyderabad waiting for the balance. At one time the firm Powell lent 200,000 pounds a year at 25%; this has not been paid and Powells are, I believe, ruined. This is old history.

The Nizam is seldom seen. I believe he tries to drown a rather monotonous existence in alcohol. Walker said nothing of this. He has crowds of wives, and they say there are 10,000 women, cousins, sisters, aunts and mothers-in-law, all living at his expense. His jewels are terrific and at the Delhi Durbar he had a wonderful cloth of pure gold covering his elephant, but he himself wore no jewels, only a little yellow plume in his turban. At Delhi he bought 7 lakhs, 45,000 pounds worth of embroidery. This got mislaid, and no one thought about it until Sergeant Hall, who teaches his boy fencing, found some old wooden cases in the stables which happen to be the purchase: he told me this himself.

Most interesting was Colonel Avasor. He was reported to have been a Persian slave's child, and he is now Commander-in-Chief of the Nizam's Army. He dined with us one day, and it was most amusing to see Walker chipping him. He gets no pay, has had no money left to him, and is very wealthy. He looks like a Spaniard and a splendid soldier, having the polish of a French courtier, and a look which makes his troops quake. He was immaculately dressed all in white, riding breeches and boots all white: if he lived in England and behaved as he does he would never be out of prison, but as it is he is always put up for all the best Clubs. What Walker was worrying him about was a complete dinner set of Wedgewood which he had bought for a farewell dinner for Sir David Barr. Avasor said it had cost Rs 20,000, but Walker says he will have to pay at least Rs 30,000, of which Avasor will pocket a good lump. The Nizam fears Avasor, he is getting very powerful, and is nearly always posted near the Nizam's door; sometimes

> when a big carouse is on he remains there for two days, and may not sleep.
>
> To go tiger shooting, which he does well, the Nizam makes a camp and always takes his old mother. They both revel in the heat and go at the hottest time of the Indian weather, and spend a lot of the daytime lying on a rock without a shade or hat, basking in the sun. Avasor hates the heat but is made to go there, and nearly dies. No ice or punkahs are allowed in camp. Yet the Nizam heaps titles on Avasor's sons. Last year his physician in camp sent word that his (the physician's) only child was very ill and could he go and see what could be done. No answer. Later, "The child is dying." No answer. "May I go and bury the child?" No answer, and he dare not go.
>
> So much for the Nizam and his State. Walker says it is not as bad as it seems, but I think he means it will not be so bad when he has finished. He is a splendid man to fight for what he believes to be right, and cares nothing for the British Govt. or his own life. The Govt. wanted to put their coinage in use in Hyderabad, but Walker fought it tooth and nail for what he terms 'abstract Justice'. The State has not been conquered, therefore the Nizam has the right to his own coins (which is one of the greatest holds a King has over his country) so he held out and the Nizam is very grateful to him. Now that his time in office is up the Nizam has asked the Govt. to get him to remain, to which Walker has consented after making a few conditions which give him greater control. Long may he flourish!

I met Mr Chubb in London after the war when he was an old, old man, still of enormous charm. He bought me miraculous meals at the Connaught Hotel when I could barely afford the price of a Lyons sandwich, and while I made a pig of myself he talked about the old days in India.

4

Pa's India

AT THE TIME when H. Emon Chubb was in Hyderabad Pa was still at Sandhurst. He had been sent back to Cork as soon as he was old enough, to be brought up by a pair of elderly aunts. As in Mama's family there were four children of his generation, Daisy the eldest, then Geoffrey, Sheila and Dorothy. Fanny and George had improved on the family planning skills of their previous generation, since George had been one of thirteen children and Fanny one of fourteen. Child-bearing in India was certainly more hazardous than in Ireland, but that wouldn't have bothered Fanny. The only plausible reason for their massive cut in output must have been that, as children had to be raised elsewhere, their number could not exceed the number of relatives willing eventually to care for them.

Pa said he loved growing up in Cork. There were two highlights, fishing in the local streams and leading a gang of boys on the train from Queenstown to Cork City in a running fight with an opposing gang. The leader of the other gang was Michael Collins, later of Republican Army fame, and when they got to Cork City they all stayed on the train and fought their way back to Queenstown.

The old aunts, though a sporting pair, felt that this pastime had its drawbacks, and he was sent to a tutor. Mr McFetteridge dealt wisely with him; he had taught a number of boys headed for public school and the army, and knew the pitfalls of headlong confrontation. He informed Pa that for every assignment properly done there would be a stated time for fishing. Pa romped through his entrance exams to St Paul's School in London, became a renowned boxer, and emerged from Sandhurst as a King's Commissioned

Officer in 1907. He served with an Irish regiment of the British Army for a short time, and then transferred to the Indian Army. For a while, in deference to his father, he was attached to the Nizam's son as minder-companion. He said that among other things it was his job to see that the sum of money allocated to the heir as a weekly allowance was spent, and that in order to achieve this, in one week, he bought seven Rolls Royces. It was the kind of thing that happened often enough in Princely circles, and the cars probably stayed forgotten in the Royal garage until they decayed.

Having been raised in India as a small child Pa was delighted to go back, but he found certain aspects of his novice period in the army difficult. Young officers might not marry until they reached a stated rank, and in general they were treated much as fags were treated in public schools, being rarely seen and never, never heard in the presence of their seniors. When they finally reached the marrying stage it couldn't be done without the approval of their Colonel, who was often far more fussy than their parents.

Although this didn't necessarily mean total celibacy in India, if you were discreet, it did make English girls look dangerously desirable once matrimony was within reach. Resident English girls were in short supply, but a steady stream arrived by boat, despatched by their families to snare a suitable husband. It was almost impossible for a girl to miss out in the matrimonial market, regardless of her defects. There was a solemn old great-uncle of ours in the Indian Civil Service who patiently took receipt of nine of his sisters, one every year, and had a positive matrimonial result every time. Whether from disillusion or exhaustion he himself never married.

There was a favourite fable of Pa's which he used to bring out for The Girls whenever he thought they needed an example of youthful virtue, and we all knew him well enough by then, young though we were, to find it patently out of character.

'Until I was a Captain I scarcely spoke to a woman. I had never asked a woman to dance, in fact it would never have crossed my mind to touch a woman, even on the dance floor. The Colonel wouldn't have allowed it. You girls are far too young to go dancing.'

'Had you ever kissed a woman, Pa?'

'Don't be damned cheeky, Jenny. Of course not!'

It has always mystified me that he avoided the clutches of the Fishing Fleet, as the husband-hunters were called, until he married Mama. They were both quite old by then, nearly thirty. It's impossible to imagine that Pa didn't cast an eye over the available girls, because his eye was far too active and expert in middle age to have been idle in his youth, but somehow he managed to dodge all permanent attachments until he met Mama.

Certainly he had to work hard. Men who wanted to make a career in India had to learn as many of the major native languages as possible; for the Army alone one had to be fluent in three. Pa was no linguist; French was beyond him because he hated the French, but in India he spoke five different languages, and could read Sanskrit. As a reward he was channelled into intelligence and spent most of his Army life on the North-west Frontier, happily engaged in what Kipling called the Great Game. He always swore that he had known the original Kim and used him as an Agent, and it was probably true. In 1911, the year of the Great Durbar, when for the first time the British Monarch, George V and Queen Mary came to receive the homage due to the King Emperor, Pa was appointed Ceremonial Attache to the King.

The Great Durbar was an extravaganza on an unprecedented scale. In a land where traditionally nothing was spared in displays of wealth and grandeur this was the ultimate opportunity for the Princes to show the Raj and each other what they were worth, and none of them was prepared to worry if they bankrupted their State in doing so. In trains and gilded carriages, and along the crowded, dusty roads of India the Princes and their entourages, their elephants and their squadrons of elite cavalry converged on Delhi. They brought with them tents the size of ballrooms, their gold dinner services, their brocades and jewels and their Maharanis and Begums, also loaded with fabulous saris and jewels which they could only wear behind the purdah screens. Delhi couldn't house them: in the end there were more than a million camped round the city, and the ordinary people grew dizzy with the scenes of splendour. Every Ruler and every member of his Court had an exact place in the Order of Precedence, and the slightest error in that Order was carried deep in the soul, an insult to be brooded on for ever. As Ceremonial Attache 'Precedence' was one of Pa's responsibilities, and his daily nightmare.

He told us of the Tattoos they held at Agra in His Majesty's honour, at night, in front of the Taj Mahal. Even in daylight the Taj makes you catch your breath. It soars out of the dust and dirt and poverty which is India, the colour and shape of a mirage. At night it floats luminous against the indigo sky and the stars, a dreaming ghost of all the loves and legends and spirits of India's past. It may be that the only ceremonial ever worthy of the Taj took place during the 1911 Durbar.

At the night Tattoos their Majesties sat enthroned, framed by torches and flanked by the most noble of their subjects, at the top of the marble steps, in front of the most perfect of all marble arches. Before them was a long line of still, marble pools bordered by soft grass, and beyond the grass tall, sentinel trees under which men of lesser importance stood to watch. The moon turned the dome of the Taj to the colour of a dove's breast, threw shadows like spears from the turrets, and mirrored itself endlessly in the water of the pools.

At the sound of a bugle a line of a thousand torches would flare on either side beneath the trees, lighting the cavalry who came galloping in ranks of four up the grass verges towards the throne, lances held high. The troops were clothed in the strong, violent colours of India, orange and pink and purple and peacock-blue, their turbans were of gold or silver silk, their uniforms buttoned with precious stones and the harness of their horses was of silver and gold. They charged out of the dark into the torchlight, glittering-drunk with their own glory and the magic of their speed, each man shouting the battle-cry of his State and raising his lance in homage to the Crown, then vanishing into the darkness again, beyond the Taj.

As the troops blazed and thundered and vanished others appeared, until the soft, watered grass turned to dust and the torches smoked, softening the hurt of colour into a mist. Then there would be fierce contests of horsemanship, tent-pegging, impossible acrobatics at full gallop, mock battles with the cream of one State's cavalry facing another's, and only a thin veneer over the desire of the troops that the fight might be real. When the Mighty had departed, with protracted ceremony, the Taj still bathed calmly in the moonlight, detached and flawless.

The Political Service, to which Pa went from the Army, was small in number and very senior in terms of prestige. It dealt with the administration and conduct of the Indian Princely States and saw that the Rulers, willingly or otherwise, behaved within the bounds of decency and the standards of the Raj. The men chosen as Politicals were required to have an encyclopedic knowledge of the country, its customs and political intricacies, its languages, and to have an unassailable reputation for integrity.

Integrity was essential because some of the Rulers, considering honesty a bad character defect, were apt to offer their Political Agent some trifle such as a handful of diamonds or a string of pigeon's blood rubies whenever a favourable decision was required. This would be brought into the Agent's presence by a senior member of the Ruler's Court. No mention would be made of the reason for the gift: the Ruler knew that the Political Agent knew, and indeed it was his job to know, what schemes his charges might be hatching.

The gift would be offered with dignity and deprecation, 'A small thing which might perhaps please the Memsahib, and His Highness would be flattered if she would accept . . .' The Agent would touch the gift with his hand, smile gravely and wave it away. The courtier would bow and withdraw without ill-will or surprise. If it had been accepted there would have been disillusion and the end of trust, and most certainly the end of the Political Agent.

The Princes were diverse and wonderful, many of them educated in England and as polished as any European Royal, yet ruling feudal kingdoms which had hardly altered in a thousand years. There were Rulers who were genuincly fcared, not only by their subjects but by people like Pa who had to deal with them. There was one who was said to have been responsible for uncounted murders, and Pa disliked taking Mama with him when he visited that State. There was one who bred, and boasted of it, over a hundred sons in order to produce the perfect polo team. There were palaces, Pa swore, which swarmed with ghosts, the spirits of people killed in every sort of macabre manner, often simply being bricked into the corner of a passage and left to suffocate, this being a tidy and economical method of disposal.

'There was one old palace I used to visit quite often,' he told us, 'Where a young woman used to come and stand beside my bed every night, and pull open the mosquito net.'

'Did you speak to her?'

'No, but she spoke to me, every time. She was English. She'd just stand there looking down at me and say, "poor old thing."'

'Why, Pa? Did you ever find out?'

'Oh, yes, the Maharajah told me. Her husband was murdered in that bed in the 1850s, during the Mutiny, and she found him.'

Mama tried very hard in India, but she was never really happy there or entirely well, and perhaps one thing caused the other. In the course of Pa's job they moved from one dreary, impersonal bungalow to the next, never settling anywhere for long. Betty and Jenny were infants and Mana would have half-mistrusted the Ayahs who looked after them.

There was an important social side to the job as well, parties and official functions which they had to attend, and she was quite unable to cope with the infamous breed of Memsahibs into whose company she was forced. Very few British wives were improved by India; whatever their former circumstances, which weren't always what they claimed, the majority were determined never to lift a finger for themselves, nor to like or understand the Indian servants who spoiled them, and in consequence they were dangerously bored.

While their husbands worked they overcame their boredom by gathering together for wholesale assassination of other peoples' characters, and for the fascinating game of out-pointing each other in their degrees of social supremacy. This entailed total contempt for anyone who could not lay claim, valid or invented, to a background which could be classed as at least County. Mama, being an Australian, was beyond the pale, socially impossible, especially as she didn't drink, There were nice Mem-Sahibs, of course, intelligent and civilised women whom Mama adored and remembered for years afterwards, but they were hopelessly outnumbered by the others who should never have been allowed beyond the narrow confines from which they came.

When our parents left India for good in 1925, Mama must have been enormously relieved, and at the same time guilty because she had never really been part of her husband's India. The future was full of uncertainties, and to make things worse she was carrying an unplanned child. Once she set foot in a country which she knew and understood, and as soon as she was delivered of her wrongly sexed afterthought she became well again, as she hadn't been for years.

She and Pa had scarcely any time together after they arrived in Australia because Pa went straight to Queensland. The situation there was critical: it was the beginning of a drought which would last seven years, sheep were dying by the thousand, and such cattle as could walk to the properties where they would be fattened for slaughter were dying on the stock routes for lack of water. Pa went straight to Isis Downs, the principal sheep property of the Partnership near Longreach. He arrived at Isisford, the local town after dark, having come by train from the coast. His introduction to Queensland was not what he expected.

Pa said, 'I was told the Manager would be there to meet me, but he wasn't. It's not much of a town, Isisford, just pubs and a wall of bottles round the outskirts; people put their bottles on the wall instead of throwing them away, and it's enormous. Anyway, I went to the nearest pub and told them where I wanted to go, and a chap said he'd drive me out.

'It was pitch dark, and after we went through the Isis Downs gate there were dead sheep everywhere. As you know, its twenty miles from the gate to the homestead and afterwards I estimated there must have been about 45,000 dead sheep along the track. Those were just the obvious ones, and it was the same all over the property.

When we finally got to the homestead and I got out of the car, I could hear someone screaming, a woman. You know the garden there, lots of trees and bushes and I couldn't see a thing. Then a woman burst out of the bushes and rushed towards us, and after her came this fellow, stark naked, laughing like a maniac and waving a carving knife.

'The chap who'd driven me and I took the knife away from him and tied him up and bundled him into the car. His wife was hysterical, we couldn't leave her alone, poor thing, so we took her too. We had to drive back to Isisford, leave the man with the police and the wife with a friend of hers. Very sad, you know, this chap had managed Isis for quite a few years, and he just couldn't stand seeing what was happening, it sent him right off his head. There were a lot of people like him in Queensland then.'

It was the opening to a life which, for Pa, could have been no more different if he'd switched planets. The Partnership was over 350,000 pounds in debt, the equivalent of millions today, and on top of that the Depression was just round the corner. The bank, which would have foreclosed if it hadn't been for the drought and the uncertainty of rural prospects, summoned Pa before them and demanded that the debt be repaid. Pa cordially invited them to accept the properties in lieu of payment, and they shook their heads. 'See what you can do, Major Walker,' they said, 'and good luck to you.'

5

Hove

BY 1928 PA HAD ASSESSED the problems facing the Queensland properties, and realised that at the very best they would take years to put right. Both the Clarke and Whiting families were heavily dependent on Queensland for their incomes, they were unused to poverty, and they found their present situation catastrophic. Harassed by the difficulties on the land Pa was equally harassed by the beneficiaries who made their discomfort known, rent their garments, metaphorically speaking, and called on him for greater efforts.

Before settling down to the exile ahead our parents decided to make a trip to England, to see Pa's family and to settle his affairs there. Fanny Walker was living in Hove, grandfather having died a little earlier, and Pa's middle sister, Sheila, whose husband had been killed in First World War, lived with her and looked after her.

Our arrival set the scene for a family gathering, with Pa's two other sisters, their husbands and children, converging on Hove. Daisy and Jim McLintock had a son named William, Barch and Dorothy Christie a daughter, Tony, and Sheila Landale had Roy and Aileen.

Of the seven cousins I was by far the youngest, the rest all within a year or two of each others' ages. For some reason, when our elders were gathered together, the subject of christenings came up, and there was grave embarrassment when they realised that this ceremony, as applied to their children, had slipped their collective minds. If asked they would all have declared themselves loyal members of the Church of England, for hadn't their Walker grandfather been a Parson? Fanny, whose attitude to religion was notoriously cool, chose to express horror and outrage on finding that her grandchildren were unbaptised. She turned on a fine Fanny drama, playing the matriarch and enjoying every moment of it.

Having been caught in dereliction of duty the parents went overboard in putting things right. The Girls told me later on that they and the others who had slipped through the baptismal net were treated like criminals, 'As though it was all our fault!' The only revenge taken on Fanny was through the parents insisting that, as she had started the thing, she must be Godmother to the lot of us. The Hove Church was booked, all available friends and acquaintances were summoned as witnesses and as an excuse for a party afterwards, and on the appointed day they filled the pews. In the front row six furiously embarrassed adolescents and one infant, held in a half-nelson by a nanny, waited for the torture to end.

Everyone waited. The Vicar looked expectantly at Aunt Sheila for the signal to start the service, but Sheila had her head turned, anxiously examining the congregation, pew by pew. She leaned towards Pa, and hissed, 'Geoff, where on earth's Fanny?' Pa rose to his feet, peered round the Church, and said ; 'Oh my God! She's gone to the bloody football!' With the old habit of command, he roared at the Vicar; 'Wait till I come back!' and disappeared down the aisle at a run. It was well known that football was higher on Fanny's list of priorities than Heaven.

The congregation, having no choice in the matter, dozed or whispered in the dusty shafts of Church sunlight. I struggled in Nanny's arms, and shouted some of the shorter, more graphic words my sisters had taught me in private. A well-meaning uncle tiptoed forward and gave me a golf ball to keep me quiet.

The atmosphere had reached a muffled boil of disapproval when Pa finally returned with Fanny. She took her time getting up the aisle, bowing with immense dignity to those on either side, settled herself beside Sheila, and nodded encouragingly to the Vicar who was mopping his brow. He had observed during the long wait that the older baptismal candidates were becoming mutinous, and decided that he had better get them over first. Being small and in custody I was more what he was used to, and could wait.

He dealt briskly with the six older ones and Fanny graciously acted as Godmother to each in turn. I'm sure there were Godfathers but our parents could never remember who they were, and later on we successfully appointed our own. At last, and with obvious relief, the Vicar turned to Nanny and reached out his arms for me.

I don't remember it but I'm told that as he went to take me, thanking God that I was the last one, I delivered the golf ball at short range with all the weight of a solid three-year-old behind it. The ball hit him squarely in the eye and he toppled backwards down the steps of the font into Fanny's arms, where she, Gibraltar-built woman that she was, laid him out gently on the floor. She straightened up and according to Aunt Sheila she smiled broadly, and when her eye met mine, she winked.

Our parents didn't see Home again until 1951, by which time even they had almost stopped speaking of it as Home. We grew up though with the myth that this year, next year, or at any rate before long, we would all go back there. There was always a sense of semi-exile, and the distant, dangled carrot of the Promised Land. Because of this we never owned a house after we left The Haven, but moved every year or two from one rented place to another.

So that we shouldn't seem like Colonials on our eventual return to England, our parents engaged an English governess to go back to Australia with us, and a nanny for me. It has always puzzled me that, if they were as poor as they said they were, they could afford such luxuries, but probably it just reflects the pittance that nannies and governesses were paid in 1928. For girls like Molly Ayers, known as Mike, governessing was the only form of employment they could hope for. Twenty years later I saw Mike again in the same narrow, dark terrace house in Hove that we'd rescued her from. She was the slave, by then, of a mad old aunt, and she told me that her time with us was the only good thing that ever happened to her.

Mike must have been in her early twenties when she came to Australia with us, and I remember her built square like a primitive wood carving, with freckles, billiard table legs, and straight, mousy hair held back by a metal slide. She had never contemplated anything so daring as make-up, and I don't think she was even particularly well educated. She came from that sad section of the British middle-class which clings to the vestiges of gentility but can no longer afford its trappings. In her family background the younger sons of younger sons had slipped gradually downhill, breeding as they went. They filtered through the Church and school-mastering and the lesser ranks of the Civil Service, underpaid and without capital, and handicapped by the small range of occupations considered suitable to their status. They grew poorer and poorer, comforted by remote relationships to famous families, and their daughters made do with whatever was left over when everything possible had been done for the sons.

Since she lived in Hove I suspect that Fanny knew Mike's family, and recommended her as our governess out of pity, but as far as The Girls and I were concerned she was a great success. We loved her and she loved us, though we didn't deserve it. She was never a dogsbody nor excluded from anything, but neither was she treated like a young woman, introduced to a few young men of her own age, or encouraged to have a life of her own. She was part of our landscape, and I don't suppose it crossed anyone's mind that her freckled body housed the hormonal urges natural to her age. Governesses weren't supposed to have things like that.

As it happened, I was present at the scene that doomed Mike to an accelerated return to the dark house in Hove. I walked in from the verandah and there was Mama standing flummoxed and speechless, with Mike on her knees in unbecoming floods of tears, her arms round Mama's legs, and her face pressed into the crutch area of Mama's skirt. It was to be years before Mama understood the term Lesbian. Probably neither she nor Mike had ever heard the word, but they both realised that something undesirable had happened; unwholesome, Mama would have called it, and Mike was sent home. There, in that horrible, repressed Hove terrace, any lingering flicker of sexuality in her must have died, as a candle flame dies without air.

In retrospect it was a tragedy for poor Mike, an unintended cruelty born of ignorance, and lack of understanding. She was warm and generous , and probably as heterosexual as Mama if the truth be known, but for the first time in her life, warmed and softened by the Australian sunshine, she had dared to look for love. Mama just happened to be the only person available and her passion was no more sinister than a schoolgirl crush.

Having been taught by governesses herself Mama thought them far more effective than schools, and the value of serious education for girls simply escaped her. Also, English governesses had an advantage over Australian governesses or schools because they insulated us against the stigma of an Australian 'twang'. The Girls, having started off in India, spoke pure Oxbridge like our parents, and I was required to do the same. Our accents were monitored in the same way one house-trains a puppy, with constant vigilance, beatings, and rubbing of noses in dirty vowels. When Pa was at home and we slipped up, he hit us over the head with a rolled-up newspaper kept specially for the purpose. When friends said to Mama, 'What wonderful English accents your children have! How d'you manage it?' she smiled modestly, and said nothing about the effort involved. Accents were important in her circle. She and her friends felt that if their children didn't sound Australian the English might overlook the fact that they were Colonials. In most cases it was a forlorn hope; their children grew up to be Australian, and proud of it.

6

The Girls

Because The Girls were so much older than me, they were both my torment and my ideal and I was their constant scourge, a perpetual background bleat of 'Wait for me! I want to come too!' They became maddened and threw things at me, yelling, 'Go home, you're too small.'

They built a brushwood cubby-house in a secret place at the end of our land, and told me that I couldn't go there, that it was theirs. That made it irresistible and I was drawn there as by a magnet, so they pulled my pants down and beat me with brushwood twigs. It didn't hurt much, and Betty cried, but not me. She could get away with tears; indeed, if she'd tried she could have got away with anything.

Betty, named Elizabeth Sheila at the mass christening, was absurdly beautiful from the day she was born, yet somehow she turned the conventional standards of beauty upside down. People judge beauty in terms of hair and features and colouring, but these can be manufactured or faked. Betty had all the basics, and never wasted a moment of her time thinking about them or trying to improve on them; more than anything they embarrassed her.

She was very tall, with hair that varied through all the shades of blond from ash to honey, and full, lovely lips that looked sad rather than sensual. People used to turn and stare after her as she passed, even when she was a child. She tried very hard to be naughty because that was what other children were and she wanted to join in, but she was naturally, inescapably good. Jenny looked forward to every wild, wicked, forbidden thing in the world as soon as she was old enough; she was in a constant hurry to start on sophisticated sin, and she wove her dreams around it. Betty wanted only to be the mother of twenty children; she spent hours trying out names in anticipation, and worrying about their characters. She neither spoke, saw, nor heard evil, and there was a kind of puzzled sadness in the way she watched the antics of the rest of us, as though she knew she was different and wanted to be the same. I make her sound priggish, but she wasn't. She made herself join in forbidden things and she never told tales, but bad things saddened her.

Jenny had been given the name of Wendy at the baptismal orgy, but someone nicknamed her Windy so Mama promptly changed it to Jenny, and forgot about the original name. It caused great trouble later on when she wanted a passport; she swore her name was Jenny, and the authorities pointed out there was no Jenny Walker recorded in our family. The same thing happened to me even later, because it turned out that I was still an unregistered female child, due to the prolonged period of waiting for me to turn into a boy. If our parents had produced a large family the confusion might have been unthinkable.

Jenny wasn't as tall as Betty, and whereas Betty had inherited the Walker genes and improved on them, Jenny had thrown to the Whiting side of the family. She was dark and straight-haired with enormous eyes, and a wide mouth in a square jaw got her the nickname of Plain Frog. It was an exotic, rather Spanish face, full of character. She went through her childhood with brows drawn blackly together, jaw set, confronting everything head-on, discipline, social niceties, sickness or being made to wear clothes she didn't like. Her face would set trap-like, and there would be silence to put your teeth on edge or else foul language, until she got over it. She spent a lot of time being punished and brooding about it, and seeing herself as a martyred figure, like Joan of Arc.

Her favourite things in life were all non-human, particularly any creature that was sick or injured; she had a genius for making them better, and the harder she had to work at it the better she liked it. I suppose one should have known she'd be a nurse, but at the time it seemed more likely that she'd be a vet. There was a tiny, disused hut outside the kitchen door of The Haven, and there were more huntsman spiders in it than you'd think possible in one place; gross, hairy spiders who gave me nightmares. When Jenny was really angry with all of us she'd sleep in the hut with them, saying that the spiders were a damn sight nicer than her family

Because she was drama-hungry at that age she often felt that the pace of life was too slow for her, and she must liven things up. These episodes usually ended in tears, more often than not mine, because being small and easily conned I was likely to be given an undesirable role in the production.

Our next door neighbours were a family called Langford who lived, during the holidays, in a large, gabled house on our southern boundary. The children went to school in Melbourne, and they thought we were odd because we had a governess, and because we lived at Sorrento all the year round. Influenced by our parents we thought they were pretty ordinary; they had the kind of voices we were supposed to keep away from. Part of their land, heavily pine-treed, ran round our fence, and we would gather down there out of sight of both houses, to throw stones and insults at each other.

Cedric Bright, whose parents lived nearer to Sorrento and were friends of our parents, was our reinforcement against the Langfords, besides being our proxy brother. He was the same age as Jenny, and in an ideal world eventually they might have married. Cedric had a round, inscrutable face, was besotted with fishing and hopelessly untidy; he reeked permanently of fish. He went to boarding school, but all through the holidays his skin, hair and clothes were encrusted with scales and old bits of bait, his shoe-laces and shirt-tails trailed behind him, and when he talked he did so with his mouth shut, and no separation between the words. We could understand him perfectly, but he drove the grown-ups to distraction. He ate with us a lot of the time, slouching in before meals to ask what we were having and then ringing up his mother to find out what was on the menu at home, either settling himself at our table or vanishing without a word depending on what food appealed to him most. The Girls and I thought he was wonderful.

He and Jenny decided that the Langford situation called for more aggression on our part, and they drew up plans for a proper war. There was an old shed known as the Boxroom down near the stables, a few feet our side of the boundary fence. Among other things it housed our coal supply, and you could get on its roof by climbing up the windmill beside it.

Jenny and Cedric, helped by Betty who was making anxious noises, laboriously shifted a large amount of coal onto the roof of the shed. They collected a coil of rope from the boatshed, and then Jenny came up to the house to tell me, with suspicious sweetness, that they wanted me to play with them. I was amazed and flattered, and with my non-existent chest stuck out I scuttled down to the shed in Jenny's wake.

The Langfords were on their side of the fence, watching the preparations with two or three of their cronies, collecting ammunition and making nasty remarks. I asked, 'What are we playing?' and Jenny said, 'You'll see. Just sit on this.'

To my outrage she produced the enamel chamber-pot I still used. Mama had not yet lost her interest in my bowel movements, and I tended to fall through the hole in the seat of our outdoor dunny, but I yearned for the day when I'd graduate to a grown-up lavatory.. It was obviously not going to be the sort of game I liked, but before I could disappear Jenny and Cedric seized me, planted me on the pot, tied my arms and legs and roped me securely to the throne. My screams alarmed them, so Jenny took off her sock and gagged me. She and Cedric then joined Betty who was on the roof, saying quite uselessly, 'Jenny, Cedric, don't! You mustn't!'

Cedric challenged the Langfords. 'Cummonyermugs,' he shouted. 'Yergottatargetterday! Tryanitit!'

The pot and I were jerked skyward on the end of the rope. Cedric, being the strongest, bounced me up and down and swung me like a pendulum, the Langfords pelted me with dirt and pine cones and The Girls bombarded them with coal. I was purple-faced, choking and shrieking behind the gag, Trixie, our Labrador bitch, was hysterical and altogether there was more noise than at Bull Run. Nemesis arrived in the shape of Mike and Mama, both making as much noise as anyone else out of sheer fury. I peed into the pot, wetting my pants which was the ultimate indignity. I was unhurt, but distraught because I was too small to kill the lot of them. For a few days afterwards The Girls were quiet and thoughtful, and Cedric was absent. Betty was the only one to be vaguely happy, because for once she had been punished too.

The Girls lived a very isolated existence for their age, and it made them self-sufficient and naive at the same time. We weren't allowed to mix with the local children, who were the only children in Sorrento outside the school holidays, because of their contaminating Australian 'twang' and, I suspect, because of a lot of other idiotic values which no longer exist. They were values which belonged to an different age and a vanished class, and even though they're incomprehensible now they were accepted then. Some values are basic, others as fickle as fashion, and fifty years on people will look back on us as we are today with wonder and contempt.

There was a Church of England church just round the corner from The Haven, a sweet, plain, limestone building. The local children went to Sunday School there, and we used to hear them singing; we could hear the hymns during the Sunday services too, but we never went to church. Church was a mystery, and tantalising, but if we asked to go Mama said, 'Goodness no, surely you 'd rather be on the beach?'

God and Jesus came as a complete surprise to me when I went to school. The Girls, at their lessons with Mike in the schoolroom, were taught something called Divinity, but that was all about missionaries in Africa who bravely saved the souls of the Natives by making them wear clothes. There were books with pictures of the missionaries standing proudly beside black people dressed in shapeless white smocks, but there was nothing much about God. I had to sit on the verandah outside the schoolroom, being forbidden to wander out of sight. I could hear the lessons, and it was horribly boring until Jenny taught me to read.

The omission of the Deity from Divinity lessons was in keeping with my family's attitude to religion in general. Being an Anglican was synonymous with being a Conservative and being British, which automatically entailed a rigid reticence about all things personal, complex or profound. Matters of the soul might be discussed by alien beings such as Roman Catholics, but our parents, and it seems to me most Anglican clergy, regarded religion as a conversational indecency. It was one of the subjects Not Discussed at Table, together with sex, which was unmentionable anywhere, and money, because talking about money was vulgar, whether one had it or not. 'And anyway,' said Pa, surrounded by women, 'No woman can ever understand money – or handle it.'

The Sorrento children were nice, knockabout kids, and they rightly looked on us as incomprehensible, stuck-up freaks. I doubt if any governess had been seen in Sorrento before Mike, and even apart from her we were branded as outcasts by our awful Pommie voices, and our clothes. Sewing was one of Mama's hobbies; she had an old Singer sewing machine, and a lot of time on her hands. She still considered a cook essential, since between her gilded youth, over-servanted India and the present she had never been in charge of a stove or a saucepan, and she believed them to be quite beyond her capabilities. As we were unable to pay any but the lowest wages a series of slovenly, evil-tempered and inefficient women ruined the food in The Haven's kitchen, and Mama kept defensively to the front of the house, rattling and banging away on the old treadle Singer.

By some evil chance she came across a pattern for bloomers, and decided that they were the perfect garment for growing girls to wear at the seaside. The bloomers were identical to the old joke-underwear of spinster schoolmarms, voluminous, elasticised at waist and knee, shapeless and hideous. The only difference between ours and the ancient chastity-type was that ours were made of luridly coloured floral cotton bought at Stringers Stores, and that while the schoolmarms kept theirs decently covered ours had to be worn on the outside. Our dresses and jumpers were stuffed in under the waist elastic, and we knew perfectly well that we looked like nothing so much as three over-decorated pumpkins on legs. The village children fell about laughing whenever they saw us, and we were green with envy at their lovely, ordinary clothes.

The only member of the family, apart from Mama, who liked the bloomers was Trixie. She was a young dog then, a black, long-coated Labrador Retriever, and after a lifetime of dogs she is still of sainted memory. In those days of her youth her charms were unlimited, and she was well aware of them; even from the confines of our garden she managed to make the combined curs of Sorrento and Portsea go mad with lust when she was on heat. Twice a year they swarmed like moths to her irresistible flame, and even though we Fort-Knoxed her in a wire run they gathered round to serenade, lament and fight, until everyone within earshot was almost demented.

It was on one of these occasions that Jenny showed a flash of the practical brilliance that would one day make her a first-class nurse. Mike, Mama and Betty were charging round the garden, shouting and hurling things at assorted dogs, Trixie was singing a dirge about unlawful confinement, dogs were fighting in the Lane, round Trixie's cage, and on the verandah. Jenny came out of the house with an old pair of bloomers and a pair of scissors, went in with Trixie, cut a hole for each of her hind legs and one for her tail, and put them on her. She said, 'Look out! I'm going to let her go.'

There was a hailstorm of suitors from every corner of the landscape, and piercing screams of triumph as Trixie disappeared under a rugger-scrum. She was a big, strong young dog, and after a few moments she surfaced and staggered across the garden, while as many of her admirers as could gain a hold clung to her hindquarters. She looked, more than anything, like and over-crowded Indian bus. As we watched her they started to drop off. One by one they fell back, their faces puzzled; one or two mounted her again, then retreated, whimpering. Trixie was getting irritated.

Hot for sex, she blamed the dogs, not the bloomers, and the next one to approach her got bitten.

We put her back in her cage and the curs gradually disappeared. Some of them hung round for a while but they'd lost confidence, and when Trixie came off heat the bloomers had become her power-totem. From then on when we went abroad in Sorrento dressed in the horrible things Trixie came with us, similarly dressed. If anyone, child or adult, laughed at us, she went for them with teeth bared and lips drawn back, because bloomers were sacred. She was never known to bite in her life, except for Alsatians which she classed as Huns, but people didn't stay around to find out whether or not she was serious

7

Fishing

FISHING RUNS IN THE WALKER BLOOD, genetically transmitted from one generation to the next, When Pa first found The Haven, and first stood on the cliff in front of the house looking across the Bay, he would have been imagining below the surface of the water the gliding, seductive shapes of his most favoured prey. In India he had hunted tiger, stuck pig, shot crocodile and deer, snipe in the marshes, and the gallant, black-horned sheep on the high passes. Innocent as savages, he and his kind destroyed the wild game of India because it was a custom, like polo, that belonged to their class. Most of them genuinely loved the things they killed, but it had never occurred to them that what is killed today cannot breed tomorrow, and must grow less in number. The Indian Princes took pride in arranging elaborate hunting parties in honour of the British, and as many of the Princes were first-class shots who regarded the shooting of game as an art-form rather than as a sport, they brought to it the added incentive of competition. This view of shooting is still widely held today, on the grouse moors of Scotland and other holy places, and Pa, having been raised in the bosom of a shooting race, might have been expected to cherish the sport for life.

There must have been a conflict in Pa's soul between his fondness for live animals and the strange compulsion to render them dead, and in the end the live animals won. He said that the fun simply went out of it, out of being the instrument that caused something to cease living, and he sounded slightly puzzled, as though he knew he'd lost something precious and could no longer remember why he'd valued it. Instead he reverted to fishing and whatever blood-lust lingered was satisfied by the pursuit of fish. The finesse inherent in dry-fly fishing suited him best of all; I have seen many fly-fishermen since I fished with my father, but never a prettier nor more skilled one. If there were no trout available, he was perfectly happy to devote himself to sea fish.

In India he had fished for Mahseer, the bravest and most powerful fighting fish of all, now almost gone from the Indian rivers, and when I was still a child he gave me the kind of gift that fairy godmothers are supposed to flick off the top of their wands when he told me about trout fishing in Kashmir. 'You must go there one day,' he said. 'It's the most beautiful place in the world to fish,' but by the time that my husband and I went there and lost our souls to the Valley Pa was dead.

He would fish for anything, anywhere, stopping just short of a bathtub which was clearly empty. Given the choice between a wide, clean-banked, well-stocked river and a narrow, overhung rivulet, he would go for the small stream every time, and get fish out of it. Several times he described to me the Anglican Heaven for which he believed he was bound, and it consisted of just such a stream, with a few nice, open pools where the fish could rise, with all his favourite dogs in attendance, and no inhibiting presence of God.

The sad part about The Haven was that Pa was in Queensland so often, and though fishing was as much part of our daily routine as meals it was not the same without him; it became pedestrian. When Pa was with us we went far out, to places otherwise forbidden and in the foulest of weather without turning a hair, always in the completely false belief that he was competent to handle a boat in the Bay. In fact he was hopeless with engines in either boats or cars, and he simply disregarded things like south-westerly changes and hidden sandbanks, but such was our trust that we ignored them too, and felt perfectly safe.

You hardly had to move offshore then, to get fish. There were no speedboats, no water-skiers and almost no pollution. The bottom of the Bay was a smorgasbord of everything fish like best, and they came in from the ocean to feed as deer come to graze on a prime meadow. Our jetty was about thirty yards long, and when you sat in the dinghy at the end of it to clean your fish the sharks would circle round you, greedy as the gulls, waiting for scraps. The Girls were allowed to use the Jack on their own at a stated distance from the shore, a hundred yards or so beyond the end of the jetty, where they would drop their lines over the side and come back half-an-hour later with enough flathead or whiting or baby schnapper to feed us all for a couple of days. There were fish in infinite variety, and because there were no freezers then you took only what you and your friends could use immediately.

The real fishing trips, to places where the big fish lived, happened either when Pa was home and we could borrow a decent boat, or when we went out with Mr Johnson, the professional fisherman. In South Channel there were King George whiting, and schnapper. At the right time of year on the right tide the schnapper were huge, taking the bait and running across the seabed like bison over the prairie, so that you could almost hear the roar of their powering through the water and the line burned your hand. They were beautiful fish when you landed them, brilliant pink and big-scaled, and not unlike a bison because all their weight was forward in their head and shoulders.

There is the forgotten ghost of a small island in the middle of South Channel. It was once fitted out as a fort to repel mythical Russian invaders, the figment of some overheated 19th century brain. The poor little island was tunnelled and shafted until it was like a Gruyère cheese; they shored up the tunnels with timber, hacked out munition stores along them, and built gun emplacements and a harbour. The mirage-Russians faded and the island was abandoned, useless for anything except the migratory mutton birds. We would take picnics out there, land on the island and sit on the harbour wall to eat, looking down into a clear, still aquarium of sheltered water. Any sea creature you can think of was apt to glide in from the depths outside and loll below you, relaxed and visible as a bull in pasture on a summers' day. If you stood on the top of the island in the rank, yellowish seagrass, it looked like a poached egg, yellow in the middle, ringed by white sand, and with a bite taken out of it at the harbour. The tunnels and weapons' stores were dark and damp; the mutton birds bred in them, leaving a smell of condensed cod liver oil, and in the breeding season a carpet of squalling, powder-puff babies.

Whales came into the Bay then, and rays bigger than our dinghy, passing slowly underneath it like huge, billowing carpets. I saw a seventeen-foot grey nurse shark landed at Sorrento pier, and was allowed to sit astride it, and two octopus, each longer than a tall man swam under Portsea pier, speckled and obscene, just as we were poised to dive.

There was a day when I was about four years old; it had been blowing hard, and the sea was murky with stirred-up sand. I went down to the beach to see what had been washed up because there was always the chance of treasure after a gale, sometimes quite disgusting things, but always worth a look. This time there was nothing interesting, and I waded out about twenty-yards until the water was round my waist, playing with the floating lumps of seaweed.

I must have trodden on the poor creature, not being able to see through the water, because something powerful and alive seized me round the legs, holding me in what felt like rubber bands and moving slowly up me at the same time. I had well-developed lungs as a child, and my yells reached Mike, who was in the garden. She screamed for Mama who called The Girls, and the whole lot came charging down the cliff into the sea. They carried me, complete with octopus, to the beach, and tried to untangle me.

The octopus was seriously disturbed, and no doubt just as disenchanted with the situation as everyone else. Panicking, it transferred its tentacles at random from me to my rescuers so that we were all knitted together, pulling, cursing, and in my case bawling. It was a fine, healthy octopus, amazingly strong and agile, and it was getting the best of things until someone had the sense to shout, 'A knife! Get a knife!' Like a giant ball of wool we staggered to the boathouse a few yards away. Someone, somehow, managed to get the jammed door open, a hand inside, and miraculously grabbed a knife. Mama and Mike hacked away at the tentacles, and as they severed them The Girls plucked them off and threw them away. In the end it was done; the operative part of the octopus lay on the ground and my rescuers, in varying stages of hysteria, could rid themselves of muck, slime, and lingering gruesome fragments. I had nightmares about things crawling up me for years.

Going fishing with Mr Johnson, the professional fisherman, was the best of all and because he charged for it we didn't go too often, but when we did everyone went because it was too good to miss. He had been fishing the Bay all his life, and when he dropped anchor on one of his marks the fish were guaranteed.

There was a great build-up before going out with Mr Johnson, packing a picnic lunch and organising all our fishing gear because it was extra if we used his, and we all got bossy and uptight with excitement. He was quite old, with a face ground by the sea and the wind until it was the same texture as the rocks on the Back Beach. I never saw him when he'd shaved, and until one particular fishing trip none of us knew that he had any teeth. His boat was an old, broad beamed, functional workman with an inboard engine and a sail in case of breakdown, and the boat, the engine and Johnson were all about the same age. Being a professional, and loving his boat, he kept it always in perfect order, up in the slips in winter for cleaning and painting, and though the engine was unbearably slow it usually worked.

Johnson supplied the bait, having plenty of it in the way of business, and brought his own lunch out of habit and because his wife knew what he liked. His bait-tin was notorious, a square, four-gallon kerosene tin full of assorted mussels, squid, pilchards and fish-pieces which had ripened in the sun for an unspecified period, and stank accordingly. Since the bait we used always came off the top we knew that the smell must come from a bottom layer which was never disturbed.

On the day of the teeth we had been drifting happily across prime fishing spots, hauling in a good catch and listening to Johnson's fishing stories, all of which we'd heard before, and all of which got better every time he told them. The sun being high overhead, and our tummies rumbling, Mama suggested lunch.

She was unpacking our basket when Johnson, who had been rummaging about in the bows, turned and said, 'Yer wouldn't bloody believe it, I've fergot me lunch. Must've left it on the pier. The wife won't 'arf larf.'

Mama gave him a sweet smile, and said, 'Don't worry, Mr Johnson, we've got far more than we need.'

'Very good of yer,' said Johnson.

Mama was starting to put things on a plate for him when Jenny grabbed her arm, made mysterious gestures towards her mouth, and shook her head vigorously.

'What on earth's the matter, Jenny?' asked Mama.

Jenny pointed to two chops, a crisp bread roll and a sausage on the plate, then to her own teeth, and shook her head again.

'Oh, I see,' said Mama. 'Mr Johnson, will these be too hard for you?'

'Too 'ard for me?' Johnson inspected the plate with evident pleasure. 'Bless yer, no. I got me teeth 'ere, 'aven't I?'

We stared at him in astonishment; it was as though Trixie had announced that she wore glasses. As we watched he reached behind him and dragged the bait-tin forward, then plunged his arm into it above the elbow. He groped round in its bottom, stirring up lethal blasts of rotting fish, then proudly withdrew his hand and brandished his dripping uppers and lowers for us to admire.

'If I keep 'em in there,' he said, 'I know I won't lose 'em.'

He popped them into his mouth, picked up the plate of food, and became happily absorbed in his lunch. Mike was leaning far out over the stern of the boat, and Mama was a very curious colour. I watched Johnson in fascination; as he ate I could see a high-watermark of maggots writhing helplessly in the hair of his forearm.

8

Cedric

WHEN CEDRIC CAME HOME from Geelong Grammar for the holidays The Girls' tempo of life changed because there were different things to do, and someone different to do them with. Cedric was nobody's dreamboat, but they weren't in a position to be fussy. I've said before that Cedric was scruffy, but it was more than that; he had developed scruff into a lifestyle. His holiday outer-wear was an encrusted record of his fishing and his meals, terminating in a pair of filthy sandshoes whose laces trailed behind him like dried-out worms.

He pursued fish from first light till last with a dedication it was pretty to watch, pausing only for sustaining intakes of food or, in springtime, when the Bay was sometimes unmanageable even for him, additions to his birds egg collection.

The birds egg collection was the exact opposite of Cedric's appearance and habits, and an early indication that he'd one day develop into a man of erudition and substance. It was lovingly arranged in boxes lined with cotton wool, each egg neatly labelled, delicately blown and varnished, more the work of a pernickety naturalist than of a maverick small boy. He was the youngest of three brothers, and like me he was the youngest by a considerable space.

Ruby, his mother, had been a beauty in her youth and was still exquisite; Alfred, his father, was very much her senior, and had reached an age where his interest in most things, Cedric included, was remote. He slept a good deal of the time, sitting in the sun in the courtyard of their two-storey house, spectacles on the end of his nose, and the great bald dome of his head shining like one of the witch's balls which the Portsea *nouveau riche* favoured as garden decoration.

Cedric regarded his father as a bad joke, no doubt resenting Alfred's indifference to him. He worked really hard during the holidays to make the old man's life hell, or perhaps to make his father notice him, and we were recruited to help. There was a balcony, handily placed above the spot where Alfred took the afternoon sun. Cedric, while bird-nesting, would stockpile a score or so of the commoner eggs, and keep them until they were at their foulest and most sulphurous. We would sneak up to the balcony en masse and bombard Alfred with a concerted volley, or else Cedric would have target practice with his shanghai.

Alfred would stir vaguely, give a buffalo snort, pass his hand over his dripping skull and go to sleep again. Ruby, who besides being beautiful was hopelessly gentle, would come to wake him up, reel back from the bad-egg fumes, and tenderly support him inside to get cleaned up, wailing, 'Oh Ceddie! You are a *naughty* boy!' When there were no bird's eggs we painted spider's webs on Alfred's bald head in Indian ink because Cedric said it kept the flies away. There was great satisfaction in sharing these harmless amusements, knowing that Pa would have beaten us half to death if we'd tried them at home.

Fishing with Cedric, if one was honoured with an invitation to do so, was apt to be unconventional. He had a long, narrow canoe, about as seaworthy as a tin bucket, and no one but Cedric could handle it. He would cruise along the foreshore just outside the line of jetties, standing upright and keeping the thing balanced with his feet. He had a great three-pronged spear like the spear traditionally carried by Neptune, and he used it to spear stingrays. He needed stingray barbs for school where they had good swap value, and his method of getting them was to spear the ray, then lift it flapping and whipping with its tail into the canoe, where he could cut off the barb.

The Girls were strictly forbidden to go out in the canoe. Anyone who has seen an enraged stingray in a confined space will appreciate the sense of this. For one thing, if their barbed sting goes into you a surgeon is needed to remove it, and when they are aggressive they use their tail with the barb in its end like a stockwhip. For another thing Cedric's canoe was designed for one expert person with nothing to disturb his balance, and not for two people dodging a stingray. Our parents took the view that if the Brights wished to encourage their son to kill himself they had every justification for doing so, but that they, personally, wanted to keep their daughters a little longer.

Betty wouldn't have dreamt of going, having been told not to. Jenny would normally have gone, forbidden or not, but she had recently overheard Mama and Ruby saying 'how nice it would be if Jenny and Cedric ... later on ... wouldn't it?' Jenny was mortified beyond belief; she had no intention of marrying anything less than Royalty, and she went through a period of treating Cedric as though he had leprosy. Cedric shrugged his shoulders, turned his back on her, and gave me serious consideration.

His problem was that although he was getting plenty of barbs he was not getting size and quality. The foreshore was a sort of promenade for the rays and there were some magnificent specimens even in shallow water, but he needed someone to stand on the flaps when he got a big one into the canoe so that he was free to grab the tail. I actually had certain advantages; not weighing very much I was less likely to capsize the canoe, but on the other hand I looked solid enough to hold down fair sized flaps, and young and silly enough not to argue about doing so. In fact, because I was always being told that I was too young and too small to do things, and because Cedric was a God, I'd have jumped off the top of a pine tree if he'd asked me to. He took me aside one afternoon and told me to meet him at the end of the jetty at first light next morning.

Leaving the house at dawn was no problem; I often went outside before the others were awake. It was one of those still, misty mornings when the sea was so flat that it almost invited you to walk on it. The silence was bottomless, and the seagulls meditated quietly along the jetty rail, waiting for the moment when the sun and the breeze would burst through the mist and compel them to flight. I heard a whisper of moving water, and Cedric's canoe slid round the end of the baths.

I still remember that morning, and light the colour of Peace rose petals gradually creeping between sea and mist, tinting the oil-still water with gold. The water was so clear, looking over the side of the canoe, that there seemed to be no separation between us and the bottom, and the stingrays came gliding along the sand, sometimes singly, sometimes in pairs, like early workmen on the way to a job. Cedric was deadly in his use of the spear; he showed me what to do, and in no time we were working as a team without a word needed between us. Cedric would heave a flailing stingray in-board, head toward me as I crouched in the stern; I would grab the spear to give me leverage and plant my feet firmly on the flaps while he caught the tail, cut off the barb, killed the ray and threw it overboard. It wasn't really either dangerous or difficult. By the time Cedric had enough barbs the sun was high, the breeze had wiped away the mist and blown the gulls skyward, and we had drifted down past Point King. We were both starving.

No one had actually told me not to go out with Cedric because it never occurred to them that he'd want me to go, and for the same reason they'd never told him not to take me. Consequently, when my family woke up and found me missing they thought of every possible disaster and tragedy, but not of Cedric. Poor Mama was frantic; neighbours were telephoned along the length of the cliff, and came running. The Sorrento police arrived and unhelpfully pointed out that my footsteps, still plain in the damp sand, led to the jetty and along it, but didn't return. They could see that my body wasn't lying under the water, but could a shark have taken me? Could I have fallen in, and the current carried me towards the dreaded Rip? Or even kidnap?

When Cedric paddled the canoe past the Langford's jetty and we saw the crowd of people on ours we were dumbfounded. Sorrento was not a place for large gatherings, much less the Walker jetty, and from the way they were all waving their arms about we realised that something important was happening. I said, 'What are they all doing, Cedric?' and he said, 'DunnoRobs.' Then we saw a police uniform, and a terrible suspicion began to dawn. 'D'yatellumyacumminfishin?'

'Of course not, they wouldn't have let me.'

'Oh! *Gawd!*' said Cedric, separating his words for once.

There is no way a canoe can vanish off the water on a clear day. One by one they turned and glared at us; Mama gave a loud wail of relief, and the police made a noise like police dogs about to 'Hold'. Even in my infant innocence I sensed impending doom as we got nearer to the jetty; from where I sat at sea level I could see innumerable feet, and rising from them like a forest, legs and bodies, all capped by furious, unsympathetic faces. Mama was in tears, and so was Mike, and The Girls registered boundless contempt. Thank Heaven Pa was away at the time.

Vengeance didn't last long at The Haven, and a couple of days later everything was back to normal. Cedric shuffled into our house at breakfast time, filthy as ever, hair stiff with salt and scales, and mumbled, 'WasferbrekfusArnAileen?'

Mama didn't even have to look up; she had heard the door slam, knew who it was and why. She said, 'Fishcakes, I think Cedric.' He moved to the phone, twirled the handle and asked for his home number. 'WasferbrekfusMa?' He listened and said, 'Fishcakesere,' hung up and seated himself happily at the table. Routine was restored.

9

Parents

ALL THROUGH THOSE INNOCENT YEARS, when The Girls legs were lengthening, their breasts, especially in Betty's case, growing like baby pumpkins, and I was graduating from chamber-pots to dunnies, Pa was changing as much as we were. His long visits to Queensland were his times of learning, a sustained effort on his part to learn all there was to know about sheep, cattle and the land.

If Pa had been a proper British Army establishment type, his transition to the management of the Queensland properties would have been a disaster. He had a few establishment characteristics, such as his views on Indian self-rule and the utter villainy of any political party other than the Conservatives, but in Queensland he kept such views to himself. Certainly there was his temper, which could explode in peoples' faces like a landmine, but he never lost it with animals or, as he used to say, 'People who can't hit back.'

Oddly enough he had humility; he was never afraid to ask questions or to admit ignorance, and this helped him a great deal. It endeared him to the proper pastoralists, the men who had spent their lives on the land, and he sought them out so that he could pick their brains. It helped him immeasurably with the managers and stockmen who worked the properties, and who nursed an in-built distrust of absentee bosses who, in their experience, knew nothing whatever about sheep or cattle. Even more deep seated was their hatred of Poms and Pommie voices, which they had learned to associate with arrogance as well as ignorance. Their initial reaction to Pa was suspicion laced with contempt.

Getting to the Queensland properties then meant long, exacting journeys by car or train. Once there, the only way of inspecting the country and the bores, or getting to the mustering camps to see the stock was on horseback, which suited Pa very well. He looked on horses as the only proper form of transport, and was totally unsympathetic to motor cars which he drove abominably. He had ridden all his life, especially in India, in the course of duty, in amateur steeplechases, playing polo, pig-sticking or just for pleasure. His years in the deserts of the North-west Frontier had taught him to navigate on horseback in every kind of inhospitable country, and the long, dusty rides across Western Queensland simply made him homesick for India.

At first the men on the properties reacted as they did to all Pommie Bastards; they set out to make life hard for him. They put him on lunatic horses, and were incensed when he didn't fall off. On trips to the bores or mustering camps, which could take several days and nights, they abandoned him on one excuse or another expecting him to get lost. He was well aware of what they were doing and why, and would camp on his own when it grew dark, track them in the morning, and rejoin them without reproach as though it had been his own choice.

This upset the stockmen because it was contrary to their beliefs. Poms weren't meant to be able to navigate their way across a twenty-acre paddock with all the fences in clear view, and few could stay on a stock horse long enough to do so. Also they were nonplussed when he didn't make a fuss about any of it. After they'd been with him a few times they found that he wasn't a bad bloke, that he was as tough as they were and they could talk to him, and from then on they began to teach him the things he wanted to know. He never told me about this, but the men themselves did, years later; they had a lot of stories about the Major.

Queensland was a hard place before aircraft opened it up. People on remote properties were so far away from other humans that they often became a little strange. Pa told a story about being off-track on his own one night on the way to a mustering camp, and of coming across a kind of humpy, surrounded by empty bottles and cans and half-wild goats. It was getting dark; three men came out, bearded and ragged, just as wild as the animals around them. One was old, the other two youngish, his sons, and they ranged themselves in front of the humpy, half-hostile, half-pleased to see someone from the outside world. The humpy was made from hammered-out kerosene tins and bits of wood with bark for a roof, and piles of dingo and 'roo skins on stretchers were drying round its walls. There was the glow of a fire inside the door, but no other light.

They inspected Pa for some time, and then the old man said, 'It's just on dark, mate. Yer'd better camp with us for the night and we'll give yer a bit of tucker, eh?' Then to one of the young men, 'Find us a bit of tucker, Wal, fast as yer can.'

He led Pa into the foul-smelling humpy which seemed to consist of a sinister mass of garbage, unidentifiable even in the light of an occasional leaping flame. Pa said the place reeked of goat and stale male, and there was no telling which was the worse. He would have ridden on but it was foolhardy in the dark, and the old man was in a fever of excitement with the dammed-up talk of years flowing out of him. Pa was offered, and refused, some rank, powerful drink out of a communal bottle. Outside a goat bleated twice, and then was silent. The old man rambled on, nonsense for the most part, but he and his sons had given up talking to each other a long time past, and for him it was like a purge.

Wal came in through the door, looking pleased with himself. He stood in the light of the fire and said, 'Got the bloody tucker, Dad.' He had a four-gallon kerosene tin of water in one hand, and in the other the gory, unskinned haunch of a newly slaughtered goat. He put the kerosene tin on the fire and thrust the goat's leg into it, hair and all. He said to Pa, 'That'll be bloody good tucker in an hour or so, mate. She were a young goat.'

In those early years when Pa and Queensland were adjusting to each other, Mama must have been dreadfully lonely. She had plenty of people around her, but no one she could talk to about her worries, and she had far too much time on her hands. She found ingenious ways to fill it, incomprehensible to us but harmless, if you exclude the conveyor belt production of bloomers.

She collected shells. The bottom of the Bay was thick with them, and every morning brought a new crop to the high-tide mark on the beaches. There were dozens of different kinds of shells, and as many variations to each species in terms of size and colour. There were cowries and conches and abalone, and the fragile nautilus, delicate as tissue paper. You could sometimes see a nautilus floating inshore, upright and brave like a miniature Grecian ghost-ship. We were made to follow Mama and Mike along the sand, mutinous in our floral bloomers, fossicking as Emus fossick among spent tickets on a racecourse. She had boxes made for her shells like Cedric's egg boxes, varnished each shell and labelled them, and the boxes followed us from house to house, unopened, until somewhere mercifully they were lost.

She collected ships. Everything that came into Australia came by sea, and everything bound for the port of Melbourne came past us, up the Channel. She had a pair of binoculars and a mound of notebooks made of hairy, brown paper, and we were all sworn to call her every time a ship went up the Bay. She would rush out and draw them in silhouette, accurate in detail to the last derrick and ventilator, the funnel and boot-topping lovingly coloured in crayon, and the name, country of register and destination filled in at the bottom of the page. For years, during our moves, the notebooks filled an unopened trunk, and when the trunk was finally needed they were burned.

She taught us French. Three days a week were French days, at meals and whenever she was present. She was fluent, and we were quite reasonable until we went to school, where our French was promptly ruined. She started a family magazine, and we were forced to contribute, but our contributions made her and Mike laugh so much that we were hurt, and it died a natural death.

Everything she did must have been time-filling between Pa's departures and returns, gallant time-filling too because she never let us think of it that way. The sad thing was that she never realised that she could have put on an apron, ejected the slut-domestics from the back of the house and occupied herself twice as happily by doing their job. It wasn't snobbery that stopped her but the honest belief in which she had been raised, that some were born to the kitchen and some to the drawing-room, and that either one in the wrong place spelled disaster.

When Pa came home she was luminous with a possessive, protective glow, and for the first few days we were warned off him as though he was an invalid, 'Don't bother your father!' It was unnecessary because his homecoming routine was anything but invalidish, and it never varied. He would unsheath and polish his swordstick, advance on the garden and demolish the geraniums round the outside loos until there was nothing left but short, bleeding stubble. Then he would get out his shanghai and airgun pellets, and if it was the time of year when the caddies from the Golf Club came over our fence to steal fruit he would hide behind an agapanthus bush and use their backsides for target practice. He'd burn anything burnable he could find, including any toys we'd accumulated during his absence because he said animals were better for us, and when the place was tidied to his liking we'd go fishing.

His lingering need for a son was manifested in the hours he spent teaching me to be one. The Girls were accepted as daughters and he was immensely proud of them, but there was still a faint question-mark over the afterthought. I think he longed for someone who would learn all the things he was fond of and good at, and because I was young enough to be taught he decided to ignore my sex and to give me a try. Some of the lessons were more successful than others.

I was a coward about loud, sudden noises, especially bangs. Thunder, guns and bursting balloons all sent me trembling under my bed. Appalled by this, Pa got out his twelve-bore and announced that I would learn to shoot. I tried to bolt, was caught by the hair and towed outside, with Pa roaring, 'Stop being such a bloody fool, Robin.' He dragged me to the edge of the cliff and tried to load the gun with one hand while holding me with the other.

'Damn you, stay still! It's not going to hurt you!'

'No! *Damn you!*'

'Don't bloody well swear!' He laid me flat, planted a knee in my neck, loaded the gun and fired it out to sea, over my head. As usual the noise did something indescribable to me and I almost stopped breathing; my mouth was full of grass, I was black in the face and hysterical. 'You see? he said, picking me up and dusting me off. 'It didn't hurt you. Have a shot yourself.'

He tried to teach me to cast a fly but his rod was too big, and the lessons always ended in Pa taking it from me and giving a virtuoso performance himself, while telling me how it was done. This was painless, and I enjoyed it.

His next step was to hire a pony from someone in the village. It was about 10-hands high and 12-hands wide, with long, dry hair dangling from every ample curve. Its eyes, small and piggy, glinted through a tangled forelock, and it had no saddle. With boring predictability, and horrible though it was, I fell in love with it and became an addict.

At the first lesson Pa explained that at Sandhurst men are required to ride without reins or stirrups in order to acquire perfect balance. He forgot to mention that most Sandhurst cadets are horsemen when they arrive there, and that perfecting their balance is just gilt on the gingerbread. Also that at Sandhurst they at least have saddles. When he lifted me onto the pony its corpulence was so great that my legs stuck out straight on either side, and I remember noticing that it laid its ears flat back against its neck. This warning had no significance for me at the time.

Pa demonstrated the Sandhurst method of knotting the reins on the pony's neck and folding my arms across my chest, then stood back to admire the result. The pony took off with astonishing speed for anything so fat. I automatically grabbed a handful of mane, which at least gave me contact, the rest of me being airborne, and a moment later had my first experience of being winded as the pony charged under the low-hanging branch of our Angelina plum tree. The first equine love of my life continued on through the gate, up the Lane, and onto the Sorrento road. Mortified, Pa banged me on the back until I got my wind, muttering, 'All ponies are sods, I should have known.' My first words, when I could speak, were, 'When can we do it again?' and for the first time he had a flicker of hope that I might be all right in the end.

10

Animals

PA'S RULE THAT WE HAD ANIMALS instead of toys didn't worry us; we thought toys were dull anyway, and animals seem to have been another genetic inheritance, like fishing. Pa was an animal fanatic, with as much of a taste for the exotic as for cats, dogs and horses. In India, on various occasions he had kept pet deer, cheetahs, python, bear, and on one posting three leopard cubs which had to be given to a zoo because they lived under the sofa and ringbarked visitors' ankles. Australia's animal options were more limited than India's, but he was apt to turn up with forbidden things like cassowaries from Papua, and had to be restrained regularly by Mama when any animal appeared without an obvious owner attached.

Almost all the land at our end of the Peninsular was uncleared ti-tree scrub, teeming with snakes, rabbits, wallabies and ringtail possums. There were even koalas, and sometimes one or two of them would take up residence in a tree in our garden, but apart from supplying them with bananas we left them alone. We always had a tribe of blue-tongue lizards, placid, thoughtful characters who accepted the old dolls' house on the schoolroom verandah as ideal lizard housing, especially as meals were laid on, and who sat motionless in our laps dreaming reptilian dreams..

The ringtail possums were the best of all. If you walked through the scrub it was common to find a castaway baby on the ground, pushed or fallen from a nest, and we took these home to rear them. Anyone who has reared a ringtail will know that when they are grown and have to be released, one's heartstrings are torn as though one had lost a child. They are gentle, wildly affectionate and extremely bright, and they have the advantage of not taking up much room. Sometimes we each had two or three of them, and in the daytime they lived down the front of our sweaters next to our hearts, the enormous eyes and pink noses poking out under our chins. We fed them with eye droppers on canned milk and water, and when they were old enough they went back to the scrub where we found them.

There were two who wouldn't go back, Chink and David. They grew up at the same time, fell hopelessly in love with each other, and apparently agreed that their idyll could be conducted better with us than among competitive possums in the bush. I suspect that the quality of our food had something to do with it. If we released them a mile away they reappeared the next day, sitting on the table outside the schoolroom window, demanding bread and bananas. Betty found their devotion to each other particularly touching, and in keeping with her motherhood obsession she decided that they must have babies.

'D'you think they're married?' asked Jenny, sarcastically.

Betty looked worried. She said, 'Oh goodness, I suppose not. You can't have babies unless you're married, can you?'

'Yes, I think so,' said Jenny. 'I think it's just that you're not supposed to.'

Things you shouldn't do worried Betty terribly; she thought for a moment and then said, 'Let's marry them.'

It was a beautiful wedding, attended by family and friends, including the Brights who brought some roses as a wedding cake. Betty made a long, trailing veil and fixed it to Chink's head with elastic under her chin, while David had a stiff, white collar like a choirboy, and a black coat. The altar was on a table, and both it and the aisle leading up to it were made of fresh ti-tree blossom. On another table was a wedding breakfast of all the things they liked best including the roses, and a jar of cream which was forbidden, and got there by mistake.

We put the bride and groom down at the end of the aisle and they ate their way to the altar; while someone read an abbreviated version of the marriage service they ate the altar too. They were carried triumphantly to the food table where Chink, who was already bulging, made a beeline for the one thing she wasn't supposed to have, seized the cream jar with both hands, and thrust her head in so hard that her ears went in too, and she was stuck.

'She'll suffocate!' yelled Betty.

'That cream'll kill her,' said Jenny. 'It's death to possums, too fatty.'

Pa grabbed a piece of wood, struck the jar a mighty blow, and broke it. Chink, creamy but unruffled, made a dive for the next item of food on the table, and Pa said to Mama, with great satisfaction, 'I told you so, darling. Much better than any damn toys.'

The Girls, mainly Jenny, of course, had the happy idea one morning of playing a harmless joke on their father, since he was so fond of animals. They took me aside before breakfast and said, 'Robs, we want to play a joke on Pa, and we want you to help.' Always the perfect sucker, I beamed happily, and waited to hear more. Jenny produced a half-grown possum from her jumper and handed it to me. She said, 'Hide under the table until Pa comes in and sits down. We'll say you're down on the beach. Then just put the possum's nose up his trouser leg and let it go. It'll be fun Robs, you'll see.'

It sounded like fun; it was the sort of joke I could imagine Pa playing on me, such as the times he'd stuffed huntsman spiders, which I loathed, down the front of my clothes. I said, 'It won't hurt the possum, will it?'

'Of course not, Pa loves them – it's only a joke. Get under the table, quick.'

I planted myself under the table, plump and trusting, nursing the possum and making no sound. The custom at breakfast time was for Mama to ring the big brass bell when it was ready. She did so; The Girls seated themselves, and there was a pause while they waited for Pa. When he arrived I could hear Jenny snorting, trying not to giggle.

'Blow your nose, Jenny,' said Mama. 'Ah, here he is.' Pa's legs settled almost across me. 'Where's Robin?'

'She's coming up from the beach,' said Jenny. 'Don't wait for her.'

'Are you sure? I'd better...'

I decided that it was then or never. I slipped the possum inside the cuff of Pa's outstretched trouser leg, and gave it a sharp push. He was of the generation that always wore long-johns. The British, in the heat of the Indian climate, believed that wool next to the skin was essential at all times, and instead of sliding on bare skin the possum had perfect purchase. It must have thought it was in some strange sort of hollow tree, and with the instinct of its kind it dashed upwards, settling with claws embedded in the T-junction of Pa's crutch.

What followed was like a preview of Hiroshima. Pa's legs convulsed, his knees hitting the edge of the table. The table gave a great heave, and a medley of eggs, milk, toast, crockery and cutlery arrived behind me on the floor. There was monstrous bellowing, as Pa expressed himself in terms unheard in the house before, and Mama's voice, in high register, shouting, 'Geoff! What is it? Stop *swearing* like that!' The crash of the front door as The Girls fled was hardly audible above the din.

I risked a look from under the tablecloth. It was before the days of zip fasteners and Pa, his face a deep plum colour, was trying to rip his fly open, hampered by well-tailored buttons. As the last one broke, there was a stirring within, and through the vent of his long-johns appeared a pink-nosed, whiskered face, eyes huge with enquiry.

'Good God, Geoff!' said Mama, shocked. 'What's *that* doing in *there?*'

There was a moment's silence, ominous and deadly; Pa went down on his hands an knees, and his face appeared under the tablecloth on a level with my own. I shut my eyes tight, and began to howl.

Our neighbour across the lane was a gentle, elderly man called Dr Davenport. He'd long since ceased to practice and he had a mysterious wife, never seen except as an outline sitting motionless behind a window. We were told never to ask about her, and wc were never invited inside the house although Davvy substituted for a vet when Jenny found injured animals, or birds with broken wings. His surgical skill was usually adequate, but his only cure for internal ailments was a massive dose of castor oil. For a long time Jenny revered him, watching his application of bandages and splints with her mouth hanging open and her eyes out on stalks, until the day when we all rushed over to his house with a mortally sick penguin we'd found on the beach.

Davvy inspected it closely, then said to Jenny, 'Don't worry, my dear. I'll fix him up in no time.' He went inside, and came back with a pint-sized bottle and a large spoon, forced open the poor bird's beak and administered a spoonful of castor oil. There was a moment of silence before the penguin gave a loud, un-penguin-like cry, rose vertically into the air and fell back dead.

'Well,' said Davvy. 'If that didn't save it nothing would.'

Jenny cradled the corpse in her arms and stalked off towards the gate, tears streaming down her face. 'Bloody old quack,' she said when we caught up with her.

Davvy's house and garden were both much larger than ours, with pine trees and flower beds and vegetables, and a cottage which housed his gardener-cum-handyman, Reilly, Reilly's wife and their swarm of children, all wild and shy as a bunch of stable rats. Reilly despised us as much as we feared him, and we avoided him, until the night when Mike lost Oej.

It was quite soon after she arrived from England that Mike acquired her treasure, a green ring-necked parrot whom she christened Oej, as a variation on Joe. Oej lived in a cage which hung from the verandah roof, developed an admirable verbal repertoire and the vilest personality imaginable in a bird of his size. He showed a modicum of tolerance for Mike, but even that was unpredictable and she bore many scars since, in the face of all evidence to the contrary she insisted that Oej loved her, and kept trying to prove it. She was the one who had to feed him and clean out his cage; none of the rest of us would go near the brute, because even a gesture of goodwill could end in the loss of a finger. We were scared of him, knew him to be lethal, and given half a chance we would have laced his birdseed with arsenic.

Mike spent a lot of time with Oej, sitting beside the cage and teaching him to talk; after the cats and canaries of Hove he seemed to her both miraculous and exotic. She even taught him to sing. Her favourite song was The Rose of Tralee which she sang to him patiently, over and over again. She had a record of it which she played to him endlessly, while we all found things to do which took us out of earshot. Oej was talented, one had to admit, and he learned The Rose of Tralee so well that he and Mike could sing a duet, and did so at the least excuse. The sickening tune was inescapable because even on his own Oej hammered it out in a tinny, maddening soprano.

Then came the terrible, tearaway night of storm when Oej escaped. The cage had been swinging wildly in the wind and perhaps the door blew open or perhaps someone helped it to open, but that was never proved. Mike went out to check on the safety of her beloved and there was a piercing wail of despair, 'Oej has gone! Oej has gone!'

We all rushed into the garden, howling wet and black as it was, all secretly praying that Oej had been blown to his destruction. Mike was already as far away as the Lane, and her cries of, 'Oej, Oej, Oej,' floated back to us on the wind. Then we heard a shriek of triumph, 'I've found him! Come quick!' and we rallied to her through the gate. Far above us in a lashing pine tree there was the sound of a squeaky, exultant voice singing The Rose of Tralee.

No one was brave enough to climb the tree in that gale, and the dark. Mike battered at the trunk, imploring her bird to come down and weeping uncontrollably. 'She was lovely and fair…' intoned Oej, his rhythm distorted by the motion of his branch, 'But it was not her beauty alone that won me…' We were all tiring rapidly of the scene, and wondering how to make Mike abandon him, when Reilly arrived.

Reilly was small and bow-legged as an old jockey. He was unshaven, grubby and malevolent, and always in one stage or another of drink. When he had enough money to embark on a full-blown binge he would beat up his wife, who was twice his size, and terrorise his litter of feral children. These occasions were clearly audible in The Haven, in spite of the boxthorn hedge and the Lane between us. Reilly's loathing of us, and of practically everybody else was well known, and it came as a surprise to find that apparently he liked Mike, perhaps sensing another underdog.

He staggered out of the darkness and went straight to her, took in the problem at a glance, and patted her on the shoulder. He said, 'Don't fret, Miss, we'll soon get the bugger down,' and then to the rest of us, 'Pick up some of them rocks and pine cones and chuck 'em at the bastard.' It was the obvious thing to do and it warmed us up, besides which there wasn't one of us who didn't want to score a bullseye. Mike screamed in protest, but we all pelted like mad, and finally The Rose of Tralee was punctuated by a violent squawk as Oej reeled out of the tree, flapped helplessly in the wind, and disappeared into the blackness over the edge of the cliff.

There was a pause while someone went to fetch a torch. When it came, we all peered downwards, hoping to see a crumpled heap of feathers at the cliff's base. By this time we had the consistency of wet blotting paper, but the possibility of a fatal accident overtaking Oej took our minds off it. Hearts sank as the torchlight showed Oej, shaken but indestructible, clinging to a ti-tree branch halfway down the cliff. His feathers were plastered against him like burnished metal, he was rendered flightless and voiceless by the gale, but still he survived.

Reilly must have been very drunk that night because he behaved like a knight errant for the first and only recorded time. He went to his house and fetched a rope, tied one end round his waist and the other to the fence, and went over the cliff's edge in a flurry of mud and stones. We heard a burst of wind-muffled curses, some sharp, satisfactory screeches from Oej, and we pulled Reilly up again, dripping with blood, the bird's beak sunk deep into his hand and gory evidence of other wounds on his face and neck. Mike embraced him, smothered Oej in a jumper for her own safety, and supported Reilly back to The Haven where we doctored him with iodine and bandages, and generous amounts of Pa's whisky.

When Mike left us to go back to England, distraught after her declaration of love for Mama, we managed to persuade her that Oej would be better off in the Zoo. It would be interesting to know whether the other occupants of his cage learned The Rose of Tralee, or whether they murdered him. It had to be one or the other...

11

Rob and Rose

WHEN MIKE LEFT I missed her badly, far more than The Girls did. She had been my middle ground between the two disciplinary factors in my life, parental wrath and judgemental siblings. Mama missed her too, especially when Pa was away; they had seen the funny side of the same things and sided together, as adults tend to do in the company of children. In retrospect it's no wonder that poor Mike, deprived of any alternative, fell in love with Mama.

A new governess was required as a matter of urgency, and Mama departed to Melbourne to inspect likely candidates. She had no sooner found one who seemed suitable than Grandfather Whiting died, fulfilling the promise of his fashionable figure by having a heart attack. Mama returned to The Haven for just long enough to deposit Miss Roberts and collect some clothes, then fled back to Melbourne to bury her father and deal with her mother. The unfortunate Miss Roberts was thrown in at the deep end without a family arbiter to act as referee, or to soften the inevitable blows.

The Girls were at what was known then as 'the difficult age', and Jenny could be very difficult, even though Betty always did her best to be co-operative. Betty's problems were different, but equally grave in the eyes of Miss Roberts. Rising 16 she was already well on the way to being 6 ft tall and most of her was leg, long, brown and skinny, and far more evident below her bloomers than was considered decent at the time. Topped by long, blond hair and blue eyes, her appearance was beginning to have an unsettling effect on the young males of Sorrento, and even though she was quite unconscious of this, guidance, or at least a change of dress, was clearly advisable. Jenny, not being a beauty, smouldered and fantasised about becoming one; she spent hours behind locked doors, gazing hopefully at herself in the mirror.

Miss Roberts was very different to what we'd been used to. She was grey-haired, with an ample figure which was confined in creaking whalebone. You could tell by the tone of each creak whether she was sitting down, getting up or just bending over. She wore glasses with steel frames, and the corners of her mouth turned downwards into her dewlap as though they were tied in a knot under her chin. Quickly she made it clear that she was deadly serious about learning, discipline and punctuality. She disapproved of animals, especially possums in jumpers, blue-tongue lizards and dogs in the house. She never fished, and thought it a sinful waste of time; she said one should buy fish from a fishmonger. In her opinion the world outside the schoolroom, the bush, the Bay, the whole sparkling, seductive wealth of land and water was a worthless distraction, specifically designed to lure pupils from their duties.

She was outraged by the things The Girls had not been taught, by their dress, their behaviour and their language, and she thought I was some kind of infant savage. Under House Rules we were each allowed two items of food which we hated and which we weren't forced to eat. Mine were liver and brains. Miss Roberts didn't believe that I was excused from eating them; she said they were very good for me, and that henceforth I would eat them. When I refused she crammed them into my mouth and clamped her hand over it; when I had to swallow for lack of breath the beastly stuff went down and came up again at the back of my nose, and I spewed everywhere. I got her tin-edged ruler across the back of my hand, and I have never been able to face liver or brains since then, raw or cooked.

Inevitably she blamed Mike for all our deficiencies, which prompted a fierce, if belated surge of outrage and loss in The Girls. They boiled visibly whenever she said, 'Do you mean to say Whatsername didn't teach you this or that?' or, 'I don't care what *she* let you do, you can't do it now.' If Mama had been there we might have had some hope together, but she was away far too long, through no fault of her own. In the end Jenny lost her temper; she screamed at Miss Roberts, 'Shut up, you bloody vile old bitch!' and threw a schoolbook. Miss Roberts grabbed her and boxed her ears, and I joined in, pummelling the fat thighs without effect. Jenny was locked in her room, and I got the tin-edged ruler until the back of my hand bled.

The next morning, after a night of sulks and misery, The Girls woke me early and we tiptoed down the path to the beach. We took the dinghy from its moorings, loaded the fishing gear, and pulled some mussels from the jetty for bait. The Girls rowed half-a-mile offshore, and we anchored and fished.

Miss Roberts appeared on the cliff in front of the house soon after we dropped anchor; probably she'd been in to wake us for further punishment, and found us gone. We could see her making beckoning gestures which quickly became threatening gestures, and then she ran into the house and came back with the big, brass bell which she swung mightily from side to side, making enough noise to bring the Fire Brigade from Sorrento if they'd been either awake or interested. We waved back impolitely and laughed, and went on fishing. Finally, she gave up, exhausted, and went back into the house. We fished on for a while, realised how hungry we were and rowed back , defiant and uncertain.

She said nothing when we appeared; she was grim, and rather pale, and we ate our breakfast in silence, feeling less pleased with ourselves every minute. She must have been terrified of being unable to manage us, and that when Mama came back horror stories would be told and she would lose her job. She must have longed to murder us; jobs for governesses were like hens teeth during the Depression, and even the miserable wage she earned with us meant the difference between survival with self-respect and destitution. It was not only us but the whole environment which was alien to her; her proper element was with some earnest suburban family whose children walked abroad in hats and glovers, on paved streets. That morning she made us feel small, and from then on we managed to live in a state of armed truce, if not of goodwill. The Haven's atmosphere changed, though; it was choppy, like the sea when the wind blows against the tide. She told us to call her Rob, told us in the manner of one bestowing a gift or sealing a friendship; we were utterly indifferent, so we called her Rob, and except for lessons and meals we kept out of her way.

When Mama came home there was another shock; her first announcement was that Rose, Granny Whiting, was coming to live with us. We knew very little about Rose, having only met her on formal, agonisingly dull visits to her house in town, but we were fairly certain that she was not Sorrento material.

The transplanting of Rose was a major operation for everyone except Rose herself. True to her lifelong role as Helpless Little Woman she relaxed, letting other people do the work. The house she left in South Yarra was a middle-sized, charming old place, probably the smallest she had ever lived in, yet The Haven would have fitted comfortably into its ground floor. The South Yarra house smelled of lavender and furniture polish; a maid in a black dress and white cap brought a loaded tea tray to the sitting-room at four-thirty sharp, and withdrew discreetly. When we went there we had to sit with our hands in our laps and our ankles crossed, and to speak only when we were spoken to. Cakes had to be eaten off plates with no finger licking, and we were given improving lectures about how girls behaved when Rose was young.

Rose was 73 when grandfather died, and it had never occurred to her that she might have to look after herself, nor to anyone else that she was capable of doing so. She had never dealt with anything more serious than the most minor transgressions of her household staff; she could add simple figures but couldn't subtract; she had never cooked so much as a boiled egg nor been responsible for paying a bill. She was quite unable to understand that there was now no money with which to pay bills, so in her own house she continued blissfully to run them up, and there was no alternative but for our parents to take her into their own household so that they could keep an eye on her. They probably thought at the time, her age being what it was, that the situation would be fairly temporary. They were wrong, and Rose was with them, her powers of reason becoming ever more erratic, until she was 90.

At least the sale of Rose's house produced some money, otherwise there was no way we could have expanded The Haven to cope with all of us. Money being a mystery handled only by men, Rose told Pa to use hers as he thought best and Pa, scrupulous as ever, used it to make life as comfortable as possible for Rose. He and Mama certainly never spent a penny of it directly on themselves, and even in the alterations to The Haven the bare minimum was used on the parts that would house the rest of us.

We were packed into the little place like sardines anyway. It was suggested that I might move in with The Girls, and that my present glorified cupboard might be put to some use, but The Girls made throwing-up gestures, and said they'd rather die than have me with them. Mama said she thought the easiest thing would be to build them a sleep-out at the back of the house. 'Or two sleep-outs,' she said. 'They're adolescents now, they could have friends to stay.'

The result was two basic 14-foot square shacks, built out of asbestos sheeting because it was safe in case of fire, as well as being cheap. Betty immediately took possession of one and Jenny of the other; it was the first time they'd ever had rooms of their own, and they behaved like dobermans over threatened bones. I stayed in my cupboard, Mama and Pa moved into The Girls old room where they could only dress at the same time if one of them dressed on the verandah, Rob had a tiny room next to the schoolroom, and Rose had the big, comfortable front bedroom looking over the Bay that had been our parents room. The schoolroom was only large enough for a table, chairs and bookcase, and that left the sitting-room which was also the dining-room, sewing-room and family-room, and in which it was impossible for everyone to sit down at once except round the table for meals.

The bathroom arrangements were even worse. A passage ran down the centre of the house and at the end of it, down a couple of dark, unsafe steps, was a primitive bathroom containing a scratched enamel bath, a wood-chip heater, and the only indoor lavatory. In the fly-wire back porch there was a well with an ancient hand-pump, and a kind of shower inside what looked like a meat safe; to use it someone had to man the pump while another showered, and the water was unnaturally cold. Some yards away, in the garden, were two wooden dunnies known as Uncles and Aunts. There was a geranium-covered trellis in front of each of them which gave a pretence of privacy, except when Pa had indulged in a pruning-frenzy with his sword-stick. They had no lighting, and on summer nights when the spiders were abroad it took courage to visit them. It was never suggested that Rose should use Aunts; the indoor facilities were hers, and the other grown-ups queued patiently outside.

The most disgraceful part of the house was what Mama was pleased to refer to as 'the maid's rooms'. These were two comfortless little weatherboard closets, a washbasin and a tub, tacked on behind the dark, unappetising kitchen. The whole of that area was monstrous as were its occupants, anonymous, nomad women, sometimes one and sometimes two at a time. They came and went mysteriously, leaving either with drama and recriminations or silently, bearing goods which belonged to us and not to them, though really there was little of value to steal. Their quarters were out-of-bounds to us children, and our paths seldom crossed. It seems terrible to me now that people lived with us, and that we simply ignored them, but I can't remember a single face or name. We accepted the boycott on maids as we accepted the boycott on the local children and other incomprehensible rules; we were too young to ask why and anyway the only answer would have been, 'Because we say so.'

Mama herself was nervous of our itinerants; she knew that we were bottom-of-the-market employers and that we got what we deserved. When we moved to Melbourne and had proper maids her whole attitude changed; they were respectable women and she loved them, was happily ruled by them, and cared for them in their old age. But in the Sorrento days a maid, however bad, was a thing one had to have as a last, shredded banner of social status. Without one our poverty would have been seen to be serious, while with one Mama could pretend that our lifestyle was a rather chic, idiosyncratic joke.

There was one disastrous occasion at The Haven when our parents took to the kitchen, the current incumbent having walked out in the late afternoon, at a moment's notice. Ruby and Alfred Bright had been asked to dinner that night in the belief that there would be someone to cook it, and Pa being at home Mama said to him, 'Darling, you'll have to ring the Brights and tell them not to come.' Pa said, 'Nonsense, of course they can come. I'll cook an omelette.'

'Can you cook an omelette?'

'Of course I can. Have we any eggs?'

Mama rummaged tentatively in the kitchen, then shouted, I can't find any.'

'Ring Ruby and ask her to bring some.'

'What about the children?'

'Give them a tin of something.'

We ate some cold baked beans, and gathered round the kitchen door to watch. We had never realised that either of our parents could produce food. The Brights arrived, very jocular and excited about this innovative dinner, Ruby with the eggs and Alfred, with his polished, bald head, looking like a giant extra egg.

The kitchen was a dark, smoke-soured room with high-up, inadequate windows, a table in its centre, cupboards like upright coffins, and a black, evil wood stove that drew downwards rather than upwards. One of the reasons we were banned from the kitchen was the language our cooks used about the stove. On this particular evening it had not had time to go out after the last cook left, and was smouldering quite nicely.

Pa brought in wood and stoked the stove with his usual passion for burning down and cutting up; he rammed logs home, opened all the draught doors, and soon the stove was making the noise of a tunnelled train. Mama found an encrusted frying pan and some bread and butter, and was putting knives and forks on the table. 'Let's have it in here,' she said.

The Brights seated themselves and were given drinks. They watched trustingly, knowing nothing about cooking themselves, and remarked happily what fun this would be and how clever Pa was to be able to cook omelettes. Ruby, always generous, had brought a dozen-and-a-half eggs, and said she hoped they'd be enough. Mama handed Pa a basin, and he broke all the eggs into it, saying, 'Put the frying pan on the stove to get hot, darling, and make some toast.'

Mama put the frying pan on the stove and opened the firebox to make the toast. This gave further impetus to the fire which was already roaring like a blacksmith's forge, and the hotplate under the frying pan became a curious shade of red. From the door we could see that a dark haze was forming below the ceiling, and there was a funny, hot smell like burning rubber. Pa was beating the eggs vigorously in the basin. Satisfied with their consistency, he said, 'Right! Aileen, put some butter in the frying pan!'

'How much?'

'All of it,' said Pa, without looking. 'Now! We've got to be quick about this.'

Mama threw a pound of butter into the red-hot pan, and simultaneously Pa threw in eighteen beaten eggs. There was the sound of a thousand enraged cobras, a shower of burning fat, and the kitchen blacked out as butter and eggs poured over the side of the frying pan onto the white-hot stove. Trixie had been lying under the table because, like all good Labradors, she considered it her duty to be as close as possible to the source of food. She was close enough to collect a smoking barrage of charred omelette, and she almost wiped us children out as she fled through the door, screaming. When we picked ourselves up the interior of the kitchen was invisible, the Brights staggered past us in a frantic search for fresh air, and Mama followed them choking dangerously, looking as if she had been made up for a minstrel show. She turned back at the door, and yelled, 'Geoff, are you all right?'

A voice replied thickly, out of the murk, 'Bloody hell, of course I'm all right. No wonder that damned woman left, there must be something wrong with this stove.'

12

Gardening

Once she had been laboriously settled in the best room in the house, Rose revived her favourite fantasy, nourished among the glowing flowerbeds of Hascombe, that she was an expert gardener. Her actual contribution had been to tell the Head Gardener what to plant, which he ignored, to order flowers for the house, and to take her guests for walks to admire what she stoutly declared to be the fruits of her own labour. Never one to miss a cliche she would invariably declare at some point, 'I always say, my God is in my garden!'

She was undeterred when she arrived at The Haven and saw that the barren, salty soil produced nothing except geraniums, agapanthus and pig-face. Ignoring the declared fact that neither Mama nor Pa had the slightest desire for ordered beds of annuals she announced that she would create a garden, and left us in no doubt that we were lucky to have an expert like herself to enrich our lives. Reilly was paid to lay out and dig the beds, and that being done Rose ordered seeds; she explored catalogues, made lists, and wrote away for enough seeds to establish a commercial nursery.

Because I was young and innocent I missed the fact that the rest of the family were all developing ailments or occupations which would make it quite impossible for them to become Rose's garden slaves. Betty took to obsessive school work for a mythical scholarship, Jenny discovered First Aid classes in the village, and Mama suffered from hay-fever for the first and only time in her life. Even Rose could see that Rob's whalebone casing prohibited gardening, which left me in the all-too-familiar role of burnt offering.

Rose brought up the subject of my appointment as apprentice gardener in front of my parents which wasn't fair; she knew very well that they'd support her. She said, with ominous sweetness, 'You'd love to help Granny in the garden, wouldn't you, dear? Think what fun that would be.'

'Say, "Yes thank you, Granny",' said Pa, sharply.

'Of course she will, mother,' said Mama.

I could see The Girls sniggering, and knew that I was trapped. 'Bloody slobs,' I hissed at them, under my breath. Pa heard me, and slapped my head. Rose retired to her room to dress herself appropriately for serious gardening.

She finally emerged and joined me beside the unpromising patches of grey sand which passed for garden beds. Pa followed her carrying a chair which he positioned in the shade, then lifted her into it. It was not a large chair, but her feet, shod in high heeled shoes, hung inches from the ground. On her head was a huge straw hat whose brim extended well beyond her shoulders, and she had covered her dress with a kind of cotton kimono. There was lace at her throat, and a double string of pearls with a diamond clasp, and pearl and diamond earrings hung from her ears. She wore white cotton gloves, to protect her hands and her rings from the sun. Trixie bounced up, welcoming this normally indoor person to the garden, and was shooed roughly away. Rose firmly believed that contact with an animal necessitated lengthy disinfection and purification, rather as a Brahmin is required to ritually cleanse himself after being touched by an Untouchable. To Rose all animals, and dogs in particular, were a minefield of germs.

She had her bag of seed packages in her lap and she examined them slowly, visualising their transformation to a future blaze of monster blooms, and hearing again the cries of praise and envy which had gladdened her heart at Hascombe. Finally decided which seed should have first planting she handed me the packet, and I went to work. It was clear that she'd read the instructions, how deep the seeds should be planted and how far apart, for she produced a ruler and made me measure each one, crumble the earth to a fine powder, and if she didn't approve I had to do it again. There was almost nothing she approved of. There was an infinity of torture until the sun moved into her shade and Rose, who regarded the sun as only slightly less lethal than animals, went inside.

In spite of lavish watering and daily visits of inspection, weather permitting, by the Master Gardener, not a seed came up. Rose said pointedly that it was a pity she didn't have someone competent to help her, and my elders and betters looked the other way.

Then she read somewhere that in barren soil seeds could be raised by planting them in half-eggshells filled with mountain soil, and transferring them to the garden when they were big enough to survive. Mountain soil was procured with great difficulty, and dozens of eggs. We endured a killer-cholesterol diet of egg dishes for some time and the shells, delicately halved, were stockpiled. There were endless sessions when I was forced to fill them with mountain soil, plant a seed in each one, and arrange them in wooden boxes. Rose supervised every move from her chair with the zeal of a galley-slave master. Eventually, at what seemed like the end of recorded time, the boxes were filled, watered, and put in a shady spot near the rainwater tanks.

I had watched the rest of the family go off fishing while I was being victimised, and when I roared with fury they said it was good for me. During the gardening period I ran away twice. On each occasion someone recognised me and brought me back, the second time with slight sunstroke. No one was sympathetic. Rose inspected the eggshells every day, and was finally overjoyed by the appearance of small, green shoots; there was great rejoicing, and she reminded us, at every opportunity, that she was indeed a gardener of genius. The seedlings looked quite healthy, and The Girls teased me about the day when I'd have to plant them out. I stamped and swore, saying it was someone else's turn.

Just before the planting-out was due, Rose made her morning visit to the garden to admire the seedlings and let out a screech of such violence that we all rushed out, thinking she must have trodden on a snake. There was a scene of devastation, boxes overturned, eggshells smashed, scattered and emptied; total disaster in fact, and Rose in tears. Everybody turned and glared at me and in spite of the ban on weeping, I wept. Punishment deserved I could accept, and I always owned up to things I'd done on the principle that it was worse if I didn't, but this was a crime of major proportions, and it wasn't me; my wickedness was not up to that standard, and I wouldn't have dared.

No-one doubted for a second that I'd done it. As they pointed out I'd done nothing but grizzle and whine about helping poor Granny with a little simple gardening, so if it wasn't me who else would do it? No one else had a motive; they all loved Granny's garden. They marched me inside, smacked me, and locked me in my room. In cold response to my screams of outrage they said it was bad enough to have ruined poor Granny's seedlings, but worse, far worse, to lie about it. No one would ever believe me again, and there would be no birthdays, no Christmas presents and no fishing until I confessed.

Rose bought more eggs, and The Girls had to do the planting because I was under a cloud; they were much more sympathetic by the time they'd finished. More green shoots appeared, and I was forbidden to go anywhere near the seed boxes, as if I'd have wanted to anyway. Then Mama paid a visit to Aunts one night when the inside loo was occupied, and she was in a hurry. As she passed the seedlings she heard a scuffling noise, and shone her torch towards it. Once again there was carnage and in the middle of it, frozen by the torchlight, was a large bushy tail possum holding an eggshell, its mouth full of delicious seedling.

My family made it up to me; I was given treats, and played up my martyrdom in the most poisonous way. Rose abandoned gardening without a sign of regret and took up crochet work. For years, until here eyesight became too bad, she produced a monotonous breed of rugs made of crocheted squares in liquorice allsort colours, all in the same stitch. She referred to them as My Work, in the manner of a great artist.

Rose was really a sweet-natured creature, with a normal number of brain cells which she deliberately smothered all her life, much as Chinese women once bound their feet to make them smaller. She knew that the more helpless and ineffectual she seemed the stronger and wiser her menfolk felt by comparison, and that the first and only duty of all females was to please men. She existed in a world of verbal and attitudinal cliches, and needed no deeper truths. She believed firmly that the Lower Classes, which included the poor, labourers, servants, waiters and shop assistants, and all those with coloured skins, belonged to a different species. One was nice to them within limits, but on no account encouraged them lest they should take advantage. When an accident, an illness or a tragedy happened to one of them she would say, comfortably, 'Never mind, dear, they don't feel it like we do.'

She clung to the maxims of her youth, and belaboured us with them. 'You must *never* wear red, dear. No *nice* woman ever wears red,' and 'promise me you will *never* paint your nails. Only negroes paint their nails.' And there were, of course, constant cries of 'Aileen! That child was kissing the dog! Aileen, that child should see a doctor! Aileen…!' If we had been older we might have found her funny; Mama and Pa could only have dealt with her for eighteen years by seeing the funny side of her, but we were too young and intolerant. She ruined my confidence and self-esteem by defining the obvious so neatly that it became a family saying, produced in public on many occasions by Mama herself.

Rose was gazing at the three of us, The Girls and me, during lunch one day, and she made a discovery. 'Betty's beautiful,' she said, 'and Jenny's handsome. *Poor* Robin!'

13

Visitors

SORRENTO COULD BE MISERABLE in winter. When the wind blew from the south-west and the rain squalls came hissing across the Bay the house took the weather full in its face, and we understood why other houses hid behind trees. Winter was black-and-white, like a bad, old-fashioned film. If you looked at the sea you saw dirty dishwater with white patches, the pines and sheoaks turned black and streamed in the wind, and great ink-and-wash clouds rolled in at cliff-top level, making the inside of the house limp with damp. Everyone tried to get as close as possible to the available sources of heat, and this led to trodden-on fingers and bad temper. Winters at The Haven had a dark, midnight quality about them which made you want to curl up and sleep until spring, like a hibernating bear.

Spring, when it came, had the sound and shape of dancing; the dance of sudden light on water, of buds and mating birds, and of moths and butterflies that tumbled in the sun-shafts like Edmund Dulac drawings of fairies. The dormant colours came out again, briefly fragile before they strengthened for the blaze of summer. We came out dancing too, pulling off sweaters, digging out fishing lines, letting the Jack down from the davits and checking her for leaks. Everything was a First at the beginning of spring; the First fishing, the First swim, the First picnic and the First visitors.

Visitors to Sorrento were seasonal creatures, and in winter they were encouraged to stay away. There was no room for them anyway, and they would only have made the discomfort worse, but their absence made our boredom deeper, and our edginess with each other more acute.

In summer there were plenty of visitors, people from India or England, who not only came themselves but passed their friends and relations on to us when they visited Australia. Some were good and some were bad, but the bad ones were not asked back. A lot of them were too old or too grand to be expected to deal with sleep-outs or outside dunnies and had to stay at the hotel, and some of them, like my self-appointed Godfather, Avenue Evans, didn't mind at all and came quite often.

Avenue Evans was Teddy Evans, Admiral Lord Mountevans or Evans of the Broke, but I was unable to handle the word Admiral. He was a small, toothy, enchanting man with an enormous, blond Norwegian wife called Elsa who laughed all the time, even at Teddy's frenetic womanising. He was quite incapable of keeping his hands off any woman within reach; his arms, like Dr Strangelove's, had a life of their own and Elsa, seeing some innocent female rise like a driven grouse from a savage grope, would be wreathed in smiles and say, 'Aaaawh, Teddy! Zat vos not nice!' Years later, when he was old and grey, and navigated solely by grace of a walking stick, he surprised me in a London taxi by squirming round Elsa's mountainous back and somehow getting a trembling hand to my suspenders. I was young and embarrassed and Elsa gently removed the hand, tapped it reprovingly and said, 'Aaaawh, poor Teddy! He vos alvays so fond of yunk gels!'

The big houses along the cliff filled up in the summer holidays, most of them with people who were friends of Pa's and Mama's, and children whom we knew. There were Baillieus and Myers, Frasers and Yenckens and Spowers, and they had their friends to stay too because their houses were so large. Our three Whiting cousins were often staying with one or the other of the families. They were Robert, Bertram and Ernest, and their respective ages were roughly the same as ours. They were dark, good-looking boys, and they came over to The Haven to fish and to climb Davvie's pine trees until Cedric, from the highest branch of a tall tree, dropped a pine cone on Robert's head and split it open. There was blood everywhere, and Robert shouting, 'I'm dead, I'm dead,

I know I'm dead!' until we dragged him along the road to Dr Camm's surgery and got him sewn up. It wasn't something we could hide, and there was drama; we said it was an accident, knowing Cedric's aim to be perfect after years of practice with his father's head.

Almost all of the holiday children were more The Girls age than mine, and the few who were my age perversely I loathed. I found the older ones fascinating, and almost drove my sisters insane by wanting to go everywhere with them. But even The Girls were restricted; they went on picnics and fishing trips with the holiday crowd but sometimes there were formal, lavish parties , birthday parties or dances, and that was a different matter. There was a set-piece scene that started with Jenny saying furiously to Mama, 'But *why* can't we go? It's not fair!' and Mama saying, 'Because we can't ask them back to a party like that, we can't compete.' Jenny would swear and Betty would weep, and neither of them would understand, any more than I can now, why we couldn't have asked them back to the kind of party we could afford, and which they'd probably have enjoyed.

Mama was very sensitive about being less well-off than her friends. She carried the chop-for-chop principle to the point where the chops exchanged had to be identical in size, shape and value. I can't remember any of us having a birthday party which our friends came to because we couldn't accept presents from them. Later on, when even I left school and the family fortunes were largely restored, Mama's attitude was still so deeply ingrained that when an invitation came she would look at it and say, automatically, 'You can't go to that, we can't compete.'

Pa was far more relaxed about relative wealth. He spent a lot of time visiting the holiday wives, most of whom were grass-widows during the week. They were a good-looking and sophisticated bunch; he would go to have a drink with them in the evenings and Mama, being a non-drinker, would stay at home. He always gave Mama reassurance by referring to whoever he'd been visiting with the preface 'poor'. 'I just had a drink with poor little

Hopey,' or 'poor little Peggy,' as though his visit had been an act of charity, when it was well-known that they were far from poor in any conceivable sense, and Pa himself came home wearing a look of well-being and satisfaction.

For some time, well into the 1930s, Pa was afflicted with a plague of would-be Jackeroos. It was the English custom then to despatch delinquent, profligate or otherwise undesirable young male relatives to the colonies, to be licked into shape. My father's friends and relations were delighted to find him connected to the pastoral industry since most of the young men they wished to get rid of were unsuited to anything but manual labour, and there was no stigma attached to a period as a Jackeroo. There was also the chance that if they were sent as far away as Australia they might stay there or even, in the fullness of time, make good.

The average Jackeroo-to-be, however nasty his record had been at Home, arrived in Australia with the fixed belief that he was doing Australia a favour by setting foot on it. He seldom came with adequate funds so he borrowed, and often failed to repay. He found the locals and their customs ludicrous, and said so. He thought the Australian accent barbaric, and was infuriated by the fact that many Australians either rudely mimicked his own accent or failed to understand a word he said. He invariably claimed to be a superior horseman.

Any illusions Pa may have had about the British rejects were dispelled by the first few samples. After that he kept them well away from Sorrento, had them met at the boat and despatched to one or other of the Queensland properties without delay, then waited resignedly for nature to take its course. Queensland stockmen were not fond of Pommie youth, especially the up-market kind who tended to patronise, and they cherished certain rogue horses whose sole function was the initiation of Jackeroos. Pa tried hard to stop this and spoke sternly to the managers about it, but as the managers had to endure the Jackeroos in their houses and at their tables they were inclined to turn a blind eye. Very few of the young imports lasted a full month before they were more or less seriously damaged and discouraged, and Pa would again be faced with medical costs, and the embarrassment of informing their family. He gave up accepting Jackeroos, well before the war arrived and substituted military service for remittance.

The highlight visit of the Sorrento years was when Aunt Sheila came to Australia, bringing Fanny and her own daughter, Aileen, with her. Fanny was still magnificent, but her mind had started to flicker and fade like a faulty striplight, one moment blinding, the next uncertain. She still dressed in the old manner, in long, dark dresses with high collars, rather like Queen Mary, and it suited her. Sheila, who was even taller than Fanny, with the same tip-tilted, smiling mouth, adored her mother. She acted as a buffer when Fanny's wit and intelligence turned to aggression and confusion, and a pathetic search for help in a world growing increasingly remote. No one but Sheila could have handled the changeling that her mother had become, but at the same time they, and Aileen, somehow made everything we did more vivid and happy than it had ever been before.

They rented a small house in Melbourne because it was to be a long visit, and we made room for them at weekends by some of us, not Rose of course, sleeping on the floor. Rose was the only person who wasn't enthusiastic about them; she was outraged by Fanny, having never met a woman like her, and hopelessly jealous. It was plain that we all adored Fanny, and that as grandmothers go Rose came a distant second. Later on, when Fanny died in England, Rose said with satisfaction, 'Now you'll have to fall back on me!' and Jenny, in tears, glared at the diminutive figure and said, 'If we do fall back on you I hope we bloody well squash you.'

Fanny flattered me by demanding my presence, but I think it was because I was the only one who could be trusted not to blink an eyelid, no matter how curious her behaviour became. She and I were left alone one day when all the others went to Sorrento in the car to shop. Fanny said, 'Let's go down to the beach,' so we wandered down the cliff path, and along the jetty.

There was a yacht belonging to some friends moored about

forty yards off the end of the jetty, in deep water; it lived there during the summer, and one got out to it and back in the dinghy. I was fully dressed, and I knew that there was a strict rule about not swimming beyond the end of the jetty, partly because of the sharks, but also because of a notorious current which swept along the shoreline down to the mouth of the Bay at ebb tide. Even grown-ups were afraid of it. When Fanny said, 'Robin, I bet you can't jump in and swim to that yacht,' it never occurred to me that she knew nothing of sharks or the current, nor that she was unqualified to judge what a small child could or couldn't do. All the same I did say, 'I'm not allowed to.'

'Not allowed to? Go on, now. I'm daring you to.'

'I've got my clothes on.'

'You're frightened to. Robin, there's one thing you've got to learn, never be frightened of anything. Now, get in with you.'

I jumped in and started swimming; I knew I swam all right for my age, and it wasn't all that far. My clothes made me a bit heavy but Fanny was giving loud shouts of approval, and I paddled on happily until I realised that the yacht, far from getting closer, was disappearing in the direction of Sorrento, and I was being swept round the end of the Langford's pier.

It was an unforgettable feeling, something between being bolted with by a horse and being a cork in a storm drain; at the time I was travelling so fast, and my mouth was so full of water that I was surprised rather than scared. By some miracle there was a dinghy anchored in my path, and a man fishing; he grabbed me as I went past, hauled me out, emptied the water from me and rowed me back. Fanny was laughing; she patted me on the back and said, 'I told you you could do it, Robin. Just remember now, I was right. You must never be afraid.'

The man who'd rescued me didn't seem amused and he waited until the family came home, then told them what had happened. Everyone was very gentle with Fanny who was still triumphant, but I was never left alone with her again. She went on giving me advice though, seeing me as unworked clay to be developed in the right mould. We were at lunch one day when she said emphatically, and out of the blue, 'Robin! You must never tell a lie!' There was instant silence and attention, and coming from Fanny who, though no liar, was the greatest decorator of the truth to come out of Ireland, it was a show stopper. I looked at her with rapt attention, and Sheila gave Mama a proud, possessive glance, delighted at this proof that her mother was still a potent moral force.

'No, you must never tell a lie,' said Fanny, thoughtfully. 'It's too damned hard to remember what you've said later on.'

She came and went from us on that visit like the sun suddenly finding a gap in the clouds, or at other times like a bolt of lightning, doing things she'd never have dreamed of doing when her mind was whole. She loved fishing, and Sheila craved days in the boat as a thirsty man craves water, so we had more fishing trips than ever before. In the boat Fanny was a different person, and behaved perfectly.

We took them to the Back Beach as often as we could, the summer they were with us. The ocean coastline behind Portsea runs clear from Point Nepean to Cape Shank at the mouth of Westernport Bay, a pure, unbroken miracle of sea and sand with never a mark on it, in those days, except for the footprints of the sea and the gulls. These days that coast is a thinly-disguised suburb, and to go there is like seeing the tiger you once saw in the jungle, proud and free, caged in a zoo. There were no roads between Portsea and the Back Beach then, only sand-tracks with deep, hidden drifts which bogged a car to the axles, and the best way to get there was to hire a horse and cart. When you hit deep sand the horse pulled, and everyone got out to push.

Long before you reached the Back Beach you could tell that the ocean was coming to meet you. The ti-tree scrub stopped standing upright and began to lie flat against the sand as a tangled ground-cover, forced prone by the south-westerlies. At about the same time as you noticed the submissive attitude of the trees you started to feel a sound in your head, much like the sound when you hold a shell to your ear. It grew in you with every yard you travelled, majestic as thunder, constant as breathing, compelling as God, meeting you full force as you topped the last high dune in a flurry of wind and sand, proving that the greatest voice of all in this world is the voice of the sea. The beach stretched away forever with its high-tide collar of kelp, and towards Point Nepean there rose massive, lonely, time-eroded pinnacles of rock, survivors of an older coastline, still standing breast-to-sea like centurions left to face an enemy's charge.

At high tide, on days of storm, the breakers hurled themselves in against the rocks like savages, the spray flew up higher than the tops of the dunes, the wind tore the breath from you and the sea-roar broke you into small pieces. On benign, sunny days when the tide was out, you could see the whole smiling length of the beach, its border of reef exposed and the waves rolling shoreward, docile and ordered as the fringe of a white silk shawl, all the blue and white and green and gold melting into a mist of distance. On those days we jumped from the top of the dunes and skidded down through the sand to the beach, hunted under stones, dived and speared fish in the rock pools of the reef and surfed, lying flat on heavy wooden surfboards. There were sandy breaks in the reef where you could paddle out on your board to catch the waves as they came in, and we knew which gaps were safe, and which to avoid.

There was a certain amount of rivalry between Mama and Aunt Sheila in the matter of surfing. Mama felt that as an Australian she should be the expert but Sheila, who was not a naturally agile person, and came from the non-aquatic climate of Ireland into the bargain, took to it like an over-sized dolphin. She was a head taller than Mama, and thanks to the Irish passion for consuming food, especially bread and cakes, at all opportunities between and during meals, she weighed a lot. Mama, on the other hand, was stout rather than fat, but quite amazingly solid. She had the solidity of granite rather than flesh, and although Pa often teased her she was proud of it.

Surfing may have been primitive compared to the art-form it has become, but it was far from risk-free. The boards were made from solid wood, not fibreglass; it took all an adult's strength to lift one, and if one lost one's board in a wave and it fell on someone else the damage could be severe.

Apart from the boards the Back Beach itself was tricky; there were no flags and no life savers to tell you where it was safe to go. The area we favoured was to claim the life of a Prime Minister, Harold Holt, who unaccountably challenged it in adverse conditions. We had enormous respect for the state of the weather, tide and undertow, and there were not too many days when all three behaved properly.

It was, however, on just such a blithe, long-promised day that Mama proved her supremacy in the surf. The waves were high, strong and uncomplicated, the tide was right, and even I was untroubled by the undertow. Mama and Sheila struggled out with their boards, discreetly bathing-suited in the fashion of the day to conceal all the curves and hollows of their sex. The gap in the rocks where they were surfing was not very wide, but the waves rolled through it evenly; they paddled their boards out again and again, and from the beach one could sense there was a contest.

Everyone knows about the seventh wave. It is higher, stronger and more difficult than the six before it, and sometimes it behaves very strangely indeed. Mama and Sheila were too fired up to bother about counting, and they launched themselves on what was obviously a potential dumper. They hovered in clear view on its crest clutching the prows of their boards, then there was a smother of foam, both boards hurtled skywards, and apart from an occasional arm or leg we saw neither surfer until they were washed up on the sand.

Mama got up straight away, and she was laughing. Sheila heaved about in the shallows, clearly distressed, and everyone, including Mama, rushed to her side. When we lifted her up and examined her we were horrified. One eye was purple and closing rapidly, her nose was bleeding, she was winded and various bits of her were turning black. Mama was distraught. She cried, 'Sheila,

Sheila, did my board hit you?' and Sheila, mopping, gasping and spitting, fixed Mama with her one open eye.

'Board be damned!' she said. 'It was you I ran into, Aileen, I could see your bathers when I hit you. And I hope to God I never do it again.'

We examined Mama closely, but she didn't have a mark on her.

14

Camels

SHEILA TOOK her mother and daughter Home at the end of the summer, and we never saw Fanny again. Our parents knew it would be the last time, and we sensed it; when they left the winter seemed to settle round us, even though the sun was still warm. Perhaps there was more to the premature threat of winter than their leaving; the big changes in life have a way of warning you, an unease, a prickling of the nerve-ends of the mind, long before the event itself happens. The Haven was getting ready to let us go, to spill us out like fledglings from a nest. It had cared for us for five years and it was tired of us. All the same it allowed us one more treasure before we left, because that winter was the winter of the camels, and Abdul Mohammed.

He had been a fixture on the Sorrento beach in summer for far longer than we had been at The Haven, materialising with his horses and camels at the beginning of the summer holidays, turbaned, bearded and smiling, with only enough English to conduct the business of selling rides. He lived in a small tent on a piece of wasteland with the animals grazing round him, bothering no one, and when the summer ended he vanished overnight. He was part of the seasonal scenery, and nobody greeted him or said goodbye, or noticed when he began to move like an old man, and his beard turned white.

Pa used to go and talk to him when he was at home in rapid, fluent Urdu. The old man regarded this as miraculous, having been starved of his own language for years, and he revered Pa as a minor God. Pa came home after one of their get-togethers and addressed Mama in the honeyed tones which always meant that he had done something which might not meet with approval.

He said, 'Darling, I've just been talking to old Abdul Mohammed down on the beach.'

'Oh, the old Afghan,' said Mama. 'Yes, he's a nice old thing, if only he didn't smell so frightful.'

'I knew you'd like him. Doesn't he remind you of those old camel-drivers in Peshawar? You used to say the camels were beautiful too, didn't you?'

'Did I?' said Mama. She looked at him suspiciously. 'Why?'

'Well, he's getting very old, Abdul Mohammed. I hadn't really noticed until today. He said it's a bit much for him, taking the camels up North for the winter. Actually, he thought he might winter down here to be ready for next summer, and it crossed my mind that there's that loft over the stables. He could live there and cook all his own meals, and the camels and horses'd keep the grass down while I'm in Queensland. Lovely things, camels, and the children could learn to ride them.'

'*YES!* 'we said, as one.

'Oh dear,' said Mama. 'Oh Geoff, how could you!'

When they arrived, swaying down the Lane in single file like a Biblical painting, Abdul Mohammed burbling reassurance to the camels in their own language, and he had installed himself with immaculate discretion in the loft, even Mama was won over. Abdul Mohammed chopped the wood, tended the garden, and bowed low whenever Mama appeared; more importantly he taught us the magic of camels. The new arrivals folded themselves down into our buffalo grass with many benign grunts and rumbling approval. They surveyed the garden through huge, liquid eyes, shadowed by Odalisque lashes, and they touched our arms and hands with lips of shorn velvet to show their gratitude. Only their breath was vile, and one learned to avoid an open mouth as one avoids the yawn of a garlic addict.

We were never conscious of the language barrier with Abdul Mohammed. He taught us to ride the camels, and because there were three of them I was allowed to ride too. He would mount one of his horses and we would pad up the road to Sorrento in line astern, turn right into the main street and along it looking down our noses, idiot-proud in our camel-given glory. We rode past the cottages with their garden gnomes, aloof as the camels themselves when people giggled and pointed at us. Jenny knew for certain that she was an Arabian Princess and Betty looked like a Valkyrie, and I was in bliss beyond thought.

When we reached the Sorrento ocean beach Abdul Mohammed would crack his stockwhip, and shout high-pitched camel commands. The camels hardly needed to be told; they loved every minute of it, and they would take off with us to the far end of the beach, their heads high and their stride so long and smooth that at the peak of each one you left the saddle and floated in mid-air, connected to the camel only by your grip on the saddle horn. Because my legs were so short Abdul Mohammed always tied me to the saddle but The Girls rode free; dark, Arabic Jenny and Betty with a yard of golden hair streaming, Abdul Mohammed on his horse singing in soprano Urdu and all of us, the camels too, drunk with joy.

When the summer came Abdul Mohammed left us. One morning he and the camels and the horses had gone, and the loft was as though he had never been there. The next time we went to the Village we saw that the camels were back on the beach, and his tent on its usual piece of wasteland. He was behaving as a bird does, or an animal, in obedience to the seasons, and he hadn't the words to explain. It was soon after he left us that our Sorrento world started to fall apart.

It happened when Mama and Pa were both away; Rose was working placidly on yet another crocheted rug, and Rob was in charge. We had shaken down with her by then, drawn and accepted the invisible boundaries that made coexistence possible. She made it her business to be helpful to Mama, and certainly she taught us more than Mike could have done, if Mike had stayed. Unfortunately, when Mama was away, Rob felt it her duty to supervise our leisure and even, at times, to join in.

Cedric had been given a new bicycle for his birthday. He brought it straight over to show us; he was wildly excited, and fishing was obviously going to take second place for a while. We inspected it with awe. It had gears, and thin, delicate tyres, and the paintwork was so beautiful it dazzled. He took it up to the high point of the garden near the Langford's fence and whizzed down past us with the speed of light. Betty had a turn, and then Jenny, and Rob, who had been shouting strange things like 'Bravo!' and 'Hurrah!' said, 'Come on, Ceddie, give me a turn.'

He looked at her in disbelief, for Rob must have weighed fourteen stone as well as being grey-haired, and said, 'YercarnridabikecanyerRob?'

'Of course I can, Ceddie, I used to ride one to school. Don't be mean.'

'Yertoobig.'

'Don't be such a rude boy!' Rob turned an ugly shade of pink. 'Its a big bike. You must learn to share, Cedric. Give it to me!'

We watched her wheel it up to the top of the slope, Cedric turning white with anxiety for his bicycle, and the rest of us speechless with wonder. She heaved herself into the saddle, grasped the handlebars and pushed off, weaving a snakelike course down the hill. As she passed Cedric she was going at high speed, and his nerve broke. He yelled, 'The wheel's buckling!' and flung himself in front of the bike.

Rob looped the loop in slow motion, and the bicycle somersaulted away from her. She lay so still that we all knew, deep and inescapable, that this was something beyond our fixing. Jenny fetched a rug, covered her, and stayed with her while Betty and Cedric telephoned the Brights who telephoned the doctor, and came straight round in their car. When they saw Rob they went white too.

The doctor arrived and they got her into the back of his car, still unconscious. There were no ambulances in Sorrento then. The Brights got in touch with Mama in Melbourne, and stayed with us until she came home. None of us talked much.

Rob had a fractured skull, and we never saw her again; no one told us whether or not she had died and we were afraid to ask, but we all believed that we had killed her. It was a long time before Mama happened to say that she'd heard from Rob, and that she was well again, and by that time The Girls and Cedric had suffered agonies of guilt. Pa was summoned from Queensland straight after it happened, and he and Mama talked interminably behind closed doors while we snapped at each other in the schoolroom, and Rose shut herself in her bedroom. Cedric, for once, was in solitary confinement at home, with the wreckage of the bicycle.

When our parents finally talked to us they had the unmistakable air of people with momentous news. We were to move to Melbourne, they said, and The Haven would be sold. The Girls would go to boarding-school until we could rent a house in town, after which they would be daygirls. We wouldn't buy a house because, after all, one of these days we'd probably go Home to England. In a year or so Robin would go to school too, but in the meantime she would have a governess. Yes, we would take Trixie. No, not the possums. No, not the lizards, no, not the Jack, it would be sold. There would be lots of things for us to do in town, and anyway The Girls would be far too busy at school to think about dinghies or possums.

Sorrento would have had to end sometime anyway. It's an accepted fact that Eden and innocence were finite, but I wonder whether Adam and Eve realised when they left there, any more than we did leaving The Haven, what they were going to and what they were leaving behind. The chances are that they were very like us, witless children idealising the future, and assuring each other that they'd outgrown the old place anyway.

We went round everything to say goodbye without really believing it was finished. Somehow we thought it would all stay with us, the Bay in the early morning, devilish or diamond-bright, the texture of wet sand on bare feet, the breath and heartbeat of water and pines. We walked our old paths along the cliff, bordered with ti-tree and festooned with periwinkles where the butterflies danced through filtered bars of sunlight, and we were bemused by the myth that the grass could be greener in a different place.

The Girls truly believed it would be greener; they were silly with excitement because the curtain was about to go up on the real world. Betty could see her future brood of angelic, golden-haired children more clearly defined; the image of their father was still unimportant, but she knew she would recognise him instantly when she found him. She declared that she would be an artist between school and motherhood. Jenny smouldered sexily, one moment Mata Hari and the next Florence Nightingale. Mama chose to ignore Mata Hari but was enthusiastic about Florence Nightingale. She said she had always wanted to be a nurse herself.

Personally I was not so sure about the grass being greener in other places. I went down to my cave in the cliff to sulk, suspecting that the glittering prizes The Girls looked forward to might not be mine. I couldn't conceive of any other world than The Haven, and I wanted to stay.

The Girls wandered about together arm in arm, singing their dreamtimes of the future in their separate minds, and their favourite song of that moment in exultant duet. It was Massenet's *Elegie*, learnt during our three-days-French-a-week, sad and haunting even when they sang it with joy, and for them, poor Girls, prophetic.

Je ne vois plus le ciel bleu,
Je n'entend plus
Les chants joyeux des oiseaux…

PART TWO

15

Melbourne

IT WAS AUTUMN when we drove off up the Lane for the last time, a scuddy, showery day with a pale sea. The fruit trees and the figtree were bare of leaves and house had closed, uncurtained windows; it wore the expressionless look of a corpse carefully laid out by an undertaker. A van left earlier with all our things, the last item to go being the chair Rose had sat on throughout, ignoring the chaos. Deprived of the chair she allowed herself to be led to the car and got into the front seat beside Mama. Trixie and I got into the back, and the engine drowned out the last sound of sea and pines. Mama kept telling me what fun it would be in town until both Trixie and I fell asleep.

Our first rented house was in Grange Road on the corner close to Toorak village. It had roses in the garden, and red-brick paths with daisies growing between the bricks, and after The Haven it seemed enormous, but like all houses that don't own you it had no soul. It did, however, have a lot of surprises.

There was a large van outside when we arrived, but not the one which had taken the things from Sorrento. Inside the house there were strange chairs and tables and large, mysterious chests against the walls. Mama immediately started telling the men from the van where to put things, Rose earmarked an armchair by the fireplace and sat in it, and I was too astonished even to ask questions. Everything was utterly different to The Haven, highly polished and rich-looking, and when the chests were unpacked amazing things came out of them, pictures and silver and china that I'd never seen before.

The Girls had been boarding at Dothegirls's Hall since the

beginning of the school year, waiting for us to move to town, and they came home for our first weekend. I'd never seen them in their school uniforms and they looked alien; they talked of matters beyond my understanding, and I was in awe of them. To my surprise they went round the house picking up the silver and the ornaments and patting the furniture as though they were old friends. When I was brave enough I asked Jenny where it had all come from, and she said, 'Don't be an idiot, it's been in store ever since we came from India. There wasn't room for it at Sorrento. You're too young to remember.' I asked where the Sorrento things were, if they were in store, and Mama said, 'They've been sold, most of them weren't worth keeping.' It was disturbing, as though besides moving we'd become different people, people my parents and sisters knew and were comfortable with, but I was a stranger.

Everything was different, especially the sounds and smells of Town. The sounds were exciting at first, keeping you awake at night; the whine of trams pulling themselves uphill, the clop of milk-cart horses in the morning, the swish of tyres on wet roads and the distant rumble of trains, but you got used to them, and then you found yourself listening for the old, lost sounds. The smells were more complex, and satisfying after a place that smelled overwhelmingly of sea. Autumn, when we moved, was a mixture of wood-smoke and leaf-mould, mown grass, wet pavements and dog-turds, all of which are very pungent when you are small and close to the ground. The house smelled different too; instead of salt and sea it was steeped in toast and Sunday roast and furniture polish.

There were days when Mama took me into the City with her to go shopping, always hatted and gloved and dressed as she'd never been at Sorrento. There were cable trams in Bourke Street with clanging bells, and brewers' drays pulled by huge, arch-necked horses, and paper-boys with voices like Cedric's who yelled, 'Pipur*Pipurr*! Readallaboutit!' and more people than there had been shells on the morning beach. I had a recurring foetal dream in which I was curled up small on the edge of the pavement, menaced by a forest of moving legs which always missed me, as though I wasn't there at all.

The Girls became daygirls after their first term at Dothegirls Hall and were at home most of the time, but they had grown up so much that I was invisible to them unless I did something wrong. I was considered too young for school, and I was farmed out to share a governess with the children of some friends of Mama's and Pa's. They were very clever children who had been intellectually stimulated since birth by parents who had advanced ideas about child-raising; I was light years behind them educationally, and our personalities clashed like Salvation Army cymbals. When they wanted to read a dictionary I wanted to climb a tree, and when I did climb a tree they ran to tell their mother, and there were long, reasoned lectures about improving my mind.

We moved to another house, in South Yarra, a two-storey house with a bigger garden, and I shared a governess with two other girls who lived across the road. They had brilliant red hair and freckles, and they were terribly clever too; they tied me to trees and beat me with ropes, and I dreaded going there in the mornings.

We moved back to Toorak, to Kooyong Road, and this was an improvement. The house was dark but there were good climbing trees in the garden, and a messy patch at the back where I was allowed to keep two pet ducks. More importantly, from my point of view, I started school. The governess-sharers were all starting school too, so there was no alternative. I was pleased about it because, naively, I thought there would be safety in numbers.

The Girls were responding to their new life by expanding like the Japanese paper flowers you could buy then. These were nondescript pieces of paper until you dropped them into a glass of water when they unfolded themselves, changed colour, and became lilies or chrysanthemums or roses. The Girls were doing the same thing gradually, but you could notice it happening. Betty was almost ready to do her School Leaving exams which no one expected her to pass, and no one cared. It was clearly her fate to charm and decorate, and the odds against her having to earn her living as a lone spinster were very long. Art school would be a perfect way for her to fill in her time before marriage, though Mama made wistful references to Finishing Schools, and the benefits of speaking perfect French. Betty sailed gently, beautifully above it all, oblivious of the effect she had on people, and fitted in with whatever anyone else wanted.

Jenny, having decided to be a nurse, was obsessed with becoming one as soon as possible. She wasn't particularly brilliant at school so she worked twice as hard as the rest of her age group. Her friendships were spasmodic and fiery, while Betty's were placid and long-lasting; increasingly, in every way, they ran on different tracks. When Betty was lying in the sun, chatting with a couple of her friends, Jenny was swotting in her room or else stretched on her bed in some fierce, personal fantasy while the gramophone played one of the sexier songs of the day. Mama adored Betty, but she was awed and intoxicated by Jenny. She could appreciate Betty and understand her, and she absorbed the nice things said about her through the very pores of her skin, but Jenny was special to Mama, her own frustrated dreams made flesh. It was impossible, in Mama's eyes, for Jenny to do wrong, and disastrously she built Jenny into a kind of saint, with the gift of immortality attached.

We moved to St Georges Road, close enough to school for me to ride there on a bicycle. The first term was distilled culture-shock, and my teachers probably thought me retarded because I was permanently open-mouthed. I had never seen so many children together at one time, all flocking to bells and roll-calls, and all sticking their hands in the air every time they were asked a question or wanted to pee. I wasn't required to learn much that term, but I did have my first lesson in anti-Semitism, Australian-style, and was frightened by it.

It happened just before Easter. There were about twenty small girls in my class and we were having Divinity which occurred with great regularity, and which concerned God and Jesus about whom I knew next to nothing. There was a girl called Dorothy in the class.

She was round and pretty, with enormous dark eyes and long, thick plaits, and it happened that she lived next door to us in St Georges Road, although I'd never spoken to her there. Our parents didn't know each other, but I'd heard Mama say that she was the granddaughter of somcone who was very famous.

The Divinity mistress was a large lady, fitting into her clothes like an over-upholstered armchair. She spoke with exaggerated care, overdoing her 'h's' and whistling through her teeth when she said 's'. She was carrying on about Easter, how it was both a sad time because He died for us and a happy time because He rose again, and suddenly she stopped and stared directly at Betty Bennett.

'But not for Dorothy, of course,' she said. 'Dorothy can't be happy because our Lord Jesus Christ rose from the dead.' We all turned to look at Dorothy, who went red.

'Who can tell me why?' asked the Divinity mistress, smiling brightly, 'Who can tell me why Betty can't feel happy about our Lord rising from the dead?'

There was silence while Dorothy's dark head sank almost to the desk top. 'Would you like to leave the room, Dorothy? No? Well, someone tell me. You've all been in my class long enough to know the answer. Thank you, Margaret. Stand up and let us all hear.'

A child at the back of the room had her hand up. She rose to her feet and said smugly, 'Please Miss, because Dorothy's one of the Christ killers.'

'That's right, dear. Dorothy's a Jew, and it was the Jews who killed our Lord Jesus Christ. And at Easter we rejoice because of His resurrection, but of course the Jews don't because that's when they killed Him Dorothy, if you're going to cry like that you'd better go to the cloakroom. Wash your face before you come back, dear, and blow your nose. Now girls…'

It worried me even though I couldn't understand it, and I told Mama about it when I got home. She looked uncomfortable and said, 'That's dreadful, but a lot of people are a bit funny about Jews, darling. You'll understand when you're older.' I remembered

Jenny saying that our Cohn relations were Jewish, and I said, 'But the Cohns are Jewish, aren't they, and Granny Whiting? Does that make us Jewish too? Are we Christ killers?' Mama went pink and said, 'It's not the same thing at all! You're only quarter Jewish, and your father's family... don't talk nonsense!'

'Well, can Dorothy come over and play with me sometimes? She's only just next door.'

'I don't think so, darling, we don't really know her parents, and I'm sure she has her own friends.'

Life was full of mysterious taboos, maintained but unexplained by Mama. I was virtually an only child by then, because The Girls were so much older, and like all children I formed brief but passionate friendships at school. I couldn't understand why some of my friends were allowed to come to play with me at home while others were rejected. Sometimes I'd appeal to Pa and he'd say, 'Do as your mother tells you,' and she'd say, 'Don't bother your father. There are plenty of other girls you can play with, but always ask me first.'

Mama worried about social contamination and her friends all worried about it too, clinging to the cooling body of a dead class system, and pretending that it was alive and well. It wasn't snobbery based on money or titles, but on style and accents and manners, on the use of certain words and phrases and the avoidance of others that were 'common', and it enabled Mama and her like to recognise each other instantly. If we had grown up in England, we were given to understand, the nuances of such things would have come to us naturally, but in Australia one couldn't be too careful. And yet Mama could be gentle and kind and loving to the very poor, to the waifs and strays, the freakish and rejected. It was the over-genteel and the pretentious who appalled her.

The Girls and I were scarcely on speaking terms by then, the age gap between an eight year-old and an eighteen year-old or a fifteen year-old being far greater than any other age gap in the average life-span, so we didn't discuss the family's social hang-ups. They must have been expected to conform, just as I was, and Betty would have done so willingly, without a second thought. She was leaving school by then, having failed her Leaving Exams, and was gliding onwards to life's next stage, swanlike and serene. She drove Mama's friends with less exemplary daughters into paroxysms of envy because she seemed indifferent to all the things their daughters craved, boyfriends, clothes and jewellery. Because of her beauty she should have loved such things, and they found it unnatural.

Most of Betty's friends were like her, tall, strong and good-looking. The main difference between them and Betty was that they, her inferiors in terms of looks, were all acutely conscious of what they wore whereas Betty was a sartorial mess. Her skirts hung down behind and rose above her knees in front, her hair was never set and she couldn't be bothered with make-up. The result, in those days of lacquered lips, crimped hair and corseted waists was sensationally different. She had full, sensual lips, her eyes were somehow sad, and the general effect was of a lost, yearning waif from another world crying out for rescue. She roused unrequited passion among the young men of her group who never realised that she hardly noticed them. She was waiting for the one person for whom she knew she was destined, the future father of her twenty children.

Jenny, on the other hand, was drawn irresistibly to make-up, clothes, and the full Hollywood-sophisticate image of the thirties. She was plump, like Mama, and hated it, seeing herself ideally as a whippet-thin, a mysterious, svelte creature designed for champagne and dim-lit night-clubs and seduction. This vision was hard to maintain in front of a mirror, but she kept on looking, in hope. It would be even harder during her nursing training, dressed in a shapeless uniform, lisle stockings and clumpy shoes, but she was determined to be a nurse, and bullied her private self-image into second place.

Even at fifteen Jenny was intrigued by sex. She must have heard about it at school, since it was never mentioned in our household, and the nearest Mama could bring herself to sex instruction was to say, in a voice of strangled distaste, 'You must never let a man touch you Down There!' This led me to believe for years that there was something filthy and shameful about a woman's body Down There, and to regard my own Down There with the utmost distrust. Betty simply dismissed the whole matter, vaguely assuming that all her conceptions would be immaculate, and anyway she had no intention of letting anyone touch her until the pre-ordained father of her children slipped the ring on her finger. Jenny, recognising the uselessness of asking Mama, pursued her own enquiries elsewhere, generously bringing home information and passing it on to Betty, who thought she was disgusting. Occasionally I'd overhear an instruction session from my own room.

Jenny: '...and then the man gets on top and the girl opens her legs and...'

Betty: 'Shut up! Shut up! I don't believe you! I don't want to know!'

Jenny: You'll have to know one day.'

Betty: 'No I won't! You're filthy, you're making it up.'

Listening on the other side of the bedroom wall I thought that she was making it up too; it sounded like some kind of silly game, but I couldn't work out why Betty thought it was filthy.

We were shaped, as children, by the attitudes of our mother's generation, and these stayed in some hidden corner of our minds, even after we had grown up and found them to be false. Sex was a forbidden subject, a mystery hinted at only in the most negative way. The legacy of Mama's attitude to sex gave me, and almost certainly my sisters as well, a disastrous tendency to link sex with guilt. Jenny rebelled against the guilt-factor from the beginning, instinctively knowing it was wrong.

The Girls and I weren't unique; Mama's views were widely held at the time, and most of our friends had been brought up on the same principles. The War would liberate our generation to a large extent; we thought we were truly emancipated after the war, and our parents were scandalised. Then came the Pill, and the revelation that sex needn't result in pregnancy and disgrace. On top of that the massive sexual revolution which followed in the 1960s made our imagined freedom of the war and post-war years seem pathetically restrictive.

Mama remained blind to every one of the changes in sexual standards and behaviour that took place during her lifetime. For her they simply didn't exist, and she would have been incapable of believing that her favourite daughter was to become, all too briefly, one of their pioneers.

16

Horses and snakes

EVEN BEFORE WE MOVED to St. Georges Rd. I'd done what innumerable boring little girls do, and become half horse. The fat pony at Sorrento had lingered in my mind as a prime object of desire, and I nagged about it. Pa found it difficult to teach me to shoot and fish in town, so when Mama heard about a riding school run by a woman in St Kilda he approved, and Mama took me off to inspect it. There were stables in the inner suburbs then and Albert Park had a riding track round the Lake, doubling back along Queen's Road beside the golf course. There was a tan track too, running round three sides of the Botanical Gardens, and considered much more fashionable than Albert Park.

Hena Kemp's stables were tucked away at the end of a cobbled lane, and when we finally found them we were greeted by a small, bow-legged woman of uncertain age. She had the battered remains of good looks, periwinkle-blue eyes and her hair, petrified by peroxide, stuck outwards stiffly, like dried grass. She addressed Mama in tones of terrifying refinement, only marred by a complete absence of H's. We were shown the hacks in their boxes, elderly, obese animals who seemed wise, benign and pampered. She took a pony into the yard, saddled it and put me on its back to walk it round saying, loud enough for me to hear, 'She sits right. She'll make a rider when I've 'ad 'er for a while, don't you worry.' I almost fainted with pride.

I spent more of my childhood with Kempie than at home, saw her boozed, eccentric, foul-tempered and foul-mouthed, loved her and feared her. I graduated from pupil to apprentice, happily arriving at her stable every holiday morning to do the early dirty work in return for unlimited riding.

All the time we lived in St Georges Road I was drearily, compulsively horsey which must have been very boring for my family, except that it kept me out of the way most of the time, when I wasn't at school. Our house had a tennis court, and The Girls had taken to tennis parties. Mixed doubles were a feature of the weekends, the mixture being drawn largely from Betty's friends and admirers. Her height, which was just on six feet, didn't seem to be a deterrent to very short men, and there were always one or two who hardly came above her midriff, but made up for their lack of height with great overdoses of ardour. Betty would give them the same dazzling smile that she gave to the Tarzans, and an equal lack of attention to their ambitions.

There was one young man whom Jenny and I approved of wholeheartedly because he was a snake-lover, and for a time it seemed that Betty might even be vaguely interested in him. He came from the Riverina, he was tall and good-looking, and when he came to Melbourne he used to stay at Illawarra, a big, ornate boarding establishment in a Crescent opposite us. It was a rather gloomy, up-market place, fully of highly respectable old people whose families used it as a sort of nursing home.

George was hardly there except for breakfast, but he seldom travelled without a selection of his snakes, mostly lethal, bundled up together in a chaff bag. He was never really happy without them, and because his passion for reptiles was so great he couldn't understand that not everyone felt the same way.

One night he failed to tie the neck of the chaff bag properly and the snakes took to the panelled, carpeted corridors of Illawarra, searching for the sheltering grass and rocks of their home. In fear and confusion they glided through open doorways and took refuge, curled up under massive pieces of Victorian furniture. George woke in the morning to find his chaff bag empty, had a hideous vision of aged feet poking into snake-filled slippers, or innocent old hands reaching under the bed for a chamber pot with fatal results, and knew he had to tell the Management.

The Management was incredulous at first, and George had to locate one of the snakes under a hall-stand to convince them; then they went berserk. The Police were called, the residents were woken up and told to stay in their beds at all costs and the reason for doing so, and their next-of-kin were summoned to be on hand for death by snakebite or the even more probable heart-attack. George crawled through room after room dragging his sack after him, restoring snakes to its depths and trying to remember how many he'd actually brought with him. His affinity with snakes was so strong that they had no fear of him, and actually seemed to like him handling them.

George wasn't arrested, partly because no one could think of a suitable charge and partly because the Management was desperate to hush the whole thing up. None of the residents had a stroke or a heart attack, and though their relatives went through the conventional motions of outrage none seemed keen to take their old people away with them. George spent the day in the missionary position, checking and rechecking to see that not a snake had been overlooked, and was told in gruesome detail what the Management would do if they ever laid eyes on him again. Then he came over the road to us for the night with his bag of snakes. Pa was enchanted when he heard the story and wanted to give the snakes a bowl of milk and some exercise in the laundry, but Mama said, 'Over my dead body!' She was never really a snake person.

The next day was a Sunday, and The Girls had a tennis party, which was the reason for George's visit. It was lovely weather, warm and sunny and perfect for watching tennis in the garden. For some reason I wasn't welded to the back of a horse but sitting on the lawn, observing my elders and betters at play.

There were about ten young men and women there that day, and among them a short, bumptious, irritating suitor of Betty's whom we all thought she could well do without. He lived close by and was constantly underfoot, almost literally so as his head came only to the level of her bosom.

George had brought his snake sack out of the house with him

and put it in the shade, under a tree. The short young man was on the court, partnering Betty; he kept shouting inane things at their opponents, and quite blatantly showing off. I saw George get up and go over to his sack, open the neck and pull out a robust-looking black snake. He retied the sack, cradled the snake gently in his arms, then walked over to the sweater which the little man had thrown on the grass when he went onto the court. For a moment or two George occupied himself with the sweater and then quietly went back to where he'd been sitting. Nobody but me had taken any notice of what he'd been doing.

The game finished and the foursome came off, the little man still making a lot of unnecessary noise. He picked up his sweater and started to put it on. Through its neck appeared a black, diamond-shaped head followed by a yard or so of shining black body; there was an unearthly scream as the sweater was thrown into the air, and its owner vanished rapidly up the drive.

'Sorry,' said George, expertly retrieving the snake. 'Must've got out when I wasn't looking. Very quiet bloke, this. Wouldn't have hurt him, but he left before I could say so. Sorry, Mrs Walker.'

I heard The Girls talking in their room later. Jenny said, 'You ought to marry George, Betty. He was brilliant, getting rid of Stewie like that.'

'D'you mean George did it on purpose? He said the snake got out.'

'Oh, for heaven's sake! George is mad about you and Stewie was behaving like an idiot . Don't you ever see what's going on?'

'Yes – I mean no!' said Betty. 'Nothing's going on. I like them both, quite, but I don't think they're keen on me. Why should they be?'

George didn't marry Betty, he married someone else, and someone else again after that. I think Pa was sorry, being a snake-man himself, but Mama was relieved; the thought of a son-in-law perpetually arriving to stay with a bag of snakes must have terrified her.

The St Georges Road house had a big garden, and we accumulated animals almost without noticing. Most of them slept together in the laundry and came on regular walks together; when we took the whole pack down the road cars swerved, and the neighbours objected. We had Trixie, now grown old and fat, two cocker spaniels, Moses the magpie, two ducks, Aaron, my pet bantam cock, two cats and an orphan lamb I'd picked up on a visit to the country. Walking them was a bit troublesome because there was always one or another of them loitering and having to be rounded up, but they all insisted on coming and enjoyed themselves. We though the accusation that it lowered the tone of St Georges Road was unjustified.

Because The Girls had defected to the adult world the animals were my family. Aaron, the bantam cock, rode on the handlebars of my bicycle wherever I went, including to school, where he spent the day in a little basket beside my desk, so perfectly behaved that no one objected. Moses the Magpie imitated our voices so well that even the dogs came when he called, and snarled at him because they'd been made to look silly. He dragged the newspapers into the house for us in the morning, had a sip of sherry at drink time in the evening, and swooned flat on his back with emotion, his eyes closed, whenever one of us was good enough to play his favourite record, 'Oh For the Wings of a Dove'.

It was a good house, the St Georges Road house, a place you remember for the sunshine and not for the shadows, busy with animals and people, and of all our houses the closest we would ever come to the days at The Haven.

17

Boarding schools

IT WAS AT ST GEORGES ROAD that our parents suddenly announced that they were going away on a trout-fishing holiday together. Pa had taught Mama to fly-fish in India, and for heaven knows how long they must have been wanting a fishing holiday together, but Pa had been too busy. They said that they had hired a caravan, that Anne, our Irish maid would look after us and Rose, and that they'd be away for ten days. I declared stridently that I wanted to go too, and The Girls told me to shut up.

Mama said, 'You'll be at school anyway. Betty's going to be in charge of you at home, and you're to do exactly as she tells you, no arguments. Jenny'll keep an eye on you at school, and you're not to make a nuisance of yourself when they have their friends round. It's only for ten days.'

Betty was far too nice to be really heavy-handed with me but she took the responsibility seriously; she may even have been practising for her own children later on. She wanted everything done on the instant, room-tidying, tooth-cleaning, homework and so on, and she kept saying, 'Remember what Mama said, Robin, do what you're told and don't argue.' She and Jenny took the opportunity to have a great many of their friends round, and when they came I was sent to my room or out into the garden. Resentment grew in me like a cancer.

One night when Betty told me to go to bed I said, 'No!' She told me again and I ignored her. She went on telling me, her voice getting higher and higher, and when I looked at her she was red in the face, almost in tears.

'Don't be an ass, Betty,' said Jenny, in a bored voice. 'Belt her.'

'I can't.'

'Well, I can. Give me that hairbrush.'

She bent me over, stripped down my pants and laid into me. I roared, and Betty wept. When she'd finished Jenny said, 'Now, get to bed, damn you.' I sat firmly on my stinging backside and said, 'No!' For the first time in my life I was determined to see how far I could go.

They carried me to bed between them, biting, kicking and swearing at them and inflicting quite satisfactory damage. They must have told Pa and Mama about it when they came home. Pa went back to Queensland, but Mama called me into her room in the voice that I knew meant serious business.

She said, 'Robin, your father and I have decided it's time you went to boarding school.'

I thought for a moment and said, 'What about riding?'

'You can ride in the holidays. We've put you down for The Hermitage in Geelong, and you start next term.'

'But I don't want to be a boarder. The Girls weren't boarders except for one term. Why can't I stay at Dothegirls Hall?'

'Because we say so,' said Mama. When she said that one knew that no argument, however reasoned, would help. 'The Girls are growing up and they want to have their own friends round. You're a nuisance, and it's not fair to them.'

I covered the whole range of self-pity and sulks until new uniforms and Mama's fictitious stories of The Hermitage's virtues distracted me. It was, she told me, a haven of leniency, tree-climbing, delicious meals and other delights, barely interrupted by tenderly taught lessons. The girls there, she said, were famous for their close comradeship and concern for new girls. My false sense of security lasted until the end of my first day there.

The Hermitage was a Church of England Girls Grammar School housed in an old, super-chilled Victorian residence on the side of a windy Geelong hill. There were about three hundred girls there at the time, and sixty of them were boarders. After Mama left I was directed to the Junior balcony which ran along the southern side of the house, on the first floor. There were twelve beds, iron-framed and with rock-hard mattresses, bare wooden floors and sliding windows which had long ceased to slide. They stayed open winter and summer, giving us full benefit of the bracing Geelong air.

The first day at any new school is traumatic, especially a new boarding school. In these enlightened days the staff take precautions to see that no new girl is victimised by the old hands, but this philosophy hadn't yet reached The Hermitage. We were herded into bed on the first night, the single light on the ceiling was turned off, and a harsh female voice said, 'No talking! If I hear anyone talking she'll be kept in tomorrow after school.'

There was a brief silence as we heard her creaking away along the passage. I lay stiffly in bed, trying to sort out the jumble of new people and places that the day had been; I had no idea of the names of the girls on the balcony with me. I could hear two or three of them whispering to each other, and low giggles. Then, suddenly there were dark figures standing all round my bed.

'What's your name?'

'Robin Walker.'

'Walker, Walker! Squawker Walker, you'll be. Silly little Squawker! Now, let's see if you'll squawk. Get up!'

'I don't want to get up.'

'Oh yes you do! Come on, give me a hand.'

They tipped me out of bed and stripped off my pyjamas, then they shoved me over to the open window. It was a dark night, and apart from the sound of a distant car the world might have been empty.

The girl behind me said, 'Now, Squawker, new girls have to do whatever we tell them. Look out of the window. See the ledge out there?' I saw a ledge where the floorboards stuck out six inches beyond the outside wall.

'You're going to get out of the window and walk along that ledge to the end of the balcony. You'll be able to hold onto things but don't look down. When you get to the other end we'll let you in again, otherwise you stay there, and if you don't get out there now we'll put you out.'

'I haven't got anything on!'

'We know that. It's part of the dare.'

'No one's dared me.'

'Same thing, all new-bugs have to do something, and we've picked this one for you. Now, get out.'

Heights didn't worry me, but I was sick with fury and humiliation. I got out of the window and found it was quite easy to shuffle along the ledge; there were plenty of handholds. When I got to the end they let me back in, shivering, and I thought it was over. I made for my bed and was barred by three figures carrying wet towels; it was my first experience of towel-lashing, and it hurt. By this time they were making a certain amount of noise, and it reached the ears of the Duty Mistress who was doubtless in front of a radiator in a warm room. The girl keeping nit at the passage door heard her coming, and let out a low whistle. The pack leapt into their beds, the towels were thrown underneath, and the balcony was sweet with innocent, childish breathing.

As with all bullying the Junior Dormitory terrorism was organised by one or two of the bigger girls, and the rest were cowed into sycophancy. The ages of the girls on that balcony ranged from five to eleven, and it gave the younger ones a fair foretaste of hell. They got tired of me as a victim quite quickly but a five-year-old arrived, homesick and tearful, and she wet her bed. I saw diabolical things happen to her, and I don't know how she survived.

I wish I could say that I stood heroically between her and the bullies, or even that I had the sense to tell someone about her, but to my eternal shame I didn't. Bullying was a proud tradition among the lower echelon, and there was no way the school staff could have escaped knowing it happened. I didn't join in, but I was as scared as the five-year-old and I kept my trap shut. Later on, when I read The Lord of the Flies, I recognised The Hermitage instantly, more particularly as it was in my second year there, for that was the year of the Polio Epidemic and the Boarding House went from the grisly to the downright horrific.

There was no Polio vaccine then, and when the epidemic took hold in Melbourne it spread like a bushfire, until the front page of the morning papers carried a casualty-list-cum-tally of the victims of the day before. Parents were advised to move their children to the country, and at all costs to keep them out of public places. When I arrived back at The Hermitage for the new school year I found that the boarders were isolated from the daygirls, barricaded into a small area at the back of the school, with what had been the little art-school building to house the lot of us as a classroom. The Headmistress assembled us there on the first day. She told us that anyone even talking to a day-girl would be severely punished, that all visits either by relatives or friends were banned, and that for those who lived in Melbourne there would be no holidays until the epidemic was over; our holidays would be spent at school.

In principle it was quite rational, and no one wanted to get Polio. In those days there were plenty of examples of what it could do to you because it was always around, and every one of us knew children with one leg or an arm shorter than the other, and had heard of people in iron lungs. In practice, sixty girls aged from five to seventeen, confined to a small area without adequate supervision, added up to misery and mayhem.

The school staff was spread very thin; there were still the same number of classrooms to be serviced for the daygirls, and they were understandably more popular with the staff than ours. In the old art-school building we were sorted roughly into age-group blocks, but as we shared a single room it was almost impossible to hear what was being taught, or to find elbow-room to write. It was hot, stuffy, and reeked of stale-schoolgirl-and-ink, and the staff quite rightly regarded their time there as a stint in the salt-mines. As soon as school was finished in the afternoons they removed themselves as far as possible from the boarders' area and left us to our own devices, secure in the belief that as we had nowhere to go we could do no harm.

Things didn't go too badly at first, but as the novelty wore off the jungle crept in; you could see little patches of savagery starting to break out, like a fungus. There was mental cruelty of great and imaginative refinement, and physical intimidation that wasn't refined at all. I remember a weekend when I was forced, by a mob of about forty girls, to fight a girl twice my size, a fat, unhappy, tearful child who was ashamed of her body, and hated it. They ringed us like jackals round a carcase, pushing us back at each other every time we tried to stop. Jessie was covered with blood and tears and snot and so was I; we had been told to use our fists and use them hard, or else. I remember the despair of knowing that a whole year lay ahead without a redeeming feature along the way.

That year dragged through its months like some obscene worm through a dark tunnel. There were letters from home every week, telling me about all the exciting things The Girls had been doing and about the animals, and one saying that Aaron had died, but not how. The gardener had always hated both him and me since I shot him in the backside with an air-rifle Pa had given me; I had dark imaginings about his fate.

The Headmistress had a hysterectomy. We were only told that she was sick in hospital, because hysterectomies were far too closely related to the sexual and reproductive organs to be discussed with girls. Uteruses and ovaries and vaginas only happened among the most senior students who were doing biology. The Headmistress came back to school to convalesce; she was a grey woman at the best of times, and she shuffled round the boarding house in a pink dressing gown, her hair colourless and straight, her face like putty, and her body bent almost double at the waist. We couldn't hear her coming in her slippers and you'd find her behind you suddenly, a queer, wild look in her eyes, and the thin mouth opening to spit vitriol.

I put my tongue out at her once, and she caught me. It was after she'd started taking the school Assembly and prayers again every morning. Boarders were still in quarantine, but she made me walk up the aisle of the hall between all the daygirls and climb onto the platform in front of her, while the school watched with awe. The boarders had been paraded outside the windows so that they could see the execution too, and when I stood in front of her she eyed me, up and down, up and down, while I shrank to insect size.

She demolished me forever, in one clear, ringing sentence. 'Never,' she said, 'Never, even in a mental home, have I seen anything as repulsive as you. You may go.' Given that I was eleven years old it was dynamite used to kill a mosquito, and I marched down the aisle between the rows of silent girls wishing I was dead.

It was near the end of the year, when the epidemic had begun to slow down, that I had my first visitor. Jenny had started her training at the Royal Melbourne Hospital and was living on Cloud Nine in spite of prehistoric conditions, lethal working hours and non-existent pay. She managed to get permission to see me by saying she was a nurse.

It was the 5th November, and she arrived with a large cardboard box which she wouldn't let me open until we were upstairs on our own, and when I looked inside it was full of the most wonderful fireworks. She said, 'I thought these might liven things up a bit, Robs. It must've been pretty dull down here all this time, but we'll have some fun when you come home.' When she left I was on my first high for months; there was life after school after all, and I might yet live it. I stashed the fireworks under my bed, and managed to steal a box of matches from Matron's office.

I told the girls on the balcony that I had a surprise for them but I wouldn't show them until after it got dark, and knowing that I'd had a visitor they all hoped that it was food. They kept nagging and simmering and trying to get at the box under my bed until I got sick of it, and about 10 o'clock I said, 'Okay, come over to the window and I'll show you.'

I lit a string of crackers first to get things going, then as quickly as possible lit the rest, bangers, candles, wheels and rockets in a blind, reckless purge of all the foul, cold, loveless months behind us. They sailed and banged and fizzed and showered sparks, and for once the dismal night air of Geelong glowed like a Chinese festival.

Directly below the Junior balcony was a plot known as the Headmistress's garden. It was a dry November, and the garden was full of highly flammable asparagus fern, right up to the wooden ground-floor verandah. The Duty Mistress that night was a timid woman, a German refugee not long arrived from Europe. She peered out of the door when she heard the noise, just in time to see the verandah catch fire from the blazing asparagus fern to the tune of almost constant explosions, and she rushed to the staff commonroom screaming that the Nazis were coming.

The Senior dormitories were in an extension at ground level, at right angles to the Junior balcony. The occupants had woken up at the first barrage, and crowded to their windows, cheering wildly. There was strenuous applause, first for the fireworks and then for the fire; the Seniors had lived through a bad year too. When the verandah burst into flames they came out through the dormitory windows, crazy as kittens on cat-nip, carrying anything they could find that would hold water and dowsing everyone and everything except what needed dowsing. From where I was standing on the balcony above them, considerably sobered, it looked like Walpurgis Night. Then the door between our balcony and the passage opened and I saw the pink dressing-gown, heard soft and gliding the approaching bedroom slippers of Nemesis.

By the time things had quietened down, the Seniors had been frog-marched back to bed and the Fire Brigade had left, I was in Solitary. It was a small room, very like a cell, in the Staff quarters, and I stayed there for three weeks until the end of term. Mama said she wrote to me, but I never got the letters. She said that the Headmistress had simply telephoned her and said that the school was not prepared to have me back the next year, but not why, and she had no idea that I was a prisoner. She drove down to collect me the day school broke up, and when she heard what had happened she sailed into the Headmistress's study like a warship. She emerged tight-lipped and fuming. She said, 'That woman! I never dreamed... I told her she isn't fit to run a school. She said it was all due to upbringing!'

There was a pre-Christmas panic to find a school that would take me on in the following year. The grapevine had been busy, and the reason why I was no longer welcome at The Hermitage had been distorted and expanded until I was high on the list on known undesirables. Mama was sorely tried; people kept telling her things I was supposed to have done, and I kept telling her I hadn't, and she didn't know who to believe. Luckily Toorak College at Mt Eliza, a school very low in the ratings then, agreed to have me. At that time, I believe, they would happily have accepted a drug-addicted moron with homicidal tendencies, had one been offered, simply to swell the numbers.

Toorak College was very different to The Hermitage. For a start it was a school which had been built for the purpose, not a worn-down old Victorian home which had been gutted, revamped and transformed into an endurance test for its occupants, and also it was close to the sea. The main building was of red brick arranged in vaguely classical form round a quadrangle with grass in the middle, bordered by red brick arches known as The Cloisters. We slept on balconies, just as open as The Hermitage balconies but the sun and sea air came into them, and there were no dark, cobwebby corners. The passages were institutional, but still more human than the sinister bluestone tunnels I had left behind.

Girls who were sent to small, private schools then were not sent there for serious education but for social contacts, the three elementary R's, and Extras which were the things you would need when you left school and entered the all-important race for a husband. At Toorak College you could take as Extras bridge, dancing, tennis, golf and piano lessons. Special teachers had to come down from Melbourne for these once or twice a week, and they were expensive. When Mama took me down to the school on the first day of term we had an interview with Miss Jones, the Bursar.

She said to Mama, 'Now, Mrs Walker, what Extras would you like Robin to take. Our standard in Extras is very high. She'll take dancing, of course, and tennis, and...'

'Thank you,' said Mama. 'I've seen the list, and they're very expensive. I'm afraid Robin won't be taking any Extras, not yet anyway.'

'Oh?" said Miss Jones. She put her glasses on, turned in her chair and eyed me as if I had two heads. 'She'll feel very out of things, you know. All our girls take *some* Extras. It's like a little club for them.'

'Perhaps later on,' said poor Mama. 'Robin, you don't want to take any Extras, do you?'

I didn't. Neither golf, cards, tennis nor dancing had any message for me, and I knew I was hopeless at music. 'I'd like to go riding,' I said. 'Someone told me there's a riding school near here, and some of the girls go there. Could I...?'

Miss Jones bared her alarmingly false teeth and gave me a glare which said quite clearly, 'One of those! I might have known!'

'If your mother gives you written permission. We take no responsibility. Riding also costs money, Mrs Walker.' She was obviously wondering if she should ask for an advance on school fees, and she had me classified as bottom-of-the-barrel material. Mama said, 'I'm perfectly happy for Robin to ride. I shall write a note of permission for her now, and I will inform the riding school that they can send the bill direct to me. Then I'll know exactly how much it costs.'

The implication that Extras were a rip-off was not lost on Miss Jones. She was a small, plump, chinless woman with a tight knob of hair scraped to the top of her head, and the look of one whose nose is permanently plagued by a bad smell. She had bad hips and rocked rather than walked, one hand clamped to her pelvis for balance and her elbow stuck aggressively out from her side. When I took to drawing to while away the hours of classroom boredom I doubled my pocket money by selling cartoons of Miss Jones and it was cruel of me, because life had simply dealt her all the wrong cards. On that first day she rocked angrily out of her office after Mama, muttering witch-warnings over her non-existent chin, and I knew that our time together wouldn't be easy.

There were only about ninety girls in the school, almost all of them boarders, and the staff were quite different to The Hermitage staff who had been serious about academic standards, and were highly qualified in their subjects. I found that a number of the Toorak College mistresses, like Miss Jones, were Old Girls of the School who had fallen on hard times and been offered a teaching job as a refuge. There were others on the staff who found it a refuge of a different kind, and I was surprised to see black-gowned women wandering round the Cloisters in pairs, their arms entwined, gazing into each others' eyes.

If the emphasis on the benefits of Extras was strong the prohibition on contact with the male sex was even stronger. Considering that we were being trained like athletes for the day when we would have to run a man down it might have helped if we'd been taught something about the nature of our quarry, or at least been allowed to see what it looked like. My own age group was utterly ignorant and smuttily curious about sex. I entranced the Junior Dormitory early on by reciting the only dirty rhyme I'd learned at The Hermitage. It was very basic.

Ma and Pa sat on the lawn,
Pa took out his hairy horn.
Ma said 'What are you going to do?'
Pa said, 'I'm going to stick it in you.'

It never got any further than that, firstly because we were all helpless with giggles, and secondly because I'd never heard the rest of it and didn't know what a hairy horn was anyway. Most of us, especially the country girls, had seen enough of mating animals to know the mechanics of the thing, but we were unable to relate it to our parents, much less to our future selves.

To confuse us even further about sex, the wing where the mistresses lived ran off at right angles to our dormitory, and their bathrooms were on our side. If we stood on our beds after lights-out we could see into the bathrooms if they forgot to pull the blinds down. There were several couples who bathed together, and they did the most mystifying things to each other. We noticed that these particular couples were always together, and we giggled about them but we didn't understand.

We were never allowed outside the school grounds unchaperoned; to walk down the empty half-mile of road to the Mt Eliza Store was a capital offence if you were caught, so we did it commando-style, cross country from bush to bush, for extra food. Our only official outings were on Sunday, after an interminable Church Service presided over by the Frankston Vicar. We formed a long line known as a Crocodile, in pairs, the youngest girls in front grading to the biggest at the back, and mistresses prowling like sheepdogs on either side. We wore hats, gloves, blazers and gartered socks or lisle stockings, and we walked in the strictest silence round an uninhabited block bordered by ti-tree scrub and derisive birds. Then we went back to Sunday lunch, the only decent meal of the week, whose leftovers would reappear in various gruesome disguises throughout Monday and Tuesday.

Toorak College was a bed of roses compared to The Hermitage during the polio year, and there was far less bullying. By then I'd observed that clowns are seldom bullied, and was busy becoming a successful clown but they still existed, the tyrants and the victims, weaving their thread of torture and misery into the long, isolated terms.

I have often marvelled at the precise, polished, perceptive cruelty which children are capable of inflicting and wondered why, if we're like that when we're young, we don't grow up as monsters, every one of us. Perhaps children need the dagger in their own ribs before they can understand its hurt, and to that end boarding school is invaluable. And I was as guilty as anyone, specially to Miss Jones, caricaturing and lampooning her until she became a comic-strip joke, and you could see her puzzling over why the girls in her classes only had to look at her to get the giggles.

Besides being the Bursar poor Miss Jones had to teach the junior forms French, to which she was a total stranger. Having been brought up on Mama's Paris-accented French I couldn't understand a word she said, not that she said much; she confined herself to grammar, giving us a page of verbs or nouns to learn and hastily boning up on the next page herself while we were doing so. Utterly bored I drew cartoons of her under the desk and took no part in the lessons. The poor woman, knowing quite well what I was doing and loathing me anyway, tried valiantly to keep her temper. Then one morning, she shouted for 'Attention!' three times, trying hard to make it sound French, and I was too absorbed to realise that it was aimed at me; I kept on drawing.

'Robin Walker!' she screamed, as her nerve finally broke. 'Gettez-vous out of here tres vite, and takez-vous an ordre mark!'

18

Acland Street and Cliveden Mansions

BY THE TIME I WENT HOME for my first holidays from Toorak College my family had moved again. This time it was to Acland Street in South Yarra, a smallish two-storey house with a garden the size of a hen coop. As usual Rose was installed in the best bedroom, Pa and Mama in the next best, The Girls in a meagre two-bed cell, and my room might once have been a large broom-cupboard.

Mama explained to me, 'St Georges Road was far too big, darling, now The Girls are grown-up and you're at school. Jenny's at the Hospital almost all the time, and Betty's off on her trip to England soon. I'm sure I told you when I wrote.'

'Yes. What happened to Trixie? Where's Moses and the lamb?'

'Poor old dog. I thought I'd tell you when you came home, darling, we had to put her down, she was just too old. And Moses must've been taken by a hawk, he simply vanished one day. The lamb's gone back to the country – that's nice, isn't it?'

We still had a cocker spaniel and a cat, but I mourned the others; I felt I'd deserted them, left them unprotected. There was a sense of things moving away from me, things kept from me, that I was watching bits of my world spin off into space. I had learned at school that if you wanted to find things out you shouldn't be too fussy about how you did it, so I listened at doors. It became plain that Betty's trip was not a Grand Tour to Finish her, but a forced separation from someone she'd fallen in love with who wanted to marry her. I picked up his name, Norman Campbell, and was avid to know more. I cornered Betty in her room.

'Betty, who's Norman?' She burst into tears.

I sat on her bed and said, 'Don't cry, tell me. Is he the childrens' father you're always looking for?'

'Yes, sobbed Betty. 'Oh, Robs, yes. I love him so much.'

'Then why go away – why can't you marry him?'

'His bloody parents, they don't like me and they don't like our family. We're not rich enough. They want him to marry a millionaire.'

'Why don't you go off together? Elope?'

'He hasn't any money of his own, he works for his parents on their sheep station. They're so mean, they don't pay him anything, and he just works and works. His mother's terribly rich, she's known as the Airey Heiress, and she looks like a witch. His father messes round in the kitchen making cakes like a woman, and Norman runs the property. Anyway, I couldn't just go off like that, think how miserable Mama would be.'

'What does Jenny say?'

'Oh – Oh! She says go to bed with him and get pregnant and they'll have to let you marry him, and I couldn't! I couldn't! It's easy for her, she's a nurse.'

There were tears, constant tears and a damp preparation for her trip, with Mama telling her again and again what fun it would be. It was that same old confidence trick of Mama's, and it didn't seem to comfort Betty much. Norman appeared from time to time, and he was both sensational to look at and nice to me, but manifestly miserable.

About a month before Betty was due to sail for England Mama had a car accident, and it led to yet another move. I was in the car with her when it happened. It was a stupid, unnecessary crash caused by our cocker spaniel who jumped over into the front seat, and Mama hit her head on the pillar of the car door trying to push it back. She knocked herself out and slid under the steering wheel onto the accelerator so that the car, normally a sober family model, developed wings.

Providentially we hit a war memorial and not another car, but Mama was dreadfully battered, and when I disentangled myself from the wreckage in the back I could see her huddled body in the front, covered with blood. I picked up the dazed spaniel and set out to walk home certain, in my fuddled state, that Mama was dead.

Someone in the crowd that gathered round the car recognised her, and against all the rules of First Aid he simply put her into his own car and drove her home, while another man, seeing me wandering bloodily along the footpath with the dog, drove me home too. I think both the spaniel and I were in shock. When I got there Pa had been summoned, and the house was in chaos.

They took Mama to hospital and she stayed there a long time, with Pa at her bedside. I was sore and miserable, blaming myself for the dog's leap, and a few days later I began to feel really ill. No one had time to worry about it until Jenny came home on her day off and took my temperature. The family Doctor was called, and said it looked like polio; Betty, only days away from her trip, was utterly demoralised by the string of disasters, and the only person who managed to rise above the general gloom was Rose. She tut-tutted a bit to show that she'd noticed that something was wrong, and placidly continued with her crochet work.

Imperceptibly things improved. I was diagnosed as mumps-meningitis which was better than polio, though no one bothered to tell me what was wrong with me at the time. I couldn't go back to school for a while, and a minder was engaged to follow me round, presumably to watch for signs of brain damage. I was puzzled and insulted, and I wasn't allowed to ride. Betty departed, tearful and protesting, on her boat, and Mama came home from hospital but kept mainly to her bed. I finally went back to school. During that term my family moved again, on the pretext that Mama wasn't well enough to run a house, and took a flat in a vast old Victorian building next to the Treasury Gardens, called Cliveden Mansions.

The Cliveden Mansions period lasted only six months, but it was memorable because we were joined there by Mama's younger sister, Dorothy, her Italian husband and their three daughters. War was a looming cloudbank over Europe, and Europeans with relatives abroad were making pilgrimages to visit them, conscious that it might be their last chance. When the letter arrived announcing her sister's intentions Mama had a relapse, Pa found urgent reasons for visiting Papua, and Jenny and I stated that we wanted no part of our cousins, regardless of the fact we had never set eyes on them. Mama had read her sister's letters to us over the years, and we knew that we could never match the brilliance, sporting prowess or beauty of the three girls described therein. According to their mother they swam to Olympic standard, rode like *Centaurs*, were in classes years beyond their age and had half the men of Italy at their feet. We didn't believe a word of it, but we hated them already. We were told to behave ourselves, to be nice.

Since we were living at Cliveden Mansions Dorothy wrote to say they'd like a flat there too, to be near us, and would Mama please arrange it. Their arrival at Cliveden had roughly the same impact as George's snakes getting loose at Illawarra.

Cliveden had originally been a very grand private house belonging to the family of the Australian Baronet who was Grandfather's partner in Queensland. When it was sold two storeys were added to it, and the interior converted to a complex of large, gloomy flats. It was full of mahogany panelling, potted palms, hideous bronzes and residents in an advanced state of decay. It was one of God's Waiting Rooms, strictly First Class. There was a central dining-room where everyone ate, a place of hushed voices, long, rich menus, elderly maids with white aprons and starched, streamered caps, and small tables where the aged and infirm were fed with spoons by expensive nurses. A raised voice was sacrilege in Cliveden, where the only permitted sound was the whine of its ancient birdcage lifts, slowly grinding between floors.

Mama went to meet the Nathans at the boat; she said that with five of them in the car there wouldn't be room for me, and she was right. When she arrived back with them hours later her car was at the head of a cavalcade of taxis, long enough for a respectable funeral. I was hanging round in the lobby, saw her car pull up, the passenger door open, and was deafened by a mixed blast of Italian and English profanity. The Cliveden Hall Porter, a dear old man, had run down the front steps to do his duty, and he reeled back as if in the face of gunfire. Still in full cry my Aunt advanced across the lobby followed by a tall, unhappy-looking man who I guessed was Uncle Joe, Mama looking limp, and three girls. Behind them, spilling out of the queued taxis came a stream of luggage.

'Merde!' shouted Aunt Dorothy, spicing up her Italian with a little French. 'Do not put it *there* you bloody *fool*, put it *there!* Pick it up! Put it down! What imbeciles! *Joe* ! You are the most bloody useless God-awful fool I ever knew! Don't just stand there with your bloody mouth open! Why do I always have to do everything myself?'

Uncle Joe slowly lowered himself into a sitting position on one of the cabin trunks, put his head in his hands and rocked backwards and forwards murmuring, 'Oh God, Oh God.' Sweet, gentle man that he was he had no protection other than God against his wife, and invoked him constantly, without success. Mama tried to reason with her sister, who didn't listen, and the three girls simply looked bored; they had seen it all before only too often, and I wished that Pa had been there to help.

The luggage was finally unloaded, and Dorothy was manoeuvred upstairs in the creaking lift to the flat Mama had rented for them. As the last piece of luggage was carried through the flat's door Dorothy decided that she didn't like it, and burst into the corridor, the hallowed, funereal corridor of muffled sounds, shrieking like a banshee.

'I might have *known*! You were always so bloody *stupid* Aileen! Even as a girl, *stupid*! No one else would get me a flat like that! A *bloody dump!* Not one night there, I tell you! What is this one?'

She pulled open the door of the flat across the passage and marched inside. A quavering, indignant voice was raised in protest from its depths, but Dorothy ignored it.

'This one is better,' she said, turning to Mama. 'You can tell the

Manager I shall have this one, it looks over the Park. You should have taken it in the first place.'

'But you can't have it, Dorothy. Old Mrs Wigthorpe lives here, she's been here for years.'

'She must move. *Joe!* Make yourself useful for once. Go to the Goddamn Manager and tell him I'm going to have this flat.' Looking more stricken than ever Joe mutely shook his head. 'I'll go myself then! Get out of my way! *God* such fools!'

The Manager, as it happened, was a woman, a cold, basilisk lady who was not impressed by her own sex, especially when they tried to stand over her. My Aunt returned after a short time, puffing slightly and with heightened colour. She went back into the original flat and began to discover virtues in it that she had missed earlier on. Mama went to bed with a bad headache.

Her return to the country of her birth persuaded Dorothy that she needed an image-change; she announced shortly after her arrival that she would forthwith be known as Peggy because it suited her better. She also tried to restore the original red of her tightly-curled hair and the result was frightening but served as a warning, like the red ribbon in the tail of a pony which habitually kicks. Her personality was unalterable, irrespective of name or hair-colour, and she existed at the epicentre of a willy-willy of temper, temperament and trouble.

The girls, Amelia, Georgina and Virginia, turned out to be perfectly nice and normal, and good-looking enough to justify their mother's superlatives in that direction at least. They were hopeless at swimming and riding, and it was hard to tell whether or not they were intellectual geniuses because English was definitely their second language, and we had no Italian. Within a few days our hearts were torn with pity for them, and even more so for Uncle Joe. It was clear that no one in Peggy's family could do anything right, except herself.

Their flat vibrated with noise; deafening gramophone records, violent voices, the occasional crash of breaking china and slamming doors. At the height of one row the flat burst open and

Amelia, the eldest daughter, flew out stark naked and screaming, followed by Peggy with her fists clenched above her head, and shortly afterwards by the other two girls and Uncle Joe, all yelling in Italian. Cliveden was rocked to its foundations and complaints flew through the stagnant air like wasps, but Peggy brushed them aside. *'Peasants* live here,' she said. 'Bloody *peasants,* all of them.' Years later I stayed with the Nathans in Rome, and realised that they had actually moderated their behaviour in Melbourne, but for Cliveden they were worse than a civil war.

When they went back to Italy, not very long before the start of the war Jo, at least, knew they were facing an uncertain future as Jewish citizens in a Fascist country, allied with Nazi Germany. Peggy, I think, imagined that not even Hitler would dare touch her, and indeed if they had ever met I wouldn't have been prepared to bet on the result. In Italy they owned a delightful villa at Tivoli and a large house in Rome which Peggy always referred to as The Palazzo, but because of Uncle Joe's Jewishness both were confiscated and they spent most of the war in hiding, sometimes with peasants in the country, sometimes in tiny tenement rooms in Rome. It is hard to imagine the horrors the girls must have endured, living at such close quarters with their mother during that time. Soon after the war ended she bullied Amelia and Virginia into marriages with men of her own choice, both of whom turned out to be unspeakably awful. The girls left them, but there was no divorce in Italy then. Georgina managed to marry an American whom Dorothy didn't even know, and was happy.

Jenny, at this time, was well on the way to becoming what she wanted to be, a high-class nurse. The Royal Melbourne Hospital had the highest reputation in Australia for nursing training, if one could survive it. The discipline would have made a penal battalion look soft, the hours were inhuman and the trainees were paid ten shillings a week. Jenny loved every moment of it, arriving home on days off in a state of exhaustion, frequently with gruesome human fragments bottled in formalin, and always with hospital anecdotes which had to be banned at meals.

Human parts had a fascination for her; we were in the car one day when a tram hit the car in front of us and Jenny leapt out to render aid, staying with the victim until the ambulance arrived. She got back into our car and sat in the front seat beside Mama cradling something in her hands. Mama, who was still slightly shaky about accidents after her own, said, 'What's that you've got, Jenny?' and Jenny proudly held up the larger section of a human ear.

She was also discovering that her healthy but incomplete interest in sex could be further developed, that many of her fellow trainees, in fact, regarded sex as a perfectly legitimate leisure pastime. Like all of us she had been saturated with dire warnings about Down There, and the ominous follow-on that 'If you're not a virgin No Decent Man Will Every Marry You.' It took a very short time as a trainee nurse to convince her that the latter was not necessarily true, and very little longer to decide that if other people got such a lot of pleasure from Down There it couldn't be as bad as Mama said it was. In addition she had become the close friend of a fellow-trainee from South Australia, Janet, who being an expatriate of sorts took up permanent residence in Betty's empty bed.

Janet was slim, blond and sexy, a good foil for Jenny's brunette lushness, and she had the lazy, sinuous movements of a sophisticated cat. Janet never sat on a sofa, she curled on it or stretched, looking as if she might lick her paws. Her father was Secretary to the Governor of South Australia, and there's no doubt that she'd been brought up on the same diet of sexual prohibitions as ourselves, but cat-like she'd disregarded them and gone her own way.

I suspect that Janet's love-life had started well before her nursing career; she had about her a confident air of know-how which is as unmistakable as the indefinable gloss that marks the very rich. Jenny was fascinated by it, and determined to achieve the same aura; she tried dressing herself in the nearest she could get to film-star clothes and painting her face until it cracked like an eggshell, and it still didn't work. After consultation with Janet she realised she must take the plunge; there were, after all, plenty of interns and doctors only too willing to oblige.

I was sitting in the bedroom with her and Janet one evening during the school holidays, Jenny getting herself ready to go out and Janet was smiling at her with an after-the-cream smile. There was an air of excitement in the room, pungent as incense.

Curious, I asked, 'Where are you off to, Jennifer? Why all the war-paint?'

She turned to me, mascara brush poised. 'Never you mind where I'm going,' she said, 'But I tell you this, I'm buggered if I'm going to die wondering. Tell Mama I've remembered I'm on duty and gone back to the hospital.'

She won the Florence Nightingale prize for the best nurse in training, and Mama was ecstatic. She asked no questions about Jenny's comings and goings because one does not question perfection, and perfection, for Mama, was inseparable from chastity. On the rare occasions when she was at home Jenny spent hours playing a record which went:

Once I loved such a ravishing physician,
Quite the best looking doctor in the State,
He looked after my physical condition
And his bedside manner was great.

In a very short time one noticed that she was achieving her objective and becoming more like Janet; she looked older than before, more self-assured, and her skin, which had been inclined to acne, was perfect.

Betty wrote from overseas that she was enjoying her Grand Tour; Austria had been exciting because the Anschluss took place when she was there, and England was lovely, but please when could she come home, she missed Norman so much? Most of the time, except for her visit to Europe, she spent in Ireland with our cousins.

There were four of them, all about her age, as close-knit as any brothers and sisters could have been, and they slotted Betty into their group as though she had been with them always. There was Aileen Landale who had come with Sheila and Fanny to Australia, and her brother, Roy. There was William who was the only child of Pa's eldest sister, Daisy McClintock, a brilliant horseman following his father, Colonel Jim McClintock, into the Army, and there was Tony, whose proper name was Cecilia. Tony's mother was Pa's youngest sister, Dorothy who had married her first cousin, Barch Christie, another professional soldier and brother to Archie Christie who became famous when his wife, Agatha, the author, staged a much-publicised fake-suicide to get rid of him.

William's mother, Daisy, was something of a mathematical genius. Her husband was a Sapper, and they spent much of their Service life in India where Daisy filled in her spare time by working out missile trajectories and other obscure problems for the Army. She was so good at it that when they returned to England and Jim was given a senior posting with the Sappers on Salisbury Plain, Daisy was as much in demand as her husband. They had a big, grey old house in Donegal, a notoriously haunted house whose ghosts were much prized as part of the family. The cousins had spent a lot of time together there, while they were growing up, and it was there that Betty spent the summer with them, the year she was away.

Betty's summer at Dunmore started idyllically; the cousins and their friends came and went, there were picnics on the Donegal beaches, visits to mad, legendary, remote relations in crumbling mansions, and an incessant Irish flow of rich, fattening food fit to explode the liver in a Bresse goose. William McClintock came home on leave and then went back to England to concentrate on the two great loves of his life, Helen, the girl to whom he'd just become engaged, and the horse which he intended to ride to victory in the Sandown Gold Cup.

I never met William, but I've seen photographs; he was tall, fair and splendid. Betty said he was wonderful to be with, fun and alive and kind, and always first into anything they wanted to do, good or bad. His parents adored him, especially his mother, though they both deprecated his charms with a fierce, protective pride. Uncle Jim's Sapper friends forecast a great future for him in the Army.

He started favourite or near favourite in the Gold Cup that year. There was a bad fall at one fence; seven horses came down in one of those awful, flailing tangles where it seems that no one has a right to be alive afterwards, and the only rider who was badly hurt was William. They took him to St Anne's Hospital, run specially for officers in H. M. Forces, and there established that he had become what we now know as a quadriplegic. In the 1930s there was very little hope for anyone in William's condition, and his parents were told that he would be in a wheelchair for the rest of his life, helpless to do anything for himself.

Daisy and Jim McClintock would have confronted the worst thing that could happen to them with stiff upper lips because their code of self-discipline, demanded it. If Daisy could have wept and torn her hair instead of bottling up her agony things might have been different. As it was she stayed in England near the hospital and her son until the doctors said he might as well go home to Dunmore, and it was arranged to have him flown to Ireland. It seems that the medicos had detected a ray of hope, the slight movement of a muscle in one of his shoulders, and thought he might develop increasing movement if he was at home, in his own surroundings. They didn't tell Daisy or Jim in case nothing came of it.

Betty was in England at the time, staying with other relations and just about to sail for home. She telephoned us at Cliveden to tell us what happened. Mama picked up the phone and said, 'Betty darling, what a lovely surprise!' Then her face changed and she said, 'Robin, go into your room for a bit,' and she called for Pa. From my room I could hear long silences and Mama sobbing, and Pa, in charge of the phone now, saying quietly, 'Oh my God.'

Daisy must have made up her mind what to do about William when he was still in hospital, when she was forced to accept that her fine, glowing son had become an immobile lump of pain-wracked flesh. Uncle Jim said that she never showed him by the flicker of an eyelash what she intended to do, but always talked as though William would get better.

They got William back to Dunmore, with a wheelchair and a nurse, and Helen, his fiancee, came over to be with him. On sunny days he was wheeled outside to sit, uncomplaining and trying to cheer everyone else up, in Dunmore's walled garden, under the fruit trees. One morning when he was out there Daisy called the nurse into the house. Then she went to Uncle Jim's gun-room, loaded a gun, walked out into the garden behind her son and shot him through the head. Without haste, or hesitation either, she retired to the other side of the wall and shot herself.

Uncle Jim heard the shots, and knowing that no one should have been shooting near the house hurried into the garden to find first the body of his son, and shortly afterwards that of his wife. Helen had been out walking somewhere, and when she came in they told her, because the truth was too terrible to tell immediately, that William had died of a haemorrhage. She didn't wait to hear any details; she must have loved him very much because she went straight to the gun-room, loaded another gun and shot herself too.

It was a tragedy that took Ireland by the throat. There were people from one end of the country to the other who knew the McClintocks, and loved them, or were related to them. There was an awesome, Celtic quality about it that made the people in the pubs and the cottages shake their heads, tell it and retell it, and compare it to ancestral stories of curses laid on families in the past.

It was not long afterwards that Aunt Sheila wrote to tell us that Uncle Jim had cancer and was dying. It must have seemed like a blessing to him, poor man, because there was nothing he wanted to live for. Sheila went to Dunmore and looked after him, and he left Dunmore to her son, Roy, in his will. Roy had joined the Royal Ulster Constabulary, and neither he nor his mother wanted to live there so it was sold to a doctor from Dublin, said to be very rich. The doctor and his wife refurnished the house, stocked the land with cattle and went to live there, but in a short time they left saying they had no peace at all with the ghosts. The ghosts in the

McClintock days had been perfectly friendly; they drove up the drive in a carriage with four horses which you could count by the sound of their hooves. They would draw up outside the front door, the carriage doors would open and close and they would drive off again, worrying nobody. It's possible that by the time the Dublin Doctor moved in there were newer, sadder ghosts.

Dunmore was never a beautiful house, and I only saw it after the end of the war when it had been empty for some time. It was like many other Irish family houses, square and grey, with lofty, forbidding windows. The rooms inside were large and high-ceilinged, empty by then, except for dust and cobwebs and the breath of ghosts. But there were marvellous trees all round it and long grass, dappled by sun, and the remains of the old, walled garden with crumbling pink bricks and fruit trees. It looked out across meadows and marshes where William and Roy used to shoot when they were boys, and the stream where they fished. Someone nameless had owned it during the war, and used it as a base for smuggling cattle across the Border.

Betty was on her way back to Australia, the sadness of what had happened in Ireland diluted by the glorious prospect of getting back to Norman. It had been agreed that if neither of them changed their minds during the time of separation they would be allowed to marry. There was no questioning Betty's fidelity; she would have died rather than go unchaste to the altar but her innocence, on the return trip, nearly brought her undone.

The Captain of her ship was a Dutchman, not that his nationality had anything to do with it; as it happened he was also a man of carnal appetites, accustomed to taking advantage of the pleasures on offer while he was at sea. Sea voyages being what they were, he normally had more pleasures on offer than he could handle.

It wasn't unusual for men to look at Betty with lust, nor for her to mistake it for harmless friendship. When she realised that her trust had been misplaced she was invariably shocked and horrified; she told the man concerned that he was a no-good so-and-so and went her way. The Dutch Captain was older and infinitely more experienced than most of Betty's men, and having decided that on this voyage nothing less than Betty would do he set about getting her like a hunter stalking his prey. She knew none of the other passengers, and a couple of days after they left England she found herself moved discreetly to the Captain's table, in fact to the seat next to him.

'He was awfully nice, you know,' she told me. 'Sort of blond and stiff, very correct in a German way, specially at meals. He asked me if I'd like to go up to the Bridge and see how things worked and I did quite often, it was fun. Then he asked me to tea in his cabin and he was still nice, he kept asking me what I'd done in Europe and so on. I told him all about Norman and what had happened to William, and he was old, forty-five at least, so of course I thought it was all right.

'Then he asked me to have drinks in his cabin one night before dinner, and I thought it'd be a party with other people, but it wasn't. He gave me some horrible Dutch stuff, Schnapps, and I didn't like it and he laughed and grabbed me and tried to kiss me! I was furious! I nearly hit him.'

'Why didn't you?'

'Well, he seemed so sorry. He apologised and swore that he hadn't meant to, he'd never done such a thing before, he was a married man – all that sort of thing, and I felt sorry for him. I hate men pawing me, except Norman, but he made me feel stupid and young and . . . Oh, just silly.'

'So you forgave him, I suppose?'

'Yes, and he went back to being sensible so I forgot about it. Then we were talking at dinner one night and he asked me if I'd ever done Swedish exercises. He said they were wonderful on board ship where you eat too much and don't take much exercise, which is true. He said he kept fit with them himself and he'd teach me, but not on deck or the Bridge because the crew would laugh at him. He said to come to his cabin in the afternoon and to wear shorts, and he'd teach me how to do them.'

'So what happened?'

'Well, nothing I thought at the time. I mean, he showed me the exercises mostly bending and stretching things, and lying down with your legs apart and sitting up suddenly, and then he made me do them myself. He was standing over by the porthole, watching me, I thought, and telling me what I was doing wrong. I didn't know he had a camera.'

'What's wrong with that?'

'Oh, Robs, you can't imagine! It's so awful! I had these shorts on, you see, and they must have shrunk or something. I knew they felt tight when I put them on, but I didn't look. When I bent over or opened my legs you could see everything – everything! And he developed his own films, can you imagine anything so beastly?'

'What happened then?'

'He asked me to come to his cabin next day, and he showed the photos to me. I thought I was going to faint. I said, 'Give them to me at once! I'll never speak to you again!' and he just laughed. He said … he said, "If you don't do vot I tell you the next person to see these vill be your vunderful Norman", and he said awful things, what a cold, silly little fool I was, and how he could teach me to grow up and be a woman. He went on and on about it! I couldn't believe it was happening to me.

'It was only a few days before we landed in Melbourne so I locked myself in my cabin and got the stewardess to bring me meals there. I sent a message to the Purser to say I'd got a cold, and would he please make my apologies in the dining-room, and I sent a cable to Pa to make sure he'd meet the ship. I was terrified of telling him, but he was the only hope of getting those awful photos back.'

Mama and Pa would have been at the wharf to meet her anyway, without the cable. They were thrilled by the thought of having her home. They'd have imagined her being on deck, waving to them as the ship berthed, and throwing herself into their arms as soon as the gangplank was lowered. Instead of that they had to run her to earth in a locked cabin, sodden with tears and shame. Betty told me about it after she'd recovered. She'd seen

Norman by then, and it had been agreed that they'd get married so her whole world was rose-coloured. The Captain and his photos seemed like an adventure rather than a disgrace.

'When I heard their voices outside my cabin,' she said, 'I honestly didn't know whether I dared let them in. You know what Mama's like about men and things, and I thought Pa'd be furious with me too. Anyway, I did unlock the door and then it all sort of poured out. Pa just grunted and disappeared, and I cried on Mama's shoulder and she said not to worry about anything, which was comforting. It was ages until Pa came back but he had the photographs and the negatives, and he made me check them to see that they were all there. And then we came home.'

'Well, how did Pa get them? What did he say to the Captain?'

'Pa said he'd just talked to the Captain, and not to worry about him any more. Maybe he punched him, I wouldn't be surprised. He said not to tell Norman, so promise you won't. If you swear not to, Robs, I'll show you something. I pinched a couple of prints.'

She produced two black-and-white photographs. The foreground of both was filled with a pair of astonishingly long, bare legs, in one they were on the floor and wide apart, in the other they led upwards to a pair of broad, white buttocks hiding a torso bent in the ostrich position. Betty had been quite right about the shorts, they must have shrunk disastrously because they left nothing at all to the imagination.

19

Rose and Shipley Street

OUR GROWING-UP YEARS seemed to pass in layers, each layer defined by yet another set of furniture vans, another rented house, each layer distinct as the colour-strata of a rainbow, but fuzzy at the edges where they merged. In each one the tempo of life was different, and each time we moved there was subtle erosion, a crumbling away of whatever it is that holds a family together.

We moved again, just after Betty came home, this time to a maisonette in South Yarra, just off Punt Road. There was a bakery opposite and a brothel on the corner. Mama firmly refused to believe it was a brothel in spite of irrefutable evidence.

Our house was small and recently built, a maisonette with its mirror-image alongside it. There were four bedrooms and a bathroom upstairs, and downstairs there was a sitting-room, dining-room, kitchen and a maid's room with a minute bathroom. It was an article of faith in the design of 1930s houses, when servants were on the way out, that all domestics were undersized or easily folded. A path ran up one side of the house leading to a small, enclosed back garden, a concrete patio and a balcony above it. The house was compact and utterly ordinary, and Mama loved it from the moment we moved in.

Rose, as usual, had the largest bedroom, next to the bathroom. She was becoming noticeably slower and deafer, more silent and detached. She was also harder for us, being young, to live with at close quarters, and our parents were constantly on the watch for signs of disrespect on our part. There had been an incident involving Rose and me before we left Cliveden, and Mama suspected me, quite wrongly, of being unkindly disposed towards my grandmother. In fact I accepted her as an inexplicable fact of life, quaint and harmless, and I was fond of her. She had gone downhill both physically and mentally during the Cliveden period, partly because of her age but also, I think, because of the trauma induced by Peggy and her family. By the time they left she had ceased to acknowledge Peggy as her daughter, or indeed to recognise her at all.

Cliveden had two lifts, the ornate wrought-iron birdcage in the front lobby and a stark, barred service lift like a zoo cage at the back. Both, but specially the service lift, were prone to spasms of wild jerking or sudden paralysis, and they were so old that there was scarcely anyone still alive in Melbourne who knew how to fix them.

Rose apparently took the wrong turning when she came out of the dining-room after lunch one day, and meandered along the passages until she came to the service lift. With rare acumen she recognised it as a lift, got into it and pressed the button for our floor. The lift went past the first floor, but halfway between that and the second floor it stuck. Rose wasn't particularly alarmed because, after all, there had been no situation in her life from which she hadn't been rescued. She wasn't a screamer and she was pleasantly full of lunch so she sank to the floor of the lift, dozed and waited.

Mama, who had been shopping in the city, arrived home a little later. I heard her come in, open Rose's door and say brightly, 'Mother, I'm back. Did you have a nice lunch?' There was a moment's silence, then she burst into my room saying, 'Robin, what's happened? Where's Granny?'

I hadn't bothered about lunch. The dining-room was so awful that I only went there at dinnertime with the family, or if I was dragged there. When Mama was out I flatly refused to eat alone with Rose, so Mama reluctantly gave me a couple of shillings to go out and buy what was known as rubbish. I'd done so on this day, bought a pie and a bag of peanuts, and come back to play with my Meccano set. Mama, having established that Rose was nowhere in our flat, was running in six different directions at once, wringing her hands and crying, 'Where can she have gone? Poor old thing, where is she?' Then furiously, 'Robin, stop playing with that damned Meccano! Go round the passages, all of them, and look for your grandmother while I go and ask in the lobby. She might have gone out into the street!'

While Mama headed towards the lift I sauntered down the corridor, unmoved; in my limited experience Rose had always been a first-class survivor. I knew the back passages of Cliveden intimately having explored them often in the boredom of flat-life. I inspected those on our floor until I came to the service lift, and pressed the button to take it down to the floor below.

It was no surprise to find that the lift had stuck between floors; it happened every week or so, usually when it was carrying irate people who yelled for help. This time there was complete silence, and I went down the fire escape to the floor below. One-third of the lift was above floor-level, and when I lay down flat and peered between the bars I saw my grandmother, peacefully asleep in a corner with pointed, buttoned shoes toed inwards and her skirt decorously draped to cover her legs. Her grey head rested on her arms and she looked for all the world like a small, sleeping animal in a zoo. I shook the bars and said, 'Hey, Granny! Wake up! It's me, Robin.'

She looked up rather blearily and said, 'Hello dear, this lift has stopped for some reason. I don't know how I got here, it isn't the usual lift. I want to get out.'

'Yes, I know. I'll go and get someone, I won't be long.'

'No! Stay here!' She was suddenly frightened, as sleep wore off. She clawed herself upright and came unsteadily across the lift to where I was lying on the floor above. She reached up to me and I held her hand; she looked as though she might cry.

I said, 'It's all right, Granny, you're quite safe but I'll have to find someone to get you out. I'll try to be quick.' Then I remembered the bag of lunch-time peanuts I still had with me; I picked one out with my free hand and gave it to her. 'Look, have a peanut, Granny, they're nice.'

Still clinging to me with one hand she took the peanut with the other, and nibbled at it. After a moment she said, 'I haven't had one of these for years. Yes, they are nice, dear, give me another one.' She held on like someone drowning while I patiently fed her peanuts, and it was like this that the rescue party, headed by a frantic Mama, found us a short while later. Perhaps because Rose had reached the age when anyone her size looks simian, and because the cage-like lift enhanced the zoo illusion, Mama refused to believe that I had been feeding Rose peanuts to comfort her and not to mock her. Rose wiped the whole thing from her mind the instant help arrived. She had a mind like a schoolroom blackboard as far as unpleasant incidents were concerned, and when she was released she shuffled happily off to bed, still clutching my bag of peanuts. When Pa came home he laughed and laughed about it, and there weren't too many times when he got a good laugh out of his mother-in-law.

The South Yarra house provided better security, as far as Rose was concerned; she ceased to think about going out, and established a routine for herself by which everybody could and did set their watches. She was getting seriously deaf, and hearing aids, in those days, were both cumbersome and unattractive. She refused to consider wearing one, but as she had arrived at the stage where one had to take a deep breath, bend down and scream into her ear to attract her attention, something had to be done. She must have found the answer herself, perhaps in some secret cache of treasures handed down by her own grandmother because I have never, before or since, seen anything remotely like it. I came home from school on holiday to see Rose sitting placidly on the sofa in the sitting-room with a single horn, like an inverted unicorn's horn, rising from the centre of her head.

As ear-trumpets go, if they still exist outside museums, it was a masterpiece. It was made of pure tortoise shell, light and pleasingly curved, and it ran on a narrow headband trimmed with gold which fitted over her head from ear to ear. If you tapped Rose on the shoulder and indicated that you had something to say she'd pull it round to her ear, and push it in. Amazingly enough, it worked. The disadvantage was that if you were telling her something she didn't want to hear, and it was usually poor Mama who had to do that, she simply slid the ear-trumpet up to its unicorn position, and heard nothing. It also had a distressing effect on visitors. Our parents were so used to it, and to Rose, that they were often quite unconscious of the distraction caused by an ancient, mute female huddled in a chair with a tortoiseshell trumpet rising from the middle of her skull. She became so cunning that it was impossible to get through to her unless she thought it would be to her advantage if she heard you.

The little patch of garden behind the house, sheltered, sunny and hidden from the neighbours, stirred her gardening instincts which had lain dormant since the fiasco at The Haven. Mama was no gardener, and when Rose started murmuring about cinerarias and carnations Mama indulged her by engaging someone to do the work. The sight of an evolving garden seemed to give Rose a lot of pleasure, and Mama pointed out to us all how perceptive she'd been to guess what her mother would like best.

'I remember so well,' she told Pa, 'How she used to adore the garden at Hascombe.'

'She never actually did anything in it, did she?'

'No, of course not. She never went outside without white gloves on. But she knew the names of a lot of the plants, and she loved showing people round it.'

'That's what I thought,' said Pa. 'But I swear I saw her squatting down and digging in one of the beds the other day. I was so surprised I went onto the balcony to make sure but she stood up again, and she wouldn't have heard me if I'd called to her.'

Mama said comfortably, 'Heaven knows what she was doing, darling, she's never dug a hole in her life. I'm just so pleased that the garden keeps her happy.'

Rose went on enjoying the garden; she spent a lot of time in it, specially when Mama was out shopping or seeing her friends.

The moment of truth came when Pa decided to change insurance companies. One of the things that had survived the family's financial disaster was Rose's jewellery, or at least enough really nice pieces to make her and grandfather, when he was still alive, feel that she wasn't forced to appear naked in public. In terms of value it added up to a substantial amount. There were some lovely strings of pearls with diamond clasps, long diamond and pearl earrings, bracelets, and some really beautiful rings and brooches; Claire and Peggy had particular items earmarked for themselves in the future, and enquired tenderly after their welfare in their letters.

When Rose first came to live with us at Sorrento she had been inclined to wear most of the jewellery most of the time, but as she grew older Mama gradually separated her from it except when we had visitors, rolling it up in velvet jewellery rolls and tucking it deep in Rose's drawers under redundant lace underwear and lavender bags. Rose treated Mama as a substitute for her Lady's Maid, on whom she had always relied to produce anything she wanted rather than to look for it herself, and it never occurred to Mama that Rose would dig deep enough to find the jewellery. She showed it to us sometimes, privately, and we dreamed secretly of wearing it, especially Jenny.

When Pa decided to switch the insurance the new company naturally demanded a revaluation of the jewellery listed on the old policy, which dated back some years. Pa, brandishing the list, said, 'Aileen, I've got to leave your mother's jewellery at Drummond's tomorrow for valuation. Would you get it for me?'

Mama said brightly, 'Yes, of course darling,' and trotted upstairs.

There was a long pause before she reappeared, holding a bundle of velvet jewellery rolls and looking very white around the gills. She dropped the rolls into Pa's lap, flapped her hands, and at last whispered hoarsely, 'Geoff! They're all empty!'

'Good God!' Pa sailed out of his chair, scattering velvet. 'How the hell could they be? Have we been burgled?' Mama shook her head.

'Then where the hell's the jewellery ? Ask her!'

They both stared at Rose who was crocheting a rug square. Mama tapped her on the shoulder, slid the ear-trumpet into position none too gently and roared into it, 'Mother! Where's your jewellery?'

'Don't shout at me, Aileen!'

'Your jewellery, Mother!' She shook the empty velvet rolls under Rose's nose. 'These were in your drawer with all your jewellery in them and now they're empty. What have you done with the jewellery?'

'Oh, those.' Rose brushed the velvet rolls away disgustedly. 'What a silly place to put good jewellery, Aileen. Anyone could have found it and taken it. Too silly for words.'

'Mother, where is it now? Geoff has to have it for the insurance company.'

'It's quite safe, dear, you don't have to worry about it. Geoff can tell the insurance people it's safe, though what it's got to do with them I don't know.'

'*Where is it, Rose?*' Pa's teeth were gritted and his moustache bristled. Rose firmly switched her ear-trumpet to the top of her head, gathered up her crochet-work with offended dignity, and shuffled off upstairs to bed. Mama and Pa stared at each other.

Our parents maintained a myth that they never exchanged a cross word during their marriage; in fact what they substituted for the normal, healthy marital row, especially in front of us, was a deadly, jaws-clenched form of self-control, and they used the word 'darling' like a scourge to prove that they weren't really fighting.

Pa said, 'Did you really leave them in her drawer rolled up in those bloody things, *darling*?'

'Yes, I did, *darling*. She never looks in her drawers, except at what's on top.'

'Well when did you last check to see if they were there? Are you sure they were there when we moved in here?'

'Of course they were! What d'you take me for? I looked at them all when I put them away, I... Robin, go to bed!' She began to cry.

'Wait a minute!' said Pa. It wasn't meant for me but I stood still anyway. He looked as though he might strangle anything that moved within his range. 'All this damned digging in the garden. When did your mother ever get her fingers dirty? When, in God's name, did she ever plant a plant? That's where they are, God-dammit. They're all buried in the garden!'

We never found them, but that is certainly where they were. We sifted the soil, scratched and dug and drove the contract-gardener mad by disturbing his work, or it may have been that he had found the treasure already. The latter is very likely because he gave our job away soon afterwards, and wasn't seen in South Yarra again.

20

Jessie

LIVING IN A HOUSE instead of a flat meant that we could have the animals back. We were still reduced to one cocker spaniel and a cat, both of whom had been fostered out during the Cliveden period and both of whom were reinstated in the new house almost before we'd unpacked. Matilda, the spaniel went on an immediate, meticulous tour of inspection, the cat curled up on the sofa and the house became a home. The recent, un-animaled past seemed like a time in the wilderness.

Shipley Street, South Yarra, was no St Georges Road; the garden was adequate for one small dog if it was walked regularly, but the animal population clearly had to be limited. We had all accepted that the quota was one dog and one cat when Jenny produced Jessie.

It was the year when she had finished her training and was doing her midwifery. It was also the year that war broke out, still months before it happened but already the future had a whiff of cordite about it, a taint of sulphur, and Jenny had declared that if war came she would be the first to join the Army as a nurse. Midwifery was not an obvious qualification for Army nursing, but she was determined to have every certificate she could get, to make sure of being accepted.

One of her friends had recently married a dentist who apparently fell short of being an ideal husband. He was also very frightened of snakes. His wife had some muddled idea that shock treatment would help, and to that end went shopping. There was a small shop behind the Myer Emporium which specialised in reptiles, and she bought one of their more impressive items, an 8ft

6in carpet snake named Jessie. In those days carpet snakes retailed at ten shillings a foot, which made Jessie an expensive animal. When the wife went home and advanced on her husband brandishing a considerable length of active reptile the husband didn't argue the point but started packing his worldly goods, something his wife hadn't reckoned on. She abandoned her position, promised to get rid of Jessie if only he would stay, and then rang Jenny.

Jenny, of course, was enchanted, and happily paid what amounted to two weeks wages on the spot. She arrived at home breathless, carrying a large wooden box with airholes in the side and put it down on the sitting-room carpet.

'Oh, darling! No more animals!' said Mama, recognising the significance of the airholes.

'What is it?' asked Pa hopefully.

'It's all right,' said Jenny, opening the box. 'She won't take up much room and she only eats every two weeks. I'll arrange about getting her fed.'

Jessie's natural curiosity was only matched by her sociability. What seemed like yards of fat, shining, beautifully marked snake flowed out of the box, coiled itself neatly on the carpet and raised a diamond-shaped head with bright, intelligent eyes to inspect the company present. Mama leapt backwards and knocked over a coffee table, Rose said vaguely, 'What have you got there, dear?' and Pa went down on his knees, doting.

'I knew you'd love her,' said Jenny.

In fact, within twenty-four hours Jessie had won over everyone in the house, including the cat and Matilda the spaniel. Rose, it's true, never acknowledged her existence; a snake in the house was so far beyond her that she refused to believe it was happening. She didn't object, she simply treated Jessie as being invisible, even when she coiled herself beside Rose on the sofa and put her head in Rose's lap. Jessie liked getting into peoples' laps because they were warm; if possible she would rest her head in the crook of your elbow, and if snakes can purr, she purred.

There were risks attached to having Jessie in the house, and we all realised that strangers were coming to the door, or old people, might be badly frightened by her. She was mad about people, and she soon learned that when the doorbell rang it meant that someone new was about to appear. There would be a concerted rush to get Jessie into her box before she had time to answer the door in person, and the faster one coiled her in the faster she'd uncoil herself out, so that by the time one got to the tail her head would be halfway across the floor. Often people got tired of waiting, decided we were out and went away.

It had never occurred to us, or we'd never thought about it, that snakes might like to play as a puppy does, or a kitten. Jessie and Matilda played together by the hour, Matilda with Jessie's head in her mouth, and Jessie wrapped round Matilda's body in as many coils as there were room for. She was far stronger than Matilda; if she had squeezed there would have been no more dog, and by the same token if Matilda had clamped her jaws there would have been no more Jessie, but they threw each other harmlessly round the room like a pair of wrestlers without a cross word between them. For the times when Matilda was absent or unwilling Jessie invented the chair-game.

Our dining-room furniture was solid; the chairs were Georgian, a set of ten that Mama and Pa had bought in England, plain and heavy. Jessie found a strange reptilian delight in wrapping herself round the leg of a chair and whipping it sharply here and there across the floor. It was quite normal to walk into the dining-room and to see a chair zigzagging around, but if one didn't know that there was a snake underneath it had a poltergeist effect that was quite eerie. Pa transformed the chair-game into a polished act; a performing snake was exactly the kind of thing he liked best.

He always had a lot of male friends he asked in for drinks, among them at that time a number of high-ranking Army and Naval officers from England who were planning, with their Australian counterparts, for the coming war. Pa would put Jessie into the dining-room before they arrived, and close the door. Then he'd take the visitor into the sitting-room, ask what they'd like to drink and leave them with Mama while he fetched it. The drink they'd asked for was seldom what they got since Pa's aim was to have them well sozzled before he exposed them to the chair-game, and he knew that most of these men were talented drinkers.

I was genuinely shocked when I saw what he was putting into the drinks one evening, but he said it was just a joke. One would have thought that a mixture of brandy, scotch and gin would be nasty enough to alert anyone, even when topped with soda, but either men lose their palates by the time they reach high rank, or else our visitors were all over-polite or abnormally thirsty. Whatever the reason I never saw one of them so much as change his expression on tasting Pa's hell-brew, and even the dullest of them became chatty and amusing after the second drink.

It was usually after the second drink that they'd make a polite move to say goodbye. Pa, very jovial, would slap them on the shoulder and say, 'No, no old boy! You can't go yet. One for the road! Come with me and get it.' He'd propel the poor man to the dining-room door, the drinks being on the sideboard, and busy himself with bottles while his stunned companion contemplated a chair doing wheelies at the end of the dining-room table.

Usually the victim would advance to investigate, meet Jessie and laugh, but occasionally one would tap Pa nervously on the shoulder, and with his eyes starting out of his head say, 'Don't think I'm mad, old boy, but that chair seems to be moving!' Pa would turn, gaze blankly down the room and say, 'What chair? What are you talking about?'

'That chair, there! Look, dammit, look!'

Pa would scan the room while the chair slid and bumped, then examine the other man with grave concern and say, 'Are you sure you're feeling all right, old boy? Like to sit down for a bit, perhaps? Have a drink – might make you feel better,' and he'd hit the poor fellow with a double scotch, so that by the time he left he'd passed the alcoholic point of no return and was thinking of taking up spiritualism.

Jessie was with us for a year. We managed to conceal her presence from all but the people we knew to be civilised enough to appreciate her, and it was hard to imagine life without her. She was no trouble; every two weeks she was driven back to the shop which had sold her, and installed in a cage with two or three white rats. She would kill and eat what she wanted, sleep it off for a couple of days and return home bright as a button, ready to play. We stopped putting her in her box at night because she much preferred to follow us upstairs to bed, and either to climb up the curtain and hang from the curtain rod or to simply curl up on one's feet.

There seemed to be no reason why she couldn't stay forever, but subconsciously we felt guilty about her. There was always that headlong rush to hide her when the doorbell rang, and the fact that we never told our neighbours about her. That was our undoing. Jenny's friend, Janet, was still living with us off and on; she had qualified as a nurse too, but we remained her second home.

One sunny day when everyone else was out Janet decided to sunbathe in the garden, and took Jessie out with her. This was quite normal, because Jessie loved a nice bask under a bush when the weather was right. Unfortunately Janet, who was always sleepy, dozed off, and Jessie took a glide round the garden fence. When Janet woke up and looked for her she was gone, and a hitherto undiscovered hole at the bottom of a paling between us and the next-door garden, was the only possible escape route.

Janet pulled a dress over her two-piece and went next door. She rang the bell, and when the lady of the house appeared she said politely, 'I'm sorry to bother you, but have you seen the Walker's snake?'

The woman looked puzzled and said, 'Their rake? No, I don't think we've borrowed their rake, but I can look.'

'No, not their rake, their snake. She's about 8 ft long, and I think she must've slipped through into your garden. May I go and see?'

The unfortunate neighbour, who was not a snake-person by any stretch of the imagination, gasped. 'A *SNAKE!* You're not serious! In our garden!' then, 'My God, they should be prosecuted! I'll ring the police.'

Janet went into the garden and retrieved Jessie who was enjoying the change of scenery. When Mama arrived home the police were already there, attended by the neighbour and her husband both registering outrage, and Janet, with Jessie draped becomingly round her neck, was trying to reason with them. The police, to the neighbours' fury, said that keeping a pet snake was not a chargeable offence, but they also warned Mama that it was not likely to promote a spirit of goodwill and understanding in our immediate vicinity, and reluctantly she had to agree.

Jessie went to a Wildlife Park where there was company of her own kind. She may have found that she preferred the carpet snakes to us, but I doubt it. It's hard to tell whether snakes show affection among themselves or not, but there was no question about Jessie's feelings when she was one of the family. She not only craved affection, but she had so much to give.

21

Adolescence

DURING OUR FIRST YEARS in the South Yarra house I was in the more hideous throes of adolescence, and all adolescents were pariahs in those days. Teenagers hadn't been invented, and it was made plain that one was in limbo, lost between childhood and becoming human. In the holidays Mama and her friends were apt to look at me and laugh, and say to each other, 'Oh, my dear! But it really *is* a frightful stage, isn't it?' as though I was deaf. Not infrequently Mama would quote Rose's Bon Mot from Sorrento, 'Betty's beautiful, Jenny's handsome...' My self-esteem hadn't quite reached its all-time low, but it was sinking fast; I consoled myself in bed at night with fantasies wherein I became beautiful and heroic.

It was a strange year, 1939. There could have been few places less exposed to the growing certainty of war than a girls boarding school at Mt Eliza yet it penetrated even there, a feeling that hovered between excitement and dread. We could sense our elders adjusting themselves, shifting gear in their approach to the future as though to ready themselves for steep, uncertain hills. Girls with elder brothers were thoughtful, and talked together in low voices; the teaching staff were edgy, and often distracted.

The actual outbreak of war was a 'what were you doing when...?' time for everyone, a moment that imprinted itself on minds as a tattoo is printed on the skin, ineradicable. No one was moving very far from their wireless, in case of news, but when the announcement came we were all upstairs, Mama and Jenny and me, and Rose was being difficult about something with Mama. Anne, our Irish maid, had the wireless on downstairs while she was cleaning. She suddenly turned the volume up full and we could hear her sobbing, and a voice graver than the grave said, '…that we are at war with Germany'.

Mama burst into tears, and we didn't know what to do; Jenny was too excited, and I was too inept. Mama, sobbing, said, 'Oh God, it can't happen again. You don't know what it's like,' and Jenny, who would finally know only too well what it was like, couldn't stop herself from grinning.

The phoney war, those first few months of stalemate in Europe, saw Mama and her friends become slightly paranoid. They felt impotent and guilty because they were so far away from Home, and because whatever horrors might come to Britain they were shamefully safe. They formed every conceivable kind of patriotic group, knitted socks and balaclavas, and as the months of anticlimax lengthened they became frustrated and confused.

Pa, as an ex-Army man and holder of a King's Commission, offered his services. He knew a lot of people in high places and they, in turn, knew his record in India, his experience in Intelligence there, and respected him for what he had done since coming to Australia. He was retrieved from retirement and seconded to the Army to organise Military Intelligence.

Jenny had finished her Midwifery Certificate, and was desperate to join up. Her aim was to go overseas as soon as possible, but it had been decreed by the Government that no nurse under the age of 24 might serve outside Australia, and Jenny was 20. There was also a problem because of her muddled Christian names, and she couldn't join up until she could produce a Birth Certificate. This inevitably had been lost during one of our moves, and the Authorities were disinclined to believe that she was who she said she was. After a lot of highly dramatised despair on her part, and a great deal of string-pulling on Pa's part, a Certificate was issued. Jenny paused only to alter the date of her birth on the Certificate from 1919 to 1915 before joining the Army Nursing Service, and requesting service overseas.

Betty was marking time. Norman's parents had agreed, reluctantly and in principle only, to their marriage. Having done so they produced, with evident relish, endless reasons why the wedding should be postponed indefinitely. They decreed that while Norman's younger brother might enlist and die for his country Norman, as their heir, must stay at home and run the property, the Land being a reserved occupation. They doubted, they said, that he would have either the time or the money to cope with a wife. As they were indecently rich, could have easily employed a Manager or paid Norman a handsome wage, this was patently unconvincing. Not only were they making excuses but they were being monstrously cruel to Norman who, being a born warrior, felt branded for life by being excluded from the war while his brother was sent to fight. Betty went mournfully to art-classes and dabbled in murals, then in stained glass, her eyes misty with longing for her love, and as soon as possible after love was legitimised for the first of the twenty-strong brood of children.

I was at school, a yeasty brew of emotion, introspection and ignorance, a condition quite common among my age-group, and far from attractive. I was eighty percent uninformed and twenty percent wrong about sex which was also fairly common; one could pick out the girls at school who really knew because they banded together and sniggered at the rest of us. Jenny could easily have educated me but it probably never dawned on her how ignorant I was, and I had been so brainwashed by Mama's taboos that I didn't dare ask.

The girls of my age had maudlin and romanticised ideas about the war and the men who fought in it. We lived in an emotional atmosphere of the greatest falsity, encouraged by the school staff who wept over the sticky-sweet songs of the time about the White Cliffs of Dover and the Nightingale in Berkeley Square. We grew weak with our longing to comfort heroic pilots, to be where the bombs were falling, and to risk our lives in some highly-sanitised situation, preferably to the sound of general applause.

When the war had started in earnest, after Dunkirk, the Headmistress heightened the emotional pressure with a night-time ritual known as 'Taps'. If the news was either very good or very bad a Taps night would be declared, and after lights-out we would gather in our pyjamas at the windows looking down on the Quadrangle. The staff would be standing behind the tall, gowned figure of the Headmistress, solemn and silent, waiting for the full weight of the occasion to sink into our childish souls.

When she judged us ready the Headmistress would step forward into the moonlight, and in her deep voice she would recite.

They who shall not grow old as we who are left grow old,
Age shall not weary them, nor the years condemn,
At the going down of the sun and in the morning
We shall remember them.

And from behind our open windows we would chant in chorus, 'We shall remember them'.

Then taps; piping young voices, shaky with emotion, and tears on cheeks.

Day is done, gone the sun,
From the sea, from the hills from the sky,
Safely rest, all is well,
God is nigh…

One of the staff would put a record of the Last Post on the gramophone, and when its last heart-rending note died away we would file off to bed, with not a dry eye between us. It was high-octane fuel for our under-developed minds, and left only a fraction of our attention free for what went on in the classroom. On top of that discipline was spasmodic, sometimes harsh, often non-existent.

Betty and Norman were married, in an austerity wartime wedding on the day Paris fell, Betty in a short blue dress and a blinding aura of joy, Norman handsome and unfamiliar in a suit, and most of the wedding guests in a state of shock at the turn the war was taking. Jenny was in the grey uniform of the Army Nursing Service at last, her hat at a strictly non-regulation angle, and her mind already on board a hospital ship. At the reception a lot of people cried, but they were almost certainly not crying about Betty and Norman; there were too many other things in the world that called for proper tears.

I had started on a gradual, unconscious divorce from my family, not through ill-will on either side but simply because we had begun to lose each other. I either spent my holidays with Kempie or with a school-friend's family on their Western District property, in a huge, rangey house reeking of permanency, riding paddocks in the wicked, cold winds which flatten the grass and bend the eucalypts double on those open plains, and coming home frozen to log fires and cocoa. Their family seemed to be far more integrated than ours; they had clotted together over the years with their house and their land, while our life was jittery and dislocated by comparison.

Pa and Mama didn't come down to school to visit me; they said it was unpatriotic to use petrol, and besides, they were busy. I was quite pleased; I was busy establishing myself as the school Enfant Terrible, and didn't fancy the staff informing my parents of this at first hand. In an undefined program of self-assertion I systematically broke rules, went Out of Bounds, mixed the staff's breakfast sugar with Epsom Salts, organised the whole school into a successful sit-down strike and demoralised the German Mistress by filling her desk to the brim with black-beetles. Because of the superior academic standard of The Hermitage I had been put into a class a year above my age-group when I first arrived; no one ever demoted me, but during classes I simply switched off and drew horses, cartoons or anything else that came to mind under the desk, getting through exams by swotting for a week beforehand. After school there was Sport, but I only appeared on the playing-field when I'd been forcibly prevented from nicking off to the riding school.

The coupling among the staff continued to flourish, encouraged by the pressure-cooker atmosphere of wartime. The established pairs clung to each other for comfort, parading round the Cloisters hand-in-hand and playing sentimental music in their rooms. It was towards the end of that year that Miss Cooke, the Games Mistress, began to take an interest in me that struck even me as strange, given that I had alienated every other member of the staff.

Miss Cooke had come to Toorak College at the same time as I had. She was a slight, muscular woman in her late twenties, her hair shingled at the back, a foxy, sharp-nosed face and lashless eyes. She strode around parade-ground style, her arms swinging, her legs bare beneath khaki shorts, followed by her Red Kelpie, Bunty, whose colouring and features were uncannily like his owner's. Miss Cooke was a singleton when she came, but the following year a new and rather superior mistress arrived, It seemed that the parents had at last rebelled against their daughters' French being ruined by Miss Jones, and demanded a replacement. The newcomer was tall and thin, and had enormous eyes with purple patches under them so that she looked like a cross between a Giant Panda and Boris Karloff. Within a week of her arrival it became apparent that she and Miss Cooke were walking out, and in no time at all they were accepted as one of the official pairs.

When Miss Cooke started to single me out for attention I was puzzled, then embarrassed, then flattered into discovering that if I concentrated on games instead of horses I could play them reasonably well. I won the school Swimming Championship, the result of a short period when Mama had tried to make me into an Olympic diver and subjected me to daily training under a crazy German coach. Praise from Miss Cooke was harder to get than teeth from a hen, and I swelled with pride when she handed me a minute silver cup and a brusque, congratulatory speech.

Her next move was to ask me to run Bunty and to feed him when she was away from school on her days off. Bunty's relationship to her was that of a sucker fish to a shark; there was a mysterious link between them, and he seldom moved beyond her shadow. No one else had ever been allowed to touch him, and once again my blind little ego sat up and purred. I was cherry-ripe, both through age and circumstance, for that hideous schoolgirl phenomenon known as a 'crush'. Crushes were rife in girls' schools before the liberating influence of co-education; they were humiliating to both the crushee and crushor, and at super-segregated Toorak College they were distressingly common.

Not only was my family becoming remote but I was increasingly conscious that in terms of looks I didn't rate alongside my sisters. It hadn't worried me much until then, but the girls of my age were starting to be obsessed with glamour, and I had to face the fact that not all grubs turned into butterflies. I had stupidly asked Mama during the last holidays whether I was going to be pretty. She studied me at length and then, as if grasping at straws, said, 'Your eldest sister says you have nice eyebrows,' and I made up my mind not to risk the subject again. With the emphasis on facial beauty both at home and school I felt that I was giving the field a long start, and as a result I was ravished by the miracle of someone of importance, like Miss Cooke, deigning to take notice of me.

Miss Cooke made no serious move towards me that year beyond turning me into her puppet, to be manipulated at will and slavishly seeking her approval. In some ways it did me a lot of good; I stopped being an Enfant Terrible and started to work, besides thundering round the playing field trying to impress. The change was so dramatic that I became a sub-prefect and captained teams, and the school staff were amazed, but grateful. My peer-group, who understood exactly what was going on, knew that I was making an idiot of myself, and gave me hell. Life became unnerving and miserable; I never knew whether Miss Cooke was going to be nice to me or snub me, and whichever it was someone would notice and tease me about it afterwards. By the end of the year I was heartily sick of the lot of them, including myself and Miss Cooke.

Jenny was home on leave at the start of the summer holidays, on the brink of her first overseas posting as a nurse on board the Hospital Ship *Oranje Nassau*, a converted Dutch liner bound for duty in the Middle East. She and Janet were both at home, and Betty had come down from Warranooke for a few days too. Mama rang me at school to say that I should come home after the school Break-up by train. She said, 'There really isn't room for you here, darling, till Betty goes back, so I've booked you a room at St Carol's.' St Carol's was a boarding house, just round the corner from where we lived. 'I know you won't get up to town until late, but you know where St Carol's is. You'll be able to carry your suitcase there from the station, and you can come round to us in the morning.'

'Couldn't you and Pa come to the Break-up?'

'No, darling, we're far too busy, and I want to be with The Girls while they're here. You'll have great fun on your own at St Carol's, it'll be good for you. The Manager's very nice, and he'll look after you. Come round here after your breakfast.'

It was a fair way from the station to St Carol's, the suitcase was heavy, and I arrived there puffing, sweating and feeling dispossessed. The Manager showed me into a large bedroom, luxurious compared to my room at home, but bleakly impersonal. I sat on the bed, reluctant to unpack; I could hear music and voices in the next room, and they heightened my isolation. Then I heard a door open and close, and there was a knock on my own door. When I opened it I was surprised to see a youngish man standing there, his finger on his lips, smiling a roguish, conspiratorial smile. Although he was clearly a man he was dressed in a long, tight skirt with a slit down one side, and a frilly white blouse. He clasped his hands, swayed from the hips like a dancer, and inspected me from head to foot.

'Welcome, darling,' he said. 'But *welcome!* We heard you were coming, Jas and I, and I said to Jas, poor little thing, I said. Fancy arriving and being all on your own in a place like this! So I came to meet you. Come into our room and have a drink with us, darling, and meet Jas. You'll love Jas.'

I thought, 'they must be dressing up, playing charades or something.' Anyway, anything was better than sitting alone in my room, so I said, 'Thank you. Are you sure it'll be all right, with Jas, I mean?'

'But of course!' He took me by the wrist and whipped me from my door to his. The room was very dark, but I could make out piled-up cushions and potted plants, and there was a strange, sweetish smell coming from some sticks which were smoking lazily in a Chinese vase. A big, soft man dressed in what looked like a brocade tent was half-lying against a heap of cushions on the floor.

'This is Jas,' said my new friend. 'And I'm Robin. What's your name, dear.

'How funny, I'm Robin too.'

'Don't *tell* me! How *quaint!* Jas, darling, do get her a drink to celebrate. We're twins!'

Jas rolled his bulk sulkily against the cushions and said, 'Get it yourself!' I sat down politely on the floor, and when Robin handed me a glass saying, 'I think this should be to your taste, love, do try it.' I tried it. It was sweet and sticky and tasted strongly of peppermint, and it settled into my depths like a hot-water bottle on a cold night.

Robin put some very weird music on the gramophone, poured himself a glass of something, and sat on the floor facing me. He talked with the uncontrollable flow of a burst water main. Every now and then he leapt to his feet, still talking, and either refilled the glasses or changed a record. At one point he said, 'Oh, *damn!* No more creme de menthe. Never mind, darling, try this, it's just as nice.' I fancy it may have been Cointreau. I was feeling no pain, and I was beyond knowing or caring what Robin was talking about. My troubles began a little later: dizziness, nausea, and when I tried to stand up a noticeable lack of directional stability. Jas heaved himself upright for the first time, looked at me closely and said, 'Now look what you've done, you bloody fool. Get her out of here, quick, she's going to throw up!'

Robin dragged me down to the Ladies Bathroom and stood outside while I threw my heart up, then escorted me back to my own room, patted me on the shoulder and shoved me inside. 'Night-night, darling,' he whispered as he left. 'You'll be fine in the morning.' Either St Carol's was empty that night or everyone there was a wonderful sleeper. I made several trips to the bathroom, and the sounds of my suffering must have carried a long way, but nobody stirred.

When I staggered over to my home next morning, pale and shaking, Mama looked at me with interest and said, 'Haven't you been well, darling? The school should have told me but never mind, the holidays'll fix you up. Did you have a lovely time at St Carol's?'

At that time neither Miss Cooke's attentions at school nor my friends at St Carol's had, for me, any connection with matters sexual, and I had no idea that in a vital part of my education I was being exposed to the exotic rather than the straight.

During the next school year I became even more confused, and considerably less trusting of my fellow human beings. To encourage my new, conformist role I was given what was known as More Responsibility. I was taking my School Leaving exams a year before the usual age, and Miss Cooke deliberately played on my nerves as though they were the keyboard of a xylophone. She missed no opportunity to pinpoint me, either for approbation or withering put-down, in shrewdly judged turns. She would touch me quite unnecessarily on the games field in front of everybody, and she secretly issued invitations for me to visit her alone at night in her room. I refused; by now I was genuinely scared of her. Her established soul-mate glared at me with open hatred, and the Headmistress gave me a lecture about not becoming too familiar with the staff. Even though I was going to great lengths to avoid her my peer-group said, rightly enough, that it was my own fault, and sneered at me. I became mildly anorexic, increasingly solitary, and more certain than ever that I must be some kind of freak. I passed my Leaving Exams but my family said that I was too young to leave school. 'You can't just sit around at home,' they said, 'And you're too young to join the Services. Go back next year and do Leaving Honours.'

There was no point in arguing; it was what Mama wanted, and Pa simply said, 'You'll do as your mother tells you.' Toorak College was still going through a lean period, and for lack of a more suitable candidate the Headmistress was forced to inform me that I would be Head Girl in the coming year.

Before the term ended, on the 7th December 1941, the Japanese attacked Pearl Harbour. The war had made a giant leap from Europe to the Pacific, and Australia watched with disbelief as a race they'd hitherto regarded as an incomprehensible, rather primitive joke proceeded to make a mockery of Britain's Far Eastern defences. The Yanks, who to most Australians were almost as foreign and remote as the Japanese, suddenly sprouted like fresh, young grass across the country, challenging and changing our perception of ourselves.

People like Mama who had nursed a lifelong reverence for everything British, the accent, the rigid self-control, the class system, were appalled by the newcomers. As a mother of daughters Mama equated them roughly with the rapist, barbarian hordes of the distant past. Young Australia on the other hand took to them with joy, embracing them and their way of life, finding both seductive. It was the beginning of the end of the old Australia, the land of the macho man and his subservient woman, of the grazier caste system and the colonial cringe. We didn't suspect that it was happening, but in 1941 our doors to the world began to creak open, and Australia would never be the same again.

22

War and Warburton

THOSE SUMMER HOLIDAYS were like coming out of a cellar into the sun, and I tried not to think about having to go down to the dark again. The *Oranje Nassau*, Jenny's Hospital Ship, had come back to Australia for a refit, and Jenny came home on leave. The ship had been carrying the men wounded in the Desert War from Alexandria down the coast of Africa to the hospitals of Durban and Cape Town, and although Jenny had been away for less than a year she had changed. She was the same on the surface, a little thinner, but there was something different about her mouth and eyes, a hardness and remoteness, and she had withdrawn from our lives to some un-shareable place of her own.

Mama was so overcome with joy and pride and excitement that she didn't seem to notice the difference, and she insisted on dragging Jenny round her own friends as though she was showing off a trophy. Jenny put up with it politely but she treated Mama with a tolerant, distant kindness, as people treat over-effusive children. One felt that she had seen and learned things which could never be explained to anyone as young and innocent as her mother.

She was different with me too, as if I had stopped being an infant sister and become a friend. Most of the friends she'd had when she left were scattered; even Janet was now an Army nurse stationed in Queensland. The girls she knew in Melbourne were doing jobs which seemed to be secondary to their absorbing love affairs and social lives, and they had lost any relevance for Jenny; she avoided them. There was nothing she could say to them about the things which haunted her, the men whose bodies and lives had been fragmented in the time it takes for a shell to explode or a bullet to strike. Tragedies devoured her, and she was twenty-two, going on forty.

We sat on the beds in her room late at night, after our parents had honoured their on-the-dot bedtime of nine-thirty and shut their door. She had brought back a couple of tall, stone bottles of Bols gin, and stacks of oval Abdullah cigarettes. She brought them out as we sat, blankets round our shoulders, poured large glasses of neat Bols, gave one to me and lit a cigarette for both of us.

She said, 'It'll be fun when the war's over, Robs, the two of us together. I'll take you out and show you round, but if you're going to come out with me you've got to learn to drink and smoke. Suck, for God's sake, don't blow! And don't chew the end. You're supposed to toss Bols off in one gulp but you'd better not, just sip.'

Made bold by Bols I asked her about the Hospital Ship and her work, sure that she wouldn't want to talk about it, but to my surprise she did, savagely butting out her cigarettes as she talked as though she was punishing them.

She said, 'They're so brave, these men, Robs. You can't imagine how brave they are. They have great holes in them that'll never heal or arms gone, or legs or they're blind. And the worst hurt ones are the bravest of all, they never complain.

'When I was training here we used to joke about men patients, how they moaned and fussed and thought they were sicker than anyone else had ever been. And they were always wanting things, even when we were flat-out busy. They were twice as much trouble as women patients. I thought this'd be the same and it isn't. Maybe it's because they've all been through it together and seen each other hurt, so they can share it, the being hurt and crippled, I mean. It's not just something that happens to one man on his own and makes him feel important. But some of them are so bloody young, just kids. You know they'll never be whole people again and so do they, but they crack jokes about it.

'I lie in my bunk at night,' she said, pouring herself another Bols, 'and I cry about them. More often about the older ones, funnily enough. The young ones only have themselves to worry about, and they'll get looked after by their families or the government, and if they're any good they'll make a life for themselves. But the married ones who've got wives and kids, what's their future? A lot of them won't be able to work any more and they'll get a pension, but their wives'll have to stay home and look after them and a lot of the wives won't do that. They'll get fed up and clear out with someone else. And there'll be kids who grow up despising their fathers because they're cripples. War heroes! Bloody hell! How I hate the rubbish people talk – all these silly, deluded old Melbourne matrons. They don't know a thing – David says...'

'David who?'

'Oh damn. Robs, forget about David. I haven't said anything about him to Mama, she wouldn't approve. I'll probably never see him again anyway.'

'Are you in love with him? Why won't you see him again?'

'He's in hospital in Cape Town, he was one of our wounded. Maybe we'll go there again on our next run, but he'll probably have been sent home.'

'Oh, Jennifer! Are you going to marry him after the war?'

'No, he's got a wife and kids in England. Don't look like that Robs, have another Bols, these things happen all the time. I don't think I'll ever get married, but for God's sake don't say so to Mama.'

'Why won't you?'

'Why not? Cleave to one man only for the rest of my life? Wash for him, cook for him, breed his brats and tell him he's wonderful five times a day? Not on your life! That's what it's like, you know, marriage, except for people like Betty who're made for it. When this is over I'm going to enjoy things. Maybe I'll go on nursing, maybe not, but I'll live my own life and if I want to have lovers I'll have them, not just one man I'll get bored with and start hating. If you breathe a word of this I'll murder you, it'd give Mama a fit. But I tell you now, all the poppycock talked about sex and marriage in this house makes me sick.'

When her leave was up and she rejoined her ship it felt to me that the house had somehow closed itself after her, in the same way that a giant clam closes its shell. Mama put framed photographs of Jenny everywhere, gazed at them and sighed over them, and invented sacrifices for us to make in small, domestic ways to match Jenny's privations at sea. She had her cooking by then to give her some distraction, and the sacrifices showed up in our meals.

She had decided soon after Dunkirk that servants were an unjustifiable luxury in wartime. Anne, the Irish maid who had been with us for years, had decided to retire anyway; she was getting old and cranky, and when she left us to go into a room in an Old People's Home, a life of blissful inactivity and gossip, Mama announced that in future she would do the cooking herself.

She took to it with alarming fervour. Recipes littered the house, she was bitterly critical of anyone who still had a cook, she bought and rapidly discarded every gadget which could possibly be used in the kitchen. Each one was a new miracle, to be superseded by a newer one. She drew the line at housework, and this was done, from scrubbing and polishing to washing and ironing, by a nice, gabby little woman called Mrs Kane. She had long, satisfactory cuppa sessions with Mama over the kitchen table, and it was impossible to avoid an intimate knowledge of Mrs Kane's extended family because Mama gave Pa and me a new episode every night.

The worst thing about Mama's cooking was her patriotism. She believed it was immoral to use more than half the prescribed amount of any ingredient, such as butter, eggs or sugar, which was on the ration list in England or might not be plentiful on board the *Oranje Nassau.* Arbitrary reductions took place in whatever recipes she happened to be following so that cakes tended to fall apart, sauces had the consistency of clag, and everything tasted flat. Pa, who always had a good lunch at the Australian Club, was immensely proud of her efforts, but said that he really preferred plain, simple food at night. Their evening meals on most nights of the week for the rest of their lives consisted of chops, potatoes and a vegetable, followed by toast and jam.

Soon after Jenny had gone back to her ship Betty had a miscarriage. It was the ultimate disaster for her, and the doctors made it worse. They said that her pregnancies would always be difficult, and that child bearing itself would be a risk. Her whole life had been built round her twenty imagined babies and their father, and the possibility of her own body betraying her dream had never occurred to her. She heard what the doctors said, refused to believe a word of it, and went back to Warranooke to try again.

I had been to Warranooke once or twice on visits, and didn't know what to make of it. There was a coldness about it, not generated by Betty and Norman but by Norman's parents and the huge, dark, concrete house they lived in. It was an imposingly ugly house, like a monstrous gun emplacement. It had been built onto the old, original bluestone kitchens and servants' quarters which still stretched behind it. There were lawns with peacocks and palms, and a huge aviary full of native birds, and sunshine, but inside the house it was dark and unwelcoming.

Betty and Norman lived in a cottage, separated from the main house by a tall, brooding cypress hedge. The cottage was very old, built of wattle and daub, with a floor that went up and down in waves so that you felt that you were walking on the deck of a moving ship. Betty had done her best with it, hanging prints and reproductions on the walls and draping bits of bright fabric here and there, but it needed money in large quantities, and they had none. The in-laws were unsympathetic; they made no secret of the fact that Norman's choice of wives had been his own, not theirs. They patronised Betty, bullied her and put her down, and when she was alone she sat on the cottage floor and wept. Norman was out all day long doing the work of three men, and his mother could torment Betty during the daylight hours at will. Jenny wouldn't have put up with it for a moment but Norman was Betty's true and only love, and she would have died rather than make trouble between him and his parents. Having longed as a child to be punished with everyone else she now reeled under punishment that was completely undeserved.

The world was full of evil spirits that year, the last year I was at Toorak College. At school one couldn't quite hear the thin wail of the Banshees but one knew that the echo was there, just out of reach. My age group was old enough to be aware that the world we knew was dying, that millions of people were dying too, among them people we knew. We felt cocooned and useless. As Head Girl I was supposed to set an example of discipline and rectitude and it all seemed irrelevant, a chore to be got through between news bulletins on the radio.

In addition, there was still Miss Cooke. In some ways it was easier to avoid her; I shared a proper bedroom with another girl, which meant there was somewhere I could shut myself away instead of being readily available in the commonroom or the corridors. Unavailability and reluctance must have made me more desirable, and Miss Cooke wasn't a woman to give up easily.

Mama telephoned me shortly before the end of the first term, and the May holidays. She didn't ring very often, and this time she had the bright, encouraging note in her voice that I had learned to mistrust.

She said, 'Darling, about the holidays…'

'Yes, Mama. What about them?'

'Well, that nice Games Mistress of yours, Miss Cooke, rang me, and I must say it's very kind of her. She says she's going hiking for a few days round Warburton at the beginning of the holidays, and because you've tried so hard at games she'd like to take you with her. It'd be lovely for you, camping out and seeing the bush. I said you'd be thrilled. Do go and thank her, darling.'

'Oh, please Mama, no. I don't want to go.'

My mother's voice ceased to be bright and encouraging, and I could hear her thinking, 'Adolescents! What on earth gets into them?'

'Why on earth not, Robin? Your father and I are busy, and there's nothing for you to do at home. You're not going to spend all your time with Kempie, you're too old for it.'

'I don't like Miss Cooke. Please, I don't want to go.'

'Oh, rubbish. A year ago you were telling me how nice she is. Anyway, I've said yes, and that's that. She's got all the camping things you'll need, so go and talk to her about it.' She rang off.

I didn't go to Miss Cooke but she came to me. She had a triumphant look in her eye and she wisely didn't elaborate too much, just told me that she'd spoken to Mama and which day we'd be leaving, then walked away with a swagger that said, 'Game, set, match.' I finished the term leaden with foreboding.

On the appointed day Mama drove me to Flinders Street Station and delivered me to Miss Cooke. She was hung about with packs and bedding rolls, a share of which she handed to me, and she looked more aggressively masculine than ever. Bunty sat at her feet, looking foxy. I was speechless, partly through fury, partly through fear, and Mama gushed overdone gratitude to cover my silence.

Miss Cooke told me that we'd get off the train at Warburton, walk up the mountain to a hut she'd stayed in before, and camp there for the night. Then she brought out a book and ignored me so that I sat, as the train rattled on, wondering why I was scared when the whole thing was so obviously harmless.

We trudged uphill through the bush. There was the silence of tall, damp trees and ferns, a winding track, and every now and then the temple-gong call of a bellbird dropping through the leaves like a stone into water. I could see Miss Cooke's iron calf-muscles pumping away ahead of me, and Bunty's tail waving just behind them. I felt humble and stupid and told myself that it'd be all right, that outside school everything was different. The hut when we reached it was small and basic with two bunks against one wall, and a fireplace. Miss Cooke sent me off to get dry wood and made a fire; it was dark by then.

When the fire was going and she had put the billy on to boil, and a frying pan for the steak, she began to talk. She had a flask of whisky, and she poured a little into a mug of tea for me, and a lot for herself. She started telling me that she'd been engaged to a man who'd been killed early in the war but the story sounded false, like something from a women's magazine. Then she began to talk about her women friends, how wonderful they were and how she loved them, then how wonderful I was, and I began to feel uncomfortable; she said things that made no sense to me at all.

She said, 'It's so nice here, just the two of us, isn't it? So lovely? I can't tell you how much I've looked forward to it, and you have too, haven't you, darling? I'm going to get undressed now and you get undressed too, and we'll get into the bunk together and keep warm.' She was stripping off her clothes as she spoke, saying, 'Quick, quick! Hurry up and get your clothes off, silly!' and laughing, and I just stood there with my mouth open, incredulous. Stark naked she flung herself into the bunk, grabbed me by the wrist and pulled me down on top of her. Her eyes closed and she wrapped her arms round me. She whispered, 'Touch my breasts, darling, please touch my breasts.'

I left the bunk as though someone had poked me with a cattle prod. I had no idea what was happening, but at least I knew why I'd been frightened of her, she was dangerously mad. Touch her breasts, indeed! What for? Why would anyone want their breasts touched? Maybe she was going to kill me, throttle me or something. I seized my jacket and a torch she'd left lying on the floor, and headed off downhill towards the lights of Warburton, slipping and scrambling on the steep track. I was half out of my mind with the fear that she might be following me.

The track ended at the station, which was cold and silent. There was an old man hunched on a chair inside the ticket office and he said to me, 'Was you wanting the milk train, Miss? It'll be 'ere in 'alf an hour.' I went onto the platform and sat on a bench, shaking, and expecting at any minute to hear Miss Cooke telling me to come back to the hut, and thinking that if she did I'd kill her first. Something touched me on the leg and I soared into the air trying not to yell, then knew unutterable relief as I found that I'd been joined by a dog

It was a red setter, collarless and skeleton thin and we sat together, leaning against each other, taking comfort. When the milk train rumbled into the station we both got on board and curled up together on the seat. I had enough money in my pocket to pay the fare when we got to Flinders Street, and they made me pay for the dog too. It was barely getting light when I telephoned home, waking my parents up. I could hear Pa grinding his teeth as he said, 'Wait on the pavement outside the station until we pick you up. You can tell us what the hell's going on then.' I forgot to mention the dog, but we were standing side by side when the car pulled up, and I could see Pa's eyes move from one to the other of us, narrowing as they did so. It was plain that his self-control was severely strained. He said, 'Where did you get that bloody dog? You can't keep it.'

'I found it on Warburton Station, it was lost.'

'What were you doing on Warburton Station? You're supposed to be camping with Miss Cooke. Well? I won't have you worrying your mother like this, d'you hear!'

At this point I began to freeze; I could think of no way to explain anything so improbable as what had actually happened, or why I had been so terrified. I'd already begun to wonder if I'd behaved like an idiot, whether it was really all right, what Miss Cooke had done, and if I was being infantile and stupid. Pa, driving erratically as usual, said, 'Well, we're waiting. D'you mind telling us what you're doing back here?'

After a long pause I said, 'Miss Cooke frightened me, she...'

'Frightened you! What d'you mean, how could she frighten you?'

'Well, it was all right till after we'd had tea, and then...'

'Yes, go on.'

'Then she got undressed, took all her clothes off, and she wanted me to do the same.'

'Good God, it was bedtime, wasn't it? What the hell's the matter with you?'

'All right!' I said, suddenly furious. 'If you must know she pulled me down on top of her on the bunk and told me to touch her breasts. I didn't want to, so I cleared out.'

'Oh, what a lot of nonsense, Robin,' said Mama, laughing with relief. 'You must have misunderstood her, why on earth would she say that? What a fuss about nothing! Poor Miss Cooke, you'll have to apologise to her. Really!'

Pa drove in total silence: I could see the outline of his cheek and jaw, and they were rigid. After a couple of minutes he said, 'I don't believe you!'

I said, 'Honestly Pa, that's exactly what happened, and it scared me.'

He said again, 'I don't believe you, you're lying. It didn't happen.' I burst into tears. Mama turned in her seat and stared at me, genuinely astonished. 'I really don't understand what all the fuss is about,' she said. 'All this silly drama when the poor woman was just trying to be kind, and anyway, Geoff, what does it matter if it did happen? I'll write to her and apologise, and you must write too Robin, and let's hope she'll just forget about it.' She turned to Pa and sighed. 'Adolescents!' she said. 'What an idiotic stage it is! Heavens knows what that poor woman must have thought!'

There is no question that my father believed me, and knew perfectly well what had happened and why, but the difficulty of explaining lesbianism to his wife was too much for him. Besides that, if he had told Mama what it was all about she would have demanded that action be taken against Miss Cooke and possibly against the school, and it would have become an open scandal. It would have been easier for me if he had said, 'Look, I believe you but there's no harm done, just forget about it,' but on the other hand, by cauterising the truth as one might a wound, he made it impossible for me to mention it to anyone and I might easily have done so, to someone at school, causing endless trouble. The only casualty was my self-confidence, already low, which now subsided in a heap.

My last two terms at school were a battle to maintain a credible front in my role of Head Girl while concealing the ugly, craven, ignorant freak which I knew lay behind the facade. Miss Cooke treated me with open hostility in public and issued urgent invitations to secret meetings if she got me alone. I learned to look through her as though she didn't exist, and to shun personal relationships of any kind since, it seemed to me, they were infinitely dangerous.

At the end of the year I'd accumulated a number of prizes, due mainly to the depleted state of the school and the lack of competition, but it persuaded my parents that they should come to the Break-up to share in their daughter's single moment of glory. All through the hypocrisy of the Headmistress's speech... 'throughout the year the School has maintained its exceptional standard of scholarship, comradeship and sporting achievement...' and '...the splendid moral standard set for the girls by the staff, to whom I extend my thanks...' I could see Mama and Pa in the front row, smiling politely. Afterwards, during the tea and sandwiches. I watched Mama moving graciously among the staff, shaking them by the hand, and I thought with a sick, helpless feeling, 'I bet she'll go and apologise for me to Miss Cooke.'

They told me Jenny's news on the way back to Melbourne, Mama's voice shaky with pride. 'She was only home for a few days, darling, and she sent you her love. She was sorry she missed seeing you, but she's wildly excited. You see, Australia has decided to set up its own Hospital Ship. It's a very small one, it only carries twelve nurses, and they say they picked the best nurses in the Army to staff it. Jenny was chosen, isn't it marvellous? Your father says they'll be operating between Australia and New Guinea, so we'll see a lot more of her when she gets Leave. The ship's being fitted out in Brisbane, so she's gone up there to join the rest of the medical staff until it's ready. It's a tremendous honour you know, to be one of the few chosen out of all the Army nurses.'

'Yes,' I said, 'It's terrific for her, I'm so glad. What's the ship called?'

'The *Centaur*,' said Mama.

23

After school

WHEN I LEFT SCHOOL at the end of 1942 I was still too young to join a Service, but it was hard to think seriously about doing anything else. Pa said, what about the University, what about doing Law, what about this and that, and I said no to all of them. I agreed to go to the Art School at the Melbourne Technical College because I knew I could drop out of it as soon as I was called up. University courses seemed irrelevant. The war was going wrong everywhere; in Europe, in the Middle East, and in our own part of the world the Japanese seemed unstoppable. The people who had been ashamed of their relative safety were discovering, with alarm and indignation, that they weren't so safe after all.

Betty, triumphantly, had produced her first son, wasting no time after her miscarriage, and was hard at work on her second child: her childbearing schedule had been upset, and she was determined to catch up. The doctors were alarmed by the urgency of her program, and insisted that she spend the last month of her second pregnancy in town so that they could keep an eye on her. Betty and Christopher were installed at home and Mama was delirious with joy. She and Betty felt the same way about babies that Pa and Jenny and I felt about animals.

Because of her size and her complete disregard for appearances Betty's pregnancies were spectacular, and I was truly shocked by the sight of my sister. I had missed seeing her in the pre-Christopher period by being at School, and I was unprepared for her sheer magnitude. She carried in front of her a bulge the size and shape of a large beer-keg, and she'd bought no maternity clothes because of the expense. She wore what she normally wore, so that her skirts hung over her vast stomach and barely covered her crutch, like inadequate awnings, while trailing down to mid-calf at the back. On anyone but Betty it would have been bizarre, but your eyes were drawn inevitably to her face which was lovelier than ever, wreathed in the seraphic smile she had worn since Christopher's birth.

Determined to be a model mother she had read every book on the subject, accumulating contradictory theories and discarding nothing. Like many mothers she would settle down with her second child but poor Christopher, while receiving the most abundant love, was a guinea pig. His mealtimes were disgusting because he was a reluctant eater; he sat in a high chair throwing up his food, and Betty grimly sat in front of him with a spoon, feeding it back to him. It reminded me of my trauma with the liver and brains at Sorrento and not even Mama could bear to watch.

While she was staying with us a lot of Betty's old friends took the chance to see something of her. One of them, Margaret, was a woman she'd known in her Art School days. She was a lot older than Betty, professional, very clever, a spinster and almost certainly a lesbian. She was devoted to Betty, but intelligent enough never to have made a move towards her other than of the most harmless and protective friendship. Betty valued and admired her and so did I, and it was she who finally enlightened Mama, me and probably Betty on the subject of homosexuality.

Miss Cooke had left Toorak College at the same time I did, whether by her own choice or the school's, I don't know. It's quite possible that her inclinations had involved someone besides myself, and that she was no longer welcome. She had taken a new job as Games Mistress at a school only half a mile from our house, and had gaily informed Mama of this during Mama's inevitable, laughing apologies for me at the School Break-up.

'I *am* so sorry, Miss Cooke! I can't imagine what came over the silly child, but of course you'd know well enough what they're like at that age.'

'Don't worry, Mrs Walker, I'll be coming past your house every day to my new job, and I'll talk it over with Robin. I'm sure I'll find out what was the matter. She might like to come to a concert or something with me, once she's got it off her chest.'

'Oh, Miss Cooke, that *is* kind of you!'

I didn't hear the conversation of course, but that's roughly how it would have gone. I was in such a state of nerves, uncertainty and self-loathing that I had become almost agoraphobic. On the rare occasions when I had to go somewhere Mama had to dose me with sal volatile, otherwise I shook and sweated so that I couldn't get dressed. The first time I walked round the corner of the house and saw Miss Cooke, eager as a bird-dog, poised outside the gate, I fled back into my room and locked the door. After that venturing into the street was my greatest terror. She never actually came to the house, but I never knew when she'd be hovering near the gate or round the corner, waiting for me.

Margaret came to see Betty one day when Miss Cooke was standing outside, gazing expectantly up the path. Margaret looked at her curiously; she saw that the woman was obviously wanting something, and she asked if she could help. Miss Cooke just glared at her, and took herself off. We were in the sitting-room, Mama and Betty and me, and when Margaret came in and said, 'Who's that odd-looking woman hanging round outside the gate?' I felt myself go white.

Mama said, 'Oh, that's just Miss Cooke. She was Games Mistress at Robin's school and she was really terribly good to Robin, but now the wretched child won't speak to her and I daren't even ask her in. The whole thing's too stupid and embarrassing, Margaret, I don't know what to do about it.'

Margaret gave me a long, appraising stare, then looked at Mama with raised eyebrows. She was much nearer Mama's age than Betty's, and I've no doubt she found Miss Cooke easily identifiable, as a type. She said, 'I'd like to have a talk to Robin if she doesn't mind. Alone. Could we use your bedroom, Betty?'

It was amazing how easy Margaret was to talk to. She sat me

down, and slowly, expertly, drew the whole story out of me, and I could tell her without shame because she believed me, even the part about Warburton.

When I'd finished she said, 'Oh dear me! Look, Robin, there's nothing so terrible about all that, really. Miss Cooke's been a fool but she can't help it, and you don't have to worry about it. Some women like other women, love them in a sexual way, and some men feel the same way about other men. I'm going to explain it all to you properly because it's high time you understood. Come to that, I wonder if Betty knows? Anyway, first of all I'd better explain the facts of life to your mother.'

Mama never mentioned their conversation to me; she would have found it too profoundly shocking, having never imagined such things could exist. However, she did keep an eye out for Miss Cooke, saw her lingering outside the gate again and charged out to confront her. She came back red in the face, found me skulking in my room and said, 'I've just told Miss Cooke that if I ever see her round here again I'll call the police. I don't think she'll be back.'

Margaret threw light on a whole lot of things for me; the interwoven couples on the school staff, my temporary friends at St Carol's and jokes I'd heard about men who were 'pansies', but she told me nothing about the mechanics of ordinary, straight sex, and I was beginning to realise that one day, sooner rather than later, I'd need to know. It was no use asking Betty or Mama; Mama genuinely couldn't bring herself to speak of it, and Betty wouldn't because she'd think that if I knew how it worked I might go out and try it, like Jenny. I promised myself that next time Jenny was home I'd tell her I didn't know, and I knew that she'd explain it all, properly. In the meantime I still didn't know any boys and I was certain that they wouldn't be interested in me if I did, so the matter wasn't urgent.

By this time Pa had relinquished his position in Army Intelligence to a younger man, and taken over the leadership of the Volunteer Defence Corps, Australia's version of Dad's Army. The VDC Headquarters were close to where we lived and Pa spent a lot of time there; he had a staff of pleasant, elderly officers, and although they all seemed to be having a wonderful time I never saw any evidence of troops. In fact Pa appeared to have more time on his hands than ever before.

He worried about me, I think, realising better than Mama that I was mortally nervous and uncertain of myself, and that I met no one except the other students at the Art School. Older women were an open book to him, but girls of my age, ingrowing and upgrowing, were a mystery. He tried hard to help, taking me to places with him on our own, and with him I always felt normal and relaxed. His sudden bursts of temper didn't worry me, nor his occasional betrayals such as his denial of Miss Cooke's advances; I understood because I was like him, and capable of the same things.

Betty had another son, Tony. Once again the birth was complicated, and the doctors shook their heads; they told Betty and Norman that it would be most unwise to try again. You could see the words going in one of Betty's ears and out the other; if she could produce two beautiful, healthy sons she could produce the other eighteen.

I was enjoying Art School; life classes absorbed me completely, and for the first time I felt that I was doing something reasonably well. Passing exams and getting prizes at school had made me feel shifty because I knew that a lot of girls had worked harder than I had, and that I was a fake. Drawing was different; everyone started from the same point with a blank sheet of paper, and the results spoke for themselves, good or bad. My drawing wasn't within miles of the way I wanted to draw and I cringed from showing my work to people, but I loved the bare, cold art-rooms and the texture of good paper, and the wonderful, rare moments when you knew that a line was exactly right. Concentration on the curve of a muscle or the shadow of a facial bone could make a morning or an afternoon pass unnoticed. I forgot myself, and even the war disappeared for hours at a time; nothing mattered but paper, and how to put life on it.

On a bleak morning, Friday the 13th of May in 1943, a few days after the Technical School had broken up for the holidays, the doorbell rang and I went to answer it. Both my parents were out, Mrs Kane, the daily, was slapping round with a duster and Rose was going through her interminable ritual of getting dressed upstairs. There was a telegraph boy at the door and he handed me a telegram in a matter-of-fact way, saying, 'Walker, is that right?'

I said, 'Yes,' and stood staring at the thing, feeling very cold and strange. I remember saying to Mrs Kane, 'Something dreadful's happened, Mrs Kane, Jenny's been killed. I've got to find my father and tell him. Could you keep Mrs Whiting upstairs until I come back?'

Mama had gone to a meeting at the Town Hall, but if I could find Pa I knew he'd fetch her and break it to her. No-one but Pa could possibly tell her. I went to VDC Headquarters, but he wasn't there. I saw his Second-in-Command, a Major Oates, and said, 'I've got to find my father. Jenny's ship's been sunk, and she's dead. Do you know where he is?' and Major Oates, who was a family friend, said, 'He's at Victoria Barracks. You go home, I'll find him and tell him for you.'

I went home and sat in my room. I could hear Mrs Kane crying, and Rose shuffling round her bedroom, mumbling to herself, and I couldn't face either of them because my ears were ringing, and I felt bloodless. Childhood training told, and I couldn't cry.

Then a car drew up outside the gate and I heard the screaming. I knew it was my mother but it sounded like an animal, an agonised, terrified animal, and I ran downstairs to the kitchen as Pa half-carried her through the door, unrecognisable in her misery. We got her upstairs and onto her bed, still screaming, '*No, no, no...*' and Pa rang the doctor who came and gave her a sedative. We turned on the radio for the midday news, not expecting it to be public property yet, but it was the first item. 'Australia's only Hospital Ship, HMS *Centaur*, was brutally torpedoed last night in Moreton Bay. She had just sailed on her return trip to New Guinea to collect Australian wounded. There are reported to be a number of survivors, among them one nurse who was on deck when the torpedo struck. All those who were below decks at the time are believed to have perished. The ship was clearly marked with the Red Cross and was showing her lights in accordance with International Regulations...'

Pa told Rose what had happened, and she understood well enough to whimper like a child and go back to bed again, while Mrs Kane made her a cup of soup. Mama was sleeping; the doctor said she'd sleep until evening, not to wake her. Pa said, 'We need something to do. Let's go for a walk and get a cake. People'll come round, they always do when these things happen, and we'll need something to give them.' It was practical, and we both wanted to get out of the house. We were halfway down the hill to the shop when Pa said, 'Where's the telegram, I'd like to have a look at it.' I remembered that I'd put it in my pocket when it arrived because I'd been going to take Matilda for a walk, and I had my coat on; I was still wearing it. I pulled out the telegram and handed it to Pa.

He stopped short, turning it over in his fingers, and looked at me oddly. He said, 'Didn't you tell Gus Oates what had happened, that Jenny's ship had been sunk and she was dead?'

Puzzled, I said, 'Yes Pa, of course I told him what had happened.'

'Well, how the hell did you know? This telegram's never been opened.'

I looked, and it was true. I felt deadly cold again, and rather sick. Pa put his arm round me and gave me a hug. 'It's all right,' he said. It's the sort of thing that happens to people in Irish families.'

PART THREE

24

More war

AFTER JENNY'S DEATH a chill came over our house. She would never have an official grave, but it felt as though we were sharing her tomb. My mother's grief took her, for a time, into an underworld beyond our reach. If Jenny had been a son she'd have been mentally prepared for disaster in wartime, but it never crossed her mind that Jenny might be vulnerable and the blow was so great that she never really got over it.

The house was already crowded with photographs of Jenny, but in the past when Mama looked at them she'd smiled to herself, as if in a private salute. Now more photographs appeared; she went from one to the other, picked them up and gazed at them for minutes on end with tears running down her cheeks, or put small, sad vases of flowers in front of them. Pa watched her miserably and tried to comfort her, but she had a wall round her. His own grief must have been great enough, but for Pa people he loved were never dead, just temporarily absent, and he always said, 'Never be sorry for people who die, they can't be hurt any more. Be sorry for the ones left behind.' With Mama he was endlessly gentle and considerate but his nerves and temper were at flashpoint, and when something had to give I was generally in its way. I understood but I hated being there; I was no good to either of them, and they would have been better on their own.

Betty brought her children to stay for a while, and it helped. Mama found children irresistible, and these were too small to know that anything was wrong; they yelled and thumped and demanded so that she was forced to think about them instead of about Jenny, and she began to thaw. Betty was too immersed in motherhood to be conscious of anything odd in Mama's behaviour, and disinclined to believe me when I told her how things had been before she arrived. She herself had changed in a way I found hard to define; she seemed to have moved, with her marriage, into another world of views and values as a chameleon changes colour in tune with its background. When we talked about Jenny she astonished me.

She said, 'Thank God Mama never knew what Jenny got up to when she was training at the Royal Melbourne. At least she can still think Jenny was perfect.'

'What d'you mean? Jenny didn't do anything so terrible.'

'Oh, don't be silly, Robin, I've heard stories about her and Janet, and I was shocked, honestly. Norman says they were no better than a couple of tarts.'

I knew how Betty felt about tarts, but before her marriage she'd never have believed that Jenny was like that, or she'd have found excuses. I remembered Jenny saying, 'I'm not going to die wondering,' and thought to myself, 'I'm damned glad she didn't, what use would all that virtue be to her now?

The Government used the sinking of the *Centaur* to inflame public hatred of the Japanese, and this made life harder for all of us. Unlike most wartime disasters, which were kept quiet for security reasons, the *Centaur* was no secret. It had all the right ingredients for flag-waving, being a mercy-ship staffed with innocent doctors and nurses. It had been sunk on the very shores of Australia, and Australians who were accustomed to their war being remote and impersonal were to be shown that it was, in fact, very close to home. For some weeks after the ship went down it was impossible to turn on the radio without some expert elaborating on the barbarism of the affair, and the probable death-agonies of those who were killed.

Outside the house it was even worse; the Government wasted no time in producing huge posters and pasting them on hoardings in prominent places. They showed the bow of the burning ship still visible above the water, and in front of it a handful of nurses frantically waving for help while being torn to pieces by sharks. We knew this to be a fiction; the survivors had confirmed that when the torpedo struck amidships the whole deck caught fire so that anyone in their cabin had died in a funeral pyre or in the explosion, but not in the sea. Mama found the posters unbearable and stayed at home behind drawn curtains; unless Pa was with her she hardly ventured out.

Australia was outraged by the sinking of the *Centaur* since hospital ships, clearly marked with the Red Cross and showing their lights at night, are supposed to be sacrosanct under International Law. Moreover, in this case, the ship had just left Brisbane and had not even cleared Moreton Bay when she was torpedoed. There seemed to be no motive other than criminal brutality for the attack since she was empty even of wounded. As many people said, in highly emotional speeches, it was proof positive of the utterly bestial nature of the enemy.

International law also states, however, that a hospital ship remains sacrosanct only so long as its cargo is confined to the wounded, and to the people and equipment necessary for their care. In fact there was a partial excuse for the sinking of the *Centaur*: a number of Ambulance personnel had joined the ship on its return voyage to Papua, and some of them carried their personal firearms on board. The rumour spread that the *Centaur* was carrying arms, and there was no shortage of enemy agents in Australia then. The Japanese may have believed that the sinking was fully justified.

At the end of those miserable May holidays I went back to Art School, this time to the Melbourne Art Gallery school under the headmastership of Daryl Lindsay. He was encouraging and kind, and a year earlier I'd have killed to work under him, but Jenny had made the war into a personal war, and I was too restless to stay. I'd be eighteen in the spring, and I had my name down for the WRANS, but there was no certainty I'd be called up straight after my birthday and in the meantime I wanted to escape from the feeling of hiding in backwaters. In the outside world I might learn some of the things I'd have to know when the time came, whatever and whenever that might be. I felt grown-up on the outside and empty on the inside, and I wasn't sure which was real.

My parents were too distracted to object when I said I was leaving the Art School; Pa had always said we must be able to earn our own living, and I used his words against him. I took a job as a script writer at a radio station where all the men were gloriously, unashamedly Gay, taught a bedridden child to read and write in a squalid, slum hovel after working hours, and dabbled with the National Theatre. It was all educational in its way, and the people I met were light years removed from the boundaries of human contact imposed on me by home and school. In the spring I left the radio station and took a job as a Land Girl on a property near Cavendish, in Western Victoria.

Kongbool was owned by Lady Smyth, the widow of a distinguished British General and ex-Governor, and she was one of the most unique and fascinating women I've known. She was in her seventies, her children grown up, one son in the Navy and her daughter married. Her property was by no means small, and like everyone on the land at that time she was short of labour. Her staff, in fact, consisted of an Italian POW, a dwarf covered with warts, and me.

I'd never met her before the day I arrived at Kongbool, on a warm spring afternoon. I walked up the drive from the bus, carrying my suitcase. On my right were sheep yards filled with ewes and lambs, the centre of activity hidden in a billowing cloud of dust. A very English female voice reached me out of the dust-cloud saying, 'Drop that suitcase and come in here. You can start work now.' It wasn't the kind of voice you ignored, no matter how inappropriately dressed you were, nor how ignorant of sheep.

They were lamb-marking. I pushed my way through the sheep, climbed the yard fence, and found my new employer with a pair of castrators in her hand, covered with blood and dust, and beaming happily. A dark, wiry man was standing in front of her holding a lamb upside down by its legs, and a dwarf the size of an eight-year-old child was shouting and shoving at ewes heavier than himself. Lady Smyth said, 'Glad you got here, I can do with another person throwing the lambs up. Just watch Angelo and do what he does.' Angelo swung a lamb onto the board in front of her with casual grace, glanced at its crutch and said, 'Bambino' or 'Bambina' as the case might be, and Lady Smyth expertly castrated the bambinos, tailed the lot and earmarked them. The dwarf continued to bully the sheep in the yards, and I swung up what seemed like endless lambs, wishing I had trousers on instead of a skirt.

When we finally finished the lambs Angelo and the dwarf moved the sheep back to the paddock, and Lady Smyth took me up to the house. It was bluestone and very big, outwardly a clone of many other Western District houses I'd seen, but inside it was quite different. The front steps led to an imposing front door and a hallway with polished wooden floors, covered with tiger-skin rugs. There were old pictures on the walls, and antique furniture; at first glance it was formal and grand, until I tripped against the snarling head of one of the tiger-skins. There was a wild cackle and a burst of feathers and a small hen stampeded out of the tiger's mouth, followed by several other hens who had been resting on a brocade settee. Other hens bolted from under an elegant mahogany table, and the whole flock left noisily through a hole in the flywire of the front door. Lady Smyth didn't seem to notice them.

She was a woman who lived at peace with her past and its grandeur and valued it, regarding the present as a rather improbable joke which had to be taken seriously. It was obvious that whatever money there had been in the past, very little of it remained. The paintings on the walls were the kind that grace rooms in the old, great houses of England, the furniture was priceless and the upholstery threadbare, there were kerosene lamps and no electricity, linoleum on the floors, and except for the blazing wood fire in the drawing-room, no trace of heating or comfort. An eskimo would have been cold; on her own she must have been fearsomely lonely, but she was a woman who radiated a mixture of goodwill, courage and humour that added up to a rare kind of grace, and made her special.

The dwarf and I started our day at four in the morning, milking cows. The dwarf was so small that he moved from cow to cow under their bellies, hardly bending his head. Angelo, the POW, spoke scarcely a word of English, but made up for it with lavish, Latin charm. He had been an acrobat before the war and was worried about losing his skills, so when I rode the paddocks in the morning, checking on the sheep and fences, it was common to come across Angelo standing on his head on top of a fencepost or turning somersaults in front of a woolly, mesmerised mob. He had a guitar, and a syrupy tenor voice, and he sang throbbing Italian love songs outside my window in the evenings without the slightest desire that I'd respond, just practising. The property was rabbit-infested to the point where sometimes the surface of the ground seemed to be moving away in front of you, and the paddocks were honeycombed with burrows and scoured by erosion. Having ridden paddocks in the mornings I waged war on the rabbits in the afternoons.

In descending numerical order of livestock on Kongbool there were the rabbits (which may have outnumbered even the flies) the sheep, the stock-ponies and the dogs. The ponies were skinny, active little beasts, and the rabbit-pack dogs ranged from dachshunds to deerhounds, with strange, unidentifiable variations in between. They lived in a state of bondage on chains, praying with their eyes for freedom whenever you went past. Last of all, except for the four house-cows, there was the bane of my rabbiting existence, an unmentionable tribe of ferrets.

Every afternoon I'd climb into a patched-up saddle held by a rotting girth, put a cage of ferrets on my back, hang a spade from my belt and let the rabbit-pack go. They'd take off blindly across-country, screaming with joy, and I'd have to go as the crow flies too, to keep track of them. Sometimes Lady Smyth would want to come and I'd saddle a pony for her, praying that the girth would hold. Her rabbiting outfit was original and dashing; a blazer with brass buttons, a yachting cap at a jaunty angle, and round her waist a string with a trowel, shears and several other implements whose purpose was obscure. The moment she was in the saddle she'd give a hunting cry, kick the pony's ribs and take off. Because of her age it terrified me, but she never fell; the ponies were like cats, and most of the fences were lying flat on the ground. Sometimes the rabbit hunts were wonderful, more often they ended after dark, in wind or drizzle, sitting at the mouth of a warren and thinking of new names for ferrets who wouldn't come out.

In the evening Lady Smyth and I would sit in front of the huge log fire and she'd talk about her husband and their life together; they had done things and seen things which patterned her stories with gold thread, and she was gifted in her telling. The fire lit and shadowed the drawing-room's walls and ceilings, and the old, gilt-framed paintings leapt with crimson and gold as the firelight touched them. The chairs we sat on were lovely, but their upholstery was full of holes. I felt something moving underneath me one night, reached under my backside and pulled out a mouse that had its extended family comfortably housed in the chair's stuffing.

Hunger defeated me at Kongbool; Lady Smyth had reached the age where she ate almost nothing while I was seventeen and healthy, starting work at 4 a.m. and finishing at dark. At breakfast there was toast and tea, at lunch whatever one could find, and at night, with horrible regularity, there was mince on toast. Sheep were never killed for the table, but if one was found dead in a paddock the dwarf would drag it into the kitchen, skin it and butcher it, and he and Angelo at least would have a square meal. They had their own quarters, and sometimes when I passed nearby and smelled roasting meat, I nearly wept.

In the end I telephoned Mama secretly, explained my problem, and asked her to invent an urgent reason for my return. It was almost my 18th birthday anyway, and I was hoping to hear that the WRANs had room for me. A month later I was in uniform.

Anyone, male or female, who had been to boarding school

started service life ahead of the rest. Young men who joined up, having never been away from home, found themselves in a bear-pit. They were thrown into dormitories, harassed, regulated and yelled at, and most of them thought they had been thrown into hell. Service life for women wasn't quite as rough, but home-raised girls still found it hard. Personally I found it very like school, but more interesting. Instruction was dealt out by Chief Petty Officers who were not only male, and therefore novel, but who were also living caricatures of what one expected CPO's to be. The CPO who drilled my intake was the shape of an inverted pear with a semi-shaven head planted between his shoulders like a hasty afterthought, and a mouth at permanent full-stretch to issue unintelligible orders and scathing rebukes.

We were housed and trained at Port Melbourne, a block inland from the sea in the shadows of the gasworks. Our time was divided between classroom and drill, and in both cases the intellectual demands were limited. I knew from the first day that the CPO loathed me and would give me a hard time; as soon as I opened my mouth and he heard my voice he stared at me as though I was a bad joke, and yelled, '*You!* Speak proper! I don't want no lah-di-dah talk 'ere!'

I said, 'I'm sorry, Chief Petty Officer, I can't help it.'

He glared at me and snarled, and from then on I was dirt but it didn't matter; I had seen enough B Class British war films to find him fascinating. He could have been type-caste in any one of them, word-perfect in the time-honoured abuse designed to stimulate recruits on the parade-ground. We had no parade-ground, but he marched us briskly up and down the windy streets of Port Melbourne, swinging our arms and tucking in our chins, '*Hep* ri' *Hep* ri' *Keep* them bloody arms swinging and *stick* them chests out and try not to look like a lotta dead bloody *flowers!*'

At the end of the course we were given our postings, decided by Higher Authority who had never laid eyes on us, and based on our written work and the CPO's assessment of our characters. I hoped to be sent to a distant Naval Base, even as a kitchen hand, because it would get me away from home. I knew that however hard I tried to be self-effacing and helpful there I was still an abrasive, a reminder to Mama of what she had lost.

The CPO told us our respective fates on the last morning, leaving me and a girl I had been at school with until last to teach us not to be lah-di-dah. He looked from the paper in his hand to us with fury, and I knew that given his way he would have condemned us to floor scrubbing for the rest of our term of service. 'Rating Walker,' he said, 'And Rating Martin. Yous two will report to HMS *Monterey* in Albert Park.'

It was clearly a shore establishment, but I'd never heard of it. 'What's *Monterey*, CPO?' I asked. 'What goes on there?'

'Never you mind what goes on there, Walker. It's 'ighly secret, and I can't tell you and you can't ask. Furthermore it's an 'ighly cushy posting what you don't deserve, and instead of living in barracks like what a Naval Rating should yous two will be billeted at your 'omes.'

'Oh God,' I thought. 'Of all the postings in Australia I had to draw this one.'

HMS *Monterey*, when Brenda Martin and I reported there, was a long, two-storey wartime building, surrounded by twelve-foot-high cyclone fencing topped with barbed wire, and the gate was manned by American guards, armed to the teeth. We had been issued with passes complete with ego-destroying photographs of ourselves, and we showed these to a gum-chewing Yank who shuddered slightly, then led us inside the building to the Commanding Officer.

Monterey was the embryo-beginning of Signals Intelligence, the monster whose installations now harness satellites, pick up the merest whisper from the inner sanctums of foreign powers, and until recently terrified the people who lived near them because of their potential as cold war nuclear targets. Monterey, in 1944, was humble, noisy and largely experimental. It was a joint American/Australian operation, with Americans in the majority although the Officer Commanding was an Australian from the regular Navy. The female complement, when we arrived, numbered only twenty-five, and we were put to work punching out cards of coded Japanese radio traffic on the clattering, primitive ancestors of IBM computers.

We worked watches, eight hours on and eight hours off, with an occasional forty-eight hour break when things were quiet. I rode a bicycle without a light from South Yarra to the middle of Albert Park and back, night and day, rain and shine, and never fell foul of a policeman, nor was I ever accosted. Melbourne, in time of war, must have been one of the safest places in the world. It was my first contact with Americans on a personal level; I had seen them everywhere around town and been amazed, firstly by the smartness of their uniforms and secondly by the size of their backsides, relative to the Australian article. It may have been only the cut of their uniform trousers, but American buttocks seemed provocatively large and rounded. Everyone had horror stories to tell about them: drink, sex, noise, brashness and too much money. I found the prospect of nights on Watch with American seamen interesting, but Mama feared the worst.

There was a certain innocence about the workplace relationships in those days; the appreciative male pat on a female bottom, the hug for a job well done or even a kiss was acceptable, not threatening. Unemancipated girls like me, longing for a little encouragement, welcomed these small attentions and were grateful for them. A wolf-whistle was appreciated, even though you tossed your head and ignored it, and it never crossed our minds that it could be classed as harassment. With the Yanks came the fear of the unknown, the possibility of orgies and massive moral corruption, pregnancies and families disgraced. It was a prospect which raised the adrenaline levels in young females to unprecedented heights, their hormones blossomed in response, and the American servicemen reaped a ready harvest.

The Americans working at HMS Monterey turned out to be simple souls, pleasant and rather childlike when they were sober, but with a habit of turning up for night watches in a state bordering on the paralytic. They were no trouble because they usually passed out, which meant more work for the female Hands and a truly dreadful duty for us when the watch ended in the morning. Because of Monterey's Top Secret Security classification no cleaners were allowed inside the building, so the girls who had been on watch had to clean out the men's lavatories as well as their own. It was typical of the chauvinism of the time; no-one would dream, in those days, of making a man do such a menial job, but it was alright for the girls. We would finish the Midnight and Morning Watch at 8 a.m. dead tired, then pick up buckets and mops and find that our Allies had distributed their intake of the previous evening, with abominable aim, from one end of their Heads, as the lavatories were called, to the other.

There were periods of frantic activity, and quiet ones when there was very little radio traffic coming in, and they were the worst because it was so hard to keep awake. Our Commanding Officer was a tall, thin man with a long, unsmiling face, eminently caricaturable, and I took to drawing cartoons of him in idle moments. In the end he either heard about it or saw some of my efforts; as I held the lowest possible rank he couldn't demote me, but he made it clear that my naval life hung by a thread which he'd dearly love to cut.

I was still sexually illiterate and I had no boyfriend; I'd been trained by Mama to regard sex as roughly comparable to leprosy but I was aware that there was a lot of sex around, and it worried me that I didn't even know what I was meant to keep away from. The Yanks and I were mutually unattracted, and when I went out it was with British Naval Officers whom Pa had brought home for drinks, most of them twenty years older than me, and married. My closest female friend was a 6ft 2in streak of blond glamour called Angela; I met plenty of men with her, but they could never tear their eyes away from her long enough to notice me. I watched Angela's cyclonic progress through the hearts and beds of men with awe and envy, and though I might have learned much from her I didn't ask; if I'd asked she'd have known that I didn't know, and instead I hinted at secret sexual adventures of my own.

The Naval officers were kindly men, and they treated me in a curious, very British way, so that I never knew whether they saw me as a younger sister or a potential lover. In off-duty hours they were seldom, if ever, entirely sober. Their gin was duty-free and absurdly cheap, and the higher the rate of gin consumption the greater the reputation of the consumer. They threw parties in their flats which ended in horse-play better suited to schoolboys, and they absent-mindedly fed me gin as if I was one of them. Luckily I'd inherited Pa's head for drink, and only occasionally found myself weaving. When they came to pick me up at home they were different people, and talked to Pa and Mama with measured gravity. Pa would say to them, 'It's terribly good of you to bother with this child. Don't let her be a nuisance,' and we would roar off in one of their cars to another gin orgy. On Victory in Europe night they threw the biggest party of all in the Officers Mess of the Australian Naval H.Q., passing me off as an officer in the English WRNS, and to this day I have no idea how I got home. It quite escaped my parents notice that I was dressing in clothes more suited to a thirty-year-old, and trying to hide the symptoms of monumental hangovers. I was half-troubled, half-relieved that none of the Royal Navy officers asked me to go to bed with them.

Mama was still far from well. Everyone seems to have some particular part of their body which is their Achilles Heel, their bowels or their chests or their hips, and for Mama it was her head. She had headaches and dizzy spells, and then she got shingles, again in her head. It was an agonisingly painful illness, and when she came home from hospital she was blind in one eye.

As usual Pa suffered almost more than she did. He always talked of her as 'Poor little Aileen', even when she was well, and her illnesses destroyed him. When she came home he fetched and carried for her, tiptoed and hushed, and I only had to close a door audibly to get my head smacked. Rose bumbled round the house, oblivious to everything, working further havoc with his nerves, and Mrs Kane clattered around in the kitchen doing emergency cooking. I came back from Monterey only to change, then to go out and stay out as long as possible, regardless of where.

Mama recovered surprisingly quickly, bravely accepting the loss of her eye but using it to shackle Pa to her side, except when he had to be in town on Clarke and Whiting affairs. He still had lunch at the Australian Club with his friends which helped to keep him sane, while Mama was given her lunch by Mrs Kane or by me. She spent her afternoons surrounded by a puzzling collection of women who, a few years earlier, she would have found laughable. They sat round her in dreadful felt hats with string bags full of knitting, saying separately or in chorus, 'Oh, Aileen, you are wonderful! You're a real Saint!' If they were still there when Pa came home he would rush upstairs, muttering about 'work', and lock himself in his room until they left. Later in the evening Mama would say to him, 'D'you know what Joan Bloggs said to me today, Geoff? She said to me, Aileen, you're a Saint. Silly, of course, isn't it?'

Fate rescued me, miraculously, one evening when I was lying on the floor reading the *Herald*. There was an article, and a photo, about one of Betty's old school friends who had married a British Army officer. He had been in Burma with the 14th Army and she, the article said, was a member of something called the Women's Auxiliary Service (Burma), and had come to Australia to recruit for it.

I said longingly, 'Gosh, I wish I could get into that.'

'Into what?' said Pa, and I handed him the paper.

He read it for a bit and then he said, 'Would you really like to go? I might be able to fix it.'

'I thought Australian women couldn't go overseas, and what about the WRANS?'

'You can still get a British passport, I've never taken out domicile papers here. If you can wangle your way out of the WRANS I'll see what I can do. It'd be good for you.'

I went to see Monterey's Commanding Officer, conscious that after my caricatures of him he was unlikely to do me any favours, and asked for a release from the Service. He eyed me nastily, and asked, 'Why?'

I want to join the Women's Auxiliary Service (Burma), Sir.'

'What? What the hell's that? Never heard of it.'

'It's a women's service in Burma, Sir, part of 14th Army.'

'Are you out of your mind? You can't go to Burma after working here! This is Top Security! What if you were captured, you could give information! Dammit girl, if you weren't the lowest rank there is I'd have you demoted. Get out of my sight!'

I bolted out of his office and went to see the Leading Hand of my Watch, CPO Britt. She was a lean, tough, kindly woman, and she had an encyclopaedic knowledge of Naval Rules and Regulations. I explained my problem.

'Didn't you tell me that your mother's not well?' she asked.

'No, she isn't. She's been a bit strange ever since Jenny was killed, and now she's lost an eye.'

'And your other sister's married up in the country, and your father works? Look, it's simple. Apply for a Compassionate Discharge in writing, give all those reasons and sent it to the Naval Board. It's going over the CO's head, but he can't stop you and you'll get it. You don't have to tell them what you're going to do afterwards. Half your luck!'

I did as she said, and it worked. The CO took it like a man, and when he said goodbye to me there was a flicker of a smile. His parting words were, 'Good luck, and I'm glad you're not *my* daughter.'

My parents were manifestly delighted to see me go, and I didn't blame them. I packed what I imagined might be useful in India and visited the WAS(B) recruiter to be signed up. There was one clause in the articles of my recruitment which made me pause . It stipulated that I must be licensed to drive a motor vehicle and experienced in doing so, and I'd never done more than steer with one hand from the passenger seat while Pa lit his pipe. The WAS(B) recruiter seemed very relaxed about everything so I signed anyway; I wasn't about to be thwarted by one small detail, and I could always pretend I hadn't read the document properly. I was told that I'd be met in Bombay and sent to Assam, and that two other recruits would be sailing with me.

Before I left I made one more attempt to unravel the mysteries of sexual technique with Mama. It seemed to me that in view of where I was going there had never been a clearer case of Need To Know, and that when you boiled it down it was her job to tell me. I was helping her make her bed, and I said, 'Mama, don't you think you'd better tell me what happens when you go to bed with a man? I mean I've never ... you know?'

'Good God!' she said, dropping her side of the blanket. 'I should hope you haven't! I can't possibly discuss it with you, Robin, I've told you before. Anyway, there's no need for you to know about that sort of thing just because you're going to Burma. I've always told you that if you're not a virgin No Decent Man Will Ever Marry You, and it's up to you to remember that.'

I had fifteen Australian pounds when I left, as my sole capital. Mama said that was all I could possibly need as I'd be met in Bombay, and Pa reinforced this, 'To my certain knowledge all ships are dry in wartime, so there'll be nothing to spend money on, not even drinks.'

'It's a lot of money, darling' said Mama. 'Be careful not to lose it.'

Pa had obviously been briefed by Mama about my embarrassing question during the bed-making, because he said, 'Don't worry about how men'll treat you when you get to Burma. All British officers know how to behave towards women. They're gentlemen, properly brought up. Wonderful fellas! I don't suppose you'll have any contact with Other Ranks, but I can tell you, if you have any trouble with men it'll be your own fault.'

Mama said, 'Yes darling, and if you always behave the way I've taught you to behave men will respect you for it. Just remember your sisters. If you think about poor Jenny and how well *she* behaved all those years when she was nursing you'll be perfectly alright.'

25

Travel

EVEN WITH THE EUROPEAN WAR ENDED there were very few ships carrying civilian passengers between Australia and India, and not many people who wanted to sail in them. The *Chyebassa*, which had peacetime accommodation for twelve passengers and was officially a cargo ship, had doubled the number of bunks in the low-caste cabins in case of emergencies. Passenger liners had been converted into troop ships, and were a thing of the past. The two-berth cabin that my companion WAS(B)s and I were to occupy had four bunks in it, and it was a small cabin anyway. The other two were already there when I went on board, trying to find somewhere to put their things. One of them was very pretty, long-haired, square-jawed and blue-eyed; the other, with carroty hair and a pale face, looked far too young and frightened to be going on anything more daring than a school picnic.

We said 'Hello', stiff-legged as strange dogs; we had no idea what to make of each other. We unpacked with hideous politeness … 'Is it okay if I put this here?'… 'Oh, please do. Are you sure this isn't in your way?' Then, suddenly, the deck under out feet came alive. There was a whistle, a rumbling, a shudder, a regular, heartbeat throb and a movement of air through an open porthole said we were under way. We dropped everything, bolted through the door and up onto the deck together laughing, touching hands and feeling like sisters.

It seemed a long haul down Port Phillip Bay; I was certain that even then something might stop me. I stayed on deck most of the time, trying to pick out The Haven, watching the shoreline and wondering when I'd see it again. Before we reached the Rip I went up to the bows and stood there, waiting for the first big wave that would signal the open sea. I felt it lift the deck beneath me, saw the bows rise up and up towards the evening sky, and then they fell with a thud and started to rise again, and all my prison gates slammed behind me as the gates of the world opened. Jenny had told me how it felt the first time she sailed on the *Oranje Nassau*, and it was true for me too. I looked for my sister through a cloud of spray as the little ship plunged, and sent her my love.

Sea voyages were far more profound experiences than are journeys to the same places by air. When you went on board a ship, not a cruise ship but a vessel of serious transport, you went into a sort of limbo for a significant period of time, suspended between all your past and all your future. You knew that whoever else was on board would mean the difference between boredom and pleasure, love and hate, joy and depression until you reached your destination. At first everyone eyed everyone else surreptitiously, made a lot of wrong judgements and painfully revised them in the course of the voyage. At first glance, which came on the first night, at dinner, the complement of the *Chyebassa* seemed unpromising.

Ngari Campbell, the pretty girl, Beth, the carroty one and I, being young, unimportant and unattached, had been seated with several of the ship's junior officers. At the head of the dining-room was the Captain's table, and when I looked at it I saw, with sinking heart, a rather grand acquaintance of my parents. I knew her daughter, and I also knew that she was the wife of the Governor of Bihar. I registered her as a possible hostile witness to what I'd hoped would be a life of liberty. There was a woman with her, too deferential to be anything but a paid travelling companion, and a squarish, military-looking man to make up the table numbers. Against the wall there was a table for two with a glamorous brunette and a tall, suave man, already kneading each other's hands as though they were alone in the room, and another rather subdued table of women, all plain as pikestaffs and dressed like school mistresses, hosted by a depressed Purser. They didn't look like the kind of women who'd enjoy India.

'Who are they?' I asked the Second Engineer, who was sitting next to me.

'Missionaries' wives,' he said. 'They've all been parked in Australia during the war, and they're meeting their husbands in Bombay. They haven't seen each other for about four years.'

'What about the couple on their own?'

'Now that's different, they're on honeymoon. He's Army I believe, and you may have heard of her, she was pretty well-known in Australia. Rhada something-or-other?'

Indeed I'd heard of her; she came from a well-known wine-making family in South Australia, and had earned a widely-publicised reputation as a wartime swinger. It was surprising, somehow, to find her on a honeymoon. She and her husband seemed oblivious to anyone or anything in the dining-room, and one wondered whether they'd be able to untangle themselves long enough to eat.

'I believe she's something to do with wine,' said the Second Engineer. 'They brought about a dozen cases of champagne on board with them. Couldn't have known the bar's open twenty-four hours a day on this ship.'

So I started on a journey so far removed from the decorous progress foreseen by my parents that I decided against trying to describe it to them. When I wrote, from Perth, I mentioned only the missionaries' wives and the Governor's wife, with a small, polite tribute to the seemliness of my fellow recruits.

Ngari and I became friends quite quickly. Beth was as young as she looked and so shy and silent that we never discovered very much about her, except that she came from a strictly Presbyterian family in Brisbane. It was a mystery why she had ever applied for or been accepted by anything so wildly unsuitable as the WAS(B)s. If I was a sexual illiterate Beth had hardly left the womb; she went scarlet at the mention of anything remotely connected to sex, she drank nothing stronger than lemonade, and once she had seen what went on at the ship's twenty-four hour bar she spent a lot of time alone in the cabin, reading the Bible.

Ngari was a different kettle of fish; not only was she pretty but she was an experienced operator, and it took me a very short time to realise that I was about to be upstaged yet again. She had been brought up on her parents plantation on Bougainville, and sent south to a well-known boarding school at the beginning of the Japanese war. She had run away from school, she said, and in the course of a hair-raising series of adventures, the details of which changed every time they were told, she learned to fly an aeroplane, drive a racing car, climb mountains and captivate men. It was impossible to mention anything Ngari hadn't done superlatively; she oozed confidence, and I could see that her career in Burma would be a breeze compared with mine. So long as I mentally divided everything she said by half and kept my mouth shut I enjoyed her company, and we made a successful team.

The bar on the SS *Chyebassa* was a total contradiction of Pa's belief that all ships were dry in wartime. After my addictive period on gin with the Royal Navy I was relieved, and stowed the bottles I had smuggled on board back in my luggage. Except for the missionaries' wives, who drank soft drinks and knitted, the bar was the social hub of the ship, patronised round the clock. The Governor's wife had a permanent seat of honour at a small table near it, and occasionally even the honeymoon couple surfaced long enough to attend.

They were apparently engaged in a marathon celebration of conjugal bliss which allowed for only the briefest of appearances, until we hit the Indian Ocean and tropical weather. Then they gave up their afternoon session in the cabin, brought rugs up on deck, and made ardent love under the Vice Regal cabin window every day between two and four o'clock. They did cover themselves with a rug, but they were active and noisy. Besides that their champagne glasses used to roll round and smash on the deck, and the Governor's wife liked to take an afternoon nap. Deck space was so limited that there was nowhere else for them to go, and their cabin was too hot.

For the first few minutes after they settled their noise would be subdued, like musicians tuning their instruments, then passion would get the better of them and they would become fully orchestrated. Immediately the head and shoulders of the Governor's wife would appear through the cabin window. Rhada's vocabulary was world class, as many people in Australia could have testified, but the Vice Regal virtuosity was astonishing, and more than held its own. The daily battle became the ship's most popular spectator sport, and the ventilators, hatches and lifeboats all served as cover for a fascinated audience . The finale was always the same; Rhada would offer, and the Governor's wife would accept, a glass of champagne, the window would close, Rhada and her husband would go to sleep, entwined like twin vines, and the rest of us knew that the show was over.

We stopped at Fremantle for longer than expected, but cargo ships were subject to changes of program in wartime. We ploughed across the Indian Ocean to Colombo and anchored in the roads there; we went to and from shore in a lighter, and we stayed there for ten days because of a submarine scare.

To my surprise the Colonel, who was the moustached, short man at the Captain's table, had been wooing me for the past week, and in Colombo he became serious and mentioned marriage. I was horribly embarrassed because it was the first time anyone had approached the subject with me, and I didn't know what to do about it without hurting his feelings. I told Ngari who said, 'Don't be silly. He only said that to you because I wouldn't have him. He asked me ages ago.'

He took us to the Galle Face Hotel where there was a swimming pool. We went to change, and when Ngari and I came out together we saw our Colonel on the diving board, in bathing costume. He was covered from head to foot in thick, brown hair, not ordinary male hair but hair so dense and wiry that he looked like a wad of coir matting. We both got the giggles so badly that we had to go back into the changing room.

Colombo was a revelation; the brown, beautiful people, even the smell of the place filled me with joy, and the red-hot curries were the most delicious food I'd ever tasted. There was a strange familiarity about it all, as though I was coming back to something I'd known before. The lone cloud on my horizon was my almost non-existent money. The fifteen pounds had dwindled to a shred. Everyone had been more than generous, but it was impossible not to insist on paying one's way occasionally, and my only hope was for some pay-in-advance when we reached Bombay. We were a day out of Colombo when the Captain came into the bar looking white and shaken, and said, 'There's a message come over the radio that you'll want to hear. The Yanks have dropped some God-awful kind of bomb on Japan, and the war's over. The Japanese have surrendered.'

Our first reaction was delight and overwhelming relief, laughter and tears. We had no inkling of the significance of the bomb, of how many it had killed or how it would change the world. The war was over and we drank too much once again, and sang sentimental songs until dawn. It wasn't till next morning, when our heads had cleared, that the three of us started to wonder what on earth we were doing in this ship, heading up the coast of India to a war that no longer existed. We were all broke, and it seemed logical that whoever met us in Bombay would turn us round and send us home again.

'Should we send a cable to someone and ask?' said Ngari.

'Well, who? I said, 'And where?'

'I wouldn't mind going home,' said Beth.

'There's nothing we can do except stay put, and see what happens when we get to Bombay.'

The ship rolled its way round the southern tip of India and up the coast in seas the colours of a butterfly's wing, white beaches and palm trees keeping us company to starboard, and little wing-sailed fishing boats bobbing in between. Peace disconcerted us; everyone was restless because a new world was waiting at the end of the journey, and we were nearly there. It had come so suddenly, and to be isolated on a small boat in the Indian Ocean when it happened made us feel rejected, robbed of something. Rhada, most of whose remedies involved alcohol, decided that we all needed cheering up.

'Stewie and I have a hell of a lot of champagne left,' she said, 'and this ship's not exactly short of drink. We ought to have a party on the last night.'

'Good idea,' said her husband. 'There's no point in lugging drink ashore.'

Ngari's personal cache of bottles, and mine, were still untouched and we offered them eagerly. The Captain came into the bar at that moment, and we put the idea to him. 'Splendid!' he said. 'We'll throw in some of the Company's grog too.' I looked over to the far corner of the room where the missionary wives sat, silently knitting, and said, 'What about them? It mightn't be their sort of party.' A dreamy look came over Rhada's face. 'Leave them to me,' she said. I'll look after it. They'll enjoy themselves all right when I've finished with them.'

Ngari and I helped her with the drinks on the night of the party. I saw that she'd wheedled some cans of concentrated fruit juice out of the Chief Steward. 'What's the juice for?' I asked her.

'Fruit punch,' said Rhada. 'I said I'd make the old bags happy. They'll never know what hit them.'

I was reminded of Pa mixing drinks for Jessie's chair-game, except that he had a lighter hand than Rhada, fewer varieties of liquor in stock to choose from, and he didn't disguise his poison with concentrated fruit juice. Rhada's punch should rightly have had smoke coming off the top, but she gave me a sip saying, 'What does that taste like?' and I had to agree that it tasted mostly like fruit juice, with some questionable undertones. 'That lot have never tasted alcohol,' said Rhada confidently. 'If I tell them it's only fruit juice they won't notice anything else.'

The missionary ladies knew there was going to be a party, of course. They had coyly approved, emphasised their teetotalism, and on the night they were in their usual corner, dressed in their best, waiting for the fun to begin. Rhada advanced on them with a tray of witch's brew and said, 'A little fruit punch, ladies? Made specially for you, and guaranteed to do you good.'

'You know that none of us touch alcohol, dear?'

'Of course I do. I said that this was made specially for you. It's lovely fruit juice, dears, do try it.'

They each took a glass and sipped tentatively. 'Oh, delicious,' said the senior wife. 'How very thoughtful of you, dear, and so clever. What kind of juice is it? Quite different to anything I've tasted before.'

Rhada had put champagne on all the tables for dinner, but the missionary ladies said virtuously that it was far too strong for them, and that they'd rather continue with their nice punch. For once they were quite rowdy; the Purser gazed round his table with his eyebrows raised, and I saw him take a glass when its owner wasn't looking, and taste it. He gave Rhada a look that spoke volumes, and shook his head.

After dinner the party moved to the bar. Someone had a set of liar dice, the younger officers produced a gramophone and records, and we settled down to make a night of it. The Captain came and went because he had things to do before we docked next morning, but he topped himself up liberally on each visit. The missionary ladies seemed to be having an hilarious time together in their corner. At one point the senior wife weaved over to us and said, 'Mishesh Shearlaw, dear, we sheem to have drunk all our punsh. Do you think . . . kin'ly . . .?'

'Of course,' said Rhada, and retired to the Steward's pantry to make more.

The liar dice game went on for a long time. I noticed that the missionary corner was empty and thought, rather relieved, that they must have gone to bed. About midnight a strange sound came to us from the deck, loud enough to make us sit upright and listen. At the same moment the bar door opened, and the Captain's face appeared. 'Come out here quick,' he said. 'This you must see.'

We went out on deck and saw, lit by a tropical moon, a conga line of five dishevelled women tripping and swaying round the ship to the tune of 'Onward Christian Soldiers', the tune recognisable if not the words. They struggled gamely up to the Bridge and down again, circumnavigated a hatch and saw us standing there, watching them.

'Oh, goodnesh!' exclaimed the senior wife. 'Wha'ever mush you think of ush? Sush fun… I don't know when… Ladiesh, I think ish time for bed.'

Trying gallantly to keep upright and clutching at whatever stable objects came their way, they vanished below decks. 'Oh my God!' said the Captain, 'How the hell are they going to be when their husbands come on board tomorrow morning?' He turned to Rhada. 'Mrs Shearlaw,' he said. 'I think you may have gone too far.'

Next morning the Captain, whose head was made of concrete, expertly manoeuvred his ship through the tangle of Bombay harbour and tied up to his allotted mooring. I was leaning over the rail, watching the bustle of lighters, tugs, small pinnaces and barges which darted about, seemingly as frantic and purposeless as water beetles on a pond. I gazed in awe at the legendary arch, The Gateway to India, which had welcomed so many of my family, and wondered what it had in store for me. The Purser ranged up and leaned on the rails beside me. 'See that?' he said, pointing to a lighter which was nearing the ship. 'See those men coming towards us?' The lighter carried a number of European men, all shading their eyes, and peering up at the *Chyebassa*'s deck. I said, 'Oh no! Don't tell me!' and the Purser said, 'That's right, it's the missionaries.'

There was just time for Rhada and Ngari and me to rush down and help the wives out on deck. They were too weak to resist, though they protested that they couldn't possibly meet their husbands, not feeling the way they did. Their hair was tousled, their faces drawn and pale, their skin shiny with the sweat of nausea. We propped them in deckchairs and covered them with rugs, seconds before the first of their husbands appeared, joyous and eager.

I don't know about Rhada, but personally I felt total shame. What should have been five touching reunions became five pathetic farces, as the worried husbands bent over their mortally ill wives. One of them knelt on the deck beside his spouse, and took her hand in both of his.

'What is it?' he implored. 'Tell me, what's the matter? Why are you all so ill?'

She opened her eyes a little, and gave him a brave smile. 'It's nothing, dear,' she murmured. 'We had a lovely party last night, and somehow the five of us must have got a bit of bad food. The fish, I think. So silly, the food's been perfect, and it's never happened before.'

There was the finality of goodbyes and going ashore, the brutal transition from seaborn cocoon to reality which marks the end of any long sea voyage. An official launch studded with gleaming ADC's arrived to take the Governor's wife to the local Government House, where she would stay before being conveyed with Vice-Regal pomp to Bihar. It came as a shock; we had become used to thinking of her as just one of us, and rather fun. The rest of us left the ship in a common lighter.

I found myself shaking as we neared the wharf with its towering, Raj-relic of the Arch. People swarmed everywhere, dressed in white, dressed like rainbows, skins tinted from ivory to ebony, bearded, veiled or even naked, and covered with ashes. They milled and eddied and spat and shouted with the confusion of an ant's nest disturbed and I, with the romantic egotism of the very young, thought ecstatically, 'This is my place. This is where I should have been born.'

26

Arrival in India

NOT ONE OF THE THREE OF US had doubted our recruiting officer's word when she told us in Australia that we'd be met in Bombay, nor had we thought to ask her who would meet us. We were young and green enough to believe what our elders said; we had a mental picture of some smart, efficient woman in jungle green who would attach importance to our arrival, and look after us. There was nobody. We wandered vaguely through the exotic, indifferent crowd, distracted and fascinated, and only half-concerned.

'Who are we looking for, d'you know?' asked Ngari.

'I haven't a clue. I thought there'd be somebody from the WASBies looking for us.'

'There's a Red Cross lady in front of that building over there,' said Beth sensibly. 'She might know.'

We made for the Red Cross woman who was looking hot and harassed, and snapping at a bunch of cowed British NCOs. We explained who we were. 'Oh God, no!' she said. 'Not more of you lot! No one told me you were coming.'

'But isn't there a WAS(B) officer here? We were told someone'd meet us and get us across to Calcutta or Assam or something.'

'There isn't a WAS(B) between here and Burma as far as I know,' said the Red Cross woman. 'I'm the dogsbody who's got to get you across, and I'm sick of coping with WAS(B) mess-ups. The best I can do is put you in an hotel tonight and get you on a train tomorrow.'

I said, 'Look, I'm sorry but I'm going to have to cable my home for some money, I'm broke. I can't move until I get some money sent to a Bank here, unless there's pay-in-advance from the WAS(B)s or something.'

'Forget it. There's no pay-in-advance and I'm not having you lot hanging round in Bombay. There's a civilian train leaving in the morning, and your fare'll be paid by the Army. Calcutta can worry about you, I've got enough on my plate.'

We hung round, deflated, while she dealt with her NCOs. Our Colonel appeared, and asked where we were going to stay. When the woman told him the name of the hotel she was taking us to he looked horrified, and said, 'But that's a flea-pit. Why there?'

'The Army's paying for them in transit, and they're only recruits, after all. If they want to pay for their own accommodation they can go where they like, as long as they're on that train in the morning.'

We shook our heads dismally. The Colonel, in a last, generous gesture, took us all to dinner at his own high-class hotel, and as we ate he asked us how much money we had between us. It amounted to three pounds, seven shillings and sixpence. The seven and sixpence was mine. He said, 'You can't possibly set off across India on that money. Did that woman actually say she was sending you on a civilian train?'

'Yes, she did. Why?'

'Europeans aren't supposed to travel on them, people are always getting robbed or murdered on civilian trains. This country's a mess you know, the Hindus and the Muslims hate each other, and they're all anti-British; the Nationalists have just been waiting for the war to end to go all-out for independence. Besides, these trains take at least two-and-a-half days to Calcutta and there's no food except what you can buy on the stations, and no washrooms or lavatories. It's inhuman.'

'Well, she sounded as though she meant it. What can we do?'

'Clear out of that dump she's put you in and go to another hotel; I'll pay. Then you can cable for your money tomorrow, Robin, and I'll try to find someone who'll see that you're sent across in a proper troop train. I know Bombay pretty well, I'll put you in an hotel she won't think of.'

He was wrong; she found us, I don't know how. We went back and collected our things and he took us to another, much nicer hotel near the seafront, paid the bill for all of us and left. We hadn't even been down for breakfast next morning when the Red Cross woman arrived with four MPs, and a face like thunder. She and the MPs stood over us in silence while we packed, then marched us down the stairs like three criminals and bundled us into a paddy-wagon. We drove to the station where the MPs formed up round us again, marched us down the platform and squeezed us and all our luggage into one small compartment, second class. There were two greasy seats, and with our luggage piled between them there was barely room to stand. Ngari said some very unladylike things to the Red Cross woman, who pretended not to hear, and the MPs stood guard outside the compartment until the train started. I was sorry about the Colonel; we didn't know where to write and thank him, and he was a kind man.

The train ride was like watching some fabulous travelogue from inside a prison cell. The windows had no glass in second class, only bars, and at night we shut and locked wooden shutters on the inside, leaving an open space at the top of the windows for the air to come in. No one tried to murder us, but at night-time station stops long poles with hooks on the end came in through the open top of the windows. They fished blindly round inside the compartment, hoping to catch onto something of value and pull it out; if you grabbed the pole you risked getting your hand torn, and the pole's owner would bang on the shutter, threatening you. We hadn't enough money to buy proper food, but we bought tea at the stations, and some oranges. There was nowhere to wash, the station lavatories were so vile that we gagged going into them and our insides turned to cement. It was hot; sweatily, unremittingly, unbelievably hot.

Outside the train windows the magic of India dazzled me from first light until dark, and at night the blackness would be broken suddenly by the lights of a village, or the moon would rise, shaping and shadowing the landscape into the fabric of dreams. In the daytime the kaleidoscope patterns formed and melted, blinding with life and colour at one moment, and at the next expanding into a vastness of empty plain and distant mountains, lonely, ruined temples and sunset, when the climax of colour was a grand finale played by the orchestras of all the world.

There were constant, inexplicable stops, because civilian trains were non-priority, and we sweltered for hours in sidings waiting for troop trains to pass. The Indian passengers got out and squatted beside the line to relieve themselves. There were no Westerners to criticise us and we were desperate, so on the second night we climbed out and joined them; it was far better than the station lavatories, and no one took the slightest notice. The journey lasted three days, and at the end of it our own mothers would have refused to recognise us.

It was about nine o'clock on the third morning when the train pulled into Howrah, Calcutta's main railway station. We put our heads through the window to look for a porter, and abruptly brought them in again. The station, as far as we could see, was covered by a shouting, flailing mob of Indians engaged in mortal combat. There was blood on the platform in significant quantities, and a number of prone figures, some moving, some not. A short distance away there was a notice that read Railway Transport Officer, and I said to Ngari, 'Let's try to make it to the RTO's office – he'll tell us what to do.'

No one even glanced at us when we got off the train; it was an Indian quarrel, and we were irrelevant. A man in a loin-cloth materialised beside us, and offered to carry our luggage, as if everything was normal. Other men milled round us, brandishing knives and hunks of wood, and screaming at each other; we ran past them to the RTO's office, followed by our porter, and it was as though we were invisible. When we reached the office it looked empty; there was a table turned on its side, and papers all over the floor.

We called out, 'Is anyone there?' and a face rose from behind the table, followed by a hand holding a revolver, and a voice said disbelievingly, 'Do you mind telling me what you three are doing here?'

'We just arrived on that train, Sir.'

'You can't have, that's a civilian train.'

'Yes, we know.'

'Oh my God! Well, you can't stay here, there's a bloody riot on. There's a YWCA round the back of the station I think, the Lady Mary Herbert Home, there's a notice at the bottom of the stairs. Round that corner over there – leave your luggage here and run like hell.' He disappeared behind the table again. We pressed a note into the porter's hand and ran like hell.

We found the flight of stairs and the notice and stumbled upwards, panting and confused. There was a doorway at the top, and two old Hindu women squatting outside it. They looked at us doubtfully, and I decided that it was time to try out the smattering of Urdu Pa had taught me.

'Burra Memsahib kidher hai?'

'Malem ne, Memsahib.'

'Burra Memsahib jeldi mangta.'

They stared at me blankly. They were old crones, toothless, wrinkled and dirty, and they chattered to each other in shrill, malevolent voices. Without understanding a word they said at the time, I realised afterwards what the gist of it must have been.

'What do these ugly, unclean daughters of pigs want?'

'What should they want in a place like this? I know nothing of that Burra Memsahib the idiot-girl asked for, but we have plenty of men. We can offer them men, but I think that our men will not want them.'

They beckoned us to follow them down the passage, and I thought they were taking us to the YWCA Supervisor, the Burra Memsahib I'd been asking for. The passage windows were cracked and the curtains were grimy, but I was relieved to see that under the grime they were standard YWCA cotton check. From the station below came a crackle of gunfire, and increased howls of rage and anguish.

Halfway down the passage the old ladies paused and threw open a door. The three of us passed through it, and stopped abruptly. It was a largish bedroom with two beds, and two mother-naked Indian men standing expectantly beside them. We backed out precipitately, and I turned on the two old women. 'Burra Memsahib!' I yelled, wishing I had a better Urdu vocabulary. 'Sahib ne mangta!' The crones waved their hands about and shook their heads, then shuffled further down the passage to open another door. This time we peered in with some caution; there was an Indian girl on the bed, and a man energetically at work on top of her. We withdrew again, and our guides squatted on the floor, shrugging their shoulders.

'What do we do now?' said Ngari.

Beth, who was looking very pale, said, 'Gosh, I'm hungry.'

'Hell!' said I, feeling helpless. 'Well, we can't go back down there – listen to it.' Then, mustering a few more words of Urdu, 'Khana mangta. Garum khana aur nimbu pani hai? Show her some money, Ngari, for God's sake! We must have some left?'

Money they understood, instantly. They tottered away to find food, and we sat ourselves down against the wall, exhausted.

They came back with hot food and cold drinks, and the food was better than any other food, ever. It was greasy unidentifiable curried something with chapattis to scrape it up into our mouths and we wolfed it messily, sitting on the filthy floor. It was our first real food for a long time, and while I ate my brain began to work. This was Calcutta, wasn't it? And Pa's friend, Dick Casey, was Governor, wasn't he, and my first cousin, Bertram Whiting, was his ADC? Having thought that the WASBies would have us transferred straight to Assam I hadn't even considered contacting Bertram; I felt horribly shy of doing so now, but there seemed to be no real choice.

We dozed miserably in the passage until early afternoon. At about two o'clock the noise from the station below started to fade and we could hear the rioters moving away, still shouting and firing the occasional shot. I said to Ngari, 'I'm going down to try to find a phone. I've got a cousin who's an ADC at Government House, and he might be able to help us.'

Downstairs the station was empty, and apart from the welter of wreckage and the bloodstains the riot might have been a dream. The RTO's office was locked but I found a telephone and a phone-book in the First Class Waiting room, and by some miracle the phone worked. My voice was shaking, because I hadn't seen Bertram for years, and I didn't know how he'd react to an unannounced young relation with two hangers-on and no visible means of support. He came to the phone quite quickly and said, 'Hello? Whiting speaking.' He sounded official, and important.

'Bertie, it's me, Robin. Robin Walker.'

'Robin! Are you in Calcutta? What are you doing here?'

I'm at Howrah Station with two other girls on the way to join the WASBies, and we're in a brothel called the Lady Mary Herbert Home, I think. The RTO here said it was a YWCA, but it isn't. We've got hardly any money left. I'm so sorry, Bertie, but could you come and get us?'

Bertie seemed deprived of speech. The silence was so long that I said, 'Bertie, are you there? I'm running out of these little coins. Can you come?'

His voice was hoarse. 'Wait where you are , I... this riot, no one's allowed on the streets. I'll have to get onto the Army, and it'll take a bit of time. Just wait there for God's sake, somewhere no one can see you.'

I went back for the others and we waited for an hour, huddled behind a column near the entrance. At last we heard a rumbling, and down the street towards us came two armoured cars with Bertie uniformed and distraught-looking in the leading car. When he saw us at close quarters his expression changed from anxiety to pure horror, and I realised for the first time how dreadful we must look after three unwashed days on the train, the riot, the brothel and our recent life-saving curry. Worse than all of that, though we'd ceased to notice it ourselves, I knew how we must smell.

We told Bertie that our luggage was locked in the RTO's office, and Bertie said, 'We can't get it now, I'll send someone for it tomorrow. There's a general curfew today, no one's allowed on the streets. How the hell did you…? No, I don't feel strong enough. You can tell me about it later. That YWCA Hostel was closed down weeks ago, by the way.'

When the armoured cars deposited us at Government House, Bertram inspected us with disgust, and gave a deep sigh. 'Now listen,' he said. 'I'm going to take you to my quarters and you'd better have a shower for a start. We have to go through the ADC room, but just follow me and don't speak to anyone yet, please. There's a party on later, so do what you can to clean yourselves up and you can come to it.'

We couldn't do much with ourselves because we had nothing to change into, but the shower was one of the wonders of the world and it changed our outlook on life. We kept sniffing to make sure our clean smell was real, and we all collapsed into chairs and went sound asleep while our hair dried. When Bertie came to fetch us our clothes were still filthy, but servants had ironed them: inside them we were scrubbed and ready to go. I noticed Bertie eyeing Ngari appreciatively, and fancied there was a reciprocal gleam in her eye. Bertie was over six-foot tall, dark, Spanish-looking, and quite unfairly endowed with charm under circumstances which didn't include young cousins turning up in Indian brothels during riots.

The contrast between the ADC's party that evening and our immediate past was so profound that it reminded me of fairy stories where pumpkins turn into coaches, and frogs into princes. Government Houses were, by definition, grand, and few were grander than that of Bengal. It was still the era of the Raj, and ADC's were still the playmates of the Princes of their generation, at polo, hunting, drinking and womanising. They aimed at the standards set by the Princes themselves, and this party achieved them.

Bertie led me up to a pleasant-faced, rather stout young man and said, 'Biyar, I'd like to present my cousin, Robin Walker. She's just arrived from Australia, via a brothel as far as I can make out, so forgive the way she looks and be nice to her.' Then, to me, 'Biyar Cooch Bihar, Robin. He's a Maharajah but he's a friend of mine, and he'll look after you.' He removed himself briskly, in the direction of Ngari.

Biyar looked at me with amusement. I realised that I should be calling him 'Your Highness', but he was too nice, and too friendly. He said, 'Tell me all about it, I can't wait to hear.'

The evening glittered and spun like the champagne bubbles in the tall, crystal glasses offered on silver trays by spectacularly uniformed servants. The other women were all beautifully dressed; they eyed us as though we were rejects from a zoo, and made wide detours to avoid having to speak to us, but the men found us quaint and made much of us, laughing. Biyar said, 'You've got to celebrate after a trip like that. I'm going to take you to a Club I own, and give you some food. Bertie and the others'll come too.'

He swept us off, his comet's-tail of State Ministers and courtiers and minders trailing behind him, and a fleet of Rolls Royces took us to his Club. It was huge and white, built in the shape of a clover-leaf, with marble floors and classic marble columns. There was a table at the top of the centre room, and other tables on either side of it; Biyar sat himself in the seat of honour and placed us round him, while his court occupied the lesser tables. Endless servants plied us with wine and the most splendid food, an orchestra played, singers sang, and when Biyar clapped his hands at the Head Waiter some curtains near us parted, and a troop of glorious half-naked girls floated through them to dance in front of our table.

We stayed at Government House that night, asleep before we had stretched out properly, and in the morning servants brought us trays with silver coffee pots, and large, indulgent breakfasts. Bertie wasn't in evidence, but he came to see us around noon, and it was clear that he'd been busy.

'I've done some checking up,' he said. 'I sent a signal to the head WAS(B) in Assam, and she managed to phone me. There seems to have been some kind of mess-up; she says she wasn't really sure if you were coming with the war ending, but she can use you. They're still running all the canteens with 14th Army, and a lot of women have left to join their husbands so they're short-handed. The thing is, they don't know when they can get you transport to Burma, and you can't stay here indefinitely.'

'No, of course we can't. You've been terribly good to us already. Is there some kind of hostel we can go to?'

'Not exactly, you've got to go to the Transit Camp at Barrackpore, and the Army'll ship you over from there. It won't be too bad, and you can get in to Calcutta by taxi – you will come in, won't you Ngari? Oh, and I sent Uncle Geoff a cable Robin, to tell him you need some money. I said to send it to my Bank, and they'll let me know when it arrives.'

I could imagine Pa grinding his teeth, and wondering how I could have managed to fritter away a sum like fifteen pounds; I hoped he wouldn't refuse to send me any more, and what would he make of a cable sent by Bertie from Calcutta? He'd undoubtedly fear the worst and assume that I'd done something disastrous; I was grateful for every mile that lay between us.

Barrackpore lasted for about ten days. There are few places less appealing than an Army Transit Camp, especially at the end of a war when it's run down and tired, but our stay there was significant both for me and for Ngari.

Ngari and Bertram embarked without a moment's pause on what promised to be a love affair of note. It lasted for about five days, during which we spent more time in Government House than in the Transit Camp, and then he introduced us to a friend of his who was passing through Calcutta on his way back to Burma. Peter was a Captain in an Indian Regiment, better looking even than Bertie and, we gathered, married. He and Ngari gave each other a long, appraising look, and from then on Bertie might not have existed; during our last five days in Calcutta she and Peter gazed into each other's eyes when together and looked tortured every time they were parted. It was during the Barrackpore period too that I met Andy.

Peter and Bertram had asked us to meet them in Calcutta for dinner at an hotel, and had set a time that was rather later than usual. Barrackpore had rigidly enforced rules about when one had to be back inside the wire at night, particularly for Other Ranks, and for female Other Ranks most of all. The camp was a sprawling, dusty, comfortless Army caravanserai staffed by disillusioned discards from the mainstream of the Army, and the only official way in or out of it was by the main gate, where sentries checked the validity of your comings and goings.

Ngari and I were well aware before we went out that we had no chance of being back at the regulation time. We were housed in one of the peas-in-a-pod brick huts, four bunks, a cement floored washroom and a lavatory bowl, but it had the advantage of being alongside the barbed-wire boundary fence. Before we left we fossicked round the camp until we unearthed three or four old gunny-sacks, and these we hung over the wire behind our hut. We knew that we'd come back either by car or taxi, and the sacks would both identify our hut for us, and give us some protection while climbing the fence. Beth never came on these excursions, much preferring the earnest, teetotal young men who stayed in camp at night, and who discussed the finer things of life with her.

When we got to the hotel where we were to meet it was crowded, and either they were late or we were early, so we sat down at a table and ordered drinks. Pa, to my surprise, had sent twenty pounds and a 'what is going on?' telegram; I hadn't yet answered the telegram, but I was feeling rich. Unaccompanied young women had scarcity value in Calcutta at the time, and before I could pay the waiter a voice said, 'May we join you? and another voice said, 'Let me pay for those drinks.'

Ngari said, 'We're waiting for friends, but have a seat till they come, they won't be long. I'm Ngari, and this is Robin.'

'Where d'you come from? You're not English.'

I said, 'How d'you know? Don't I sound English?'

'Yes, but you don't look it, you're both different to English girls. I'm Andy, by the way.

Andy was tall and thin, narrow shouldered and he wore glasses, but he had a nice grin; he was attractive, I thought, in a funny way, and he showed signs of finding me more interesting than Ngari which endeared him to me. When Bertie and Peter arrived, Peter and Ngari immediately became limp as two invertebrates, and I introduced Bertie to Andy. Andy's friend looked bored, and wandered off.

The evening was utterly predictable; dinner, a great deal to drink at the bar afterwards, and a game of liar dice. Andy told me he was a Captain in a Signals Unit with one of the Indian Divisions, and had been at Imphal during the fighting there. He was on his way back to his Unit in Burma after being on Leave. It was nearly midnight when we realised that we should have been back at Barrackpore two hours earlier.

'We'll have to take you back by taxi,' said Bertie. 'I can't risk being nabbed by MPs in a Government House car with a couple of Absent Without Leave WASBies on board. Come on Peter – Andy, do you want to come?'

We found an ancient, rickety taxi outside with a Sikh driver, and managed to pack into it by putting a willing Ngari onto Peter's knee. As we drove off Andy said, 'Keep an eye out for an MP's jeep. I spent a few nights at Barrackpore once and they're bastards. If they catch us they'll arrest the lot of us.' Bertie said, 'Oh God, that'd be the end of me,' and twisted round to peer out of the rear window.

The Sikh driver drove like all Sikhs, which is to say like a homicidal maniac goaded by red-hot pokers. He careered round corners and down every road on the wrong side at maximum speed, clutching the steering wheel to his chest and muttering into his beard. He found the Transit Camp in record time, but quite understandably came to a noisy halt right in front of the gate and the guardhouse. 'Make him go round the back!' I yelled. 'We'll have to go over the fence!' The driver, believing he'd fulfilled his contract, stopped the engine.

Andy and Bertram, with passable Urdu, persuaded the driver

that he must do a circuit of the camp. He gunned the engine into deafening life and took off again in a shower of gravel, activating a jeep full of MPs who had been waiting inside the gates, hoping for something like us to brighten up their duty shift.

The camp was set on a large, square block of land with roads all round it. Our taxi had a head start and a driver possessed of a devil. We screamed round the first corner and up a mile of tree-lined dirt road, skidding from side to side, with the lights of the MP's jeep dancing behind us.

'Where's your hut? We'll have to make him slow down and just chuck you two out. I can't get arrested, H.E.'d sack me on the spot. There's sure to be a ditch beside the road so roll into it and keep your heads down, and we'll try to lose the MPs.

'We've got sacks over the wire along the back fence so try to get ahead of them round the next corner, and we'll bale out. Then go like hell!'

The jeep wasn't making much ground as we rounded the corner into the back stretch; we could see their lights, but it was hard to make out the distance through the dust. I thought we were about level with our hut, and I yelled, 'Now!' Andy screamed at the Sikh to stop, and he slowed down just long enough for the back door to open, and for Ngari and me to be pushed out onto the road. We hit fairly hard, but we both rolled towards the edge and down into the storm ditch.

The sound of the taxi faded into the distance but another noise, and headlights, took its place as the MP's jeep came to a stop above us. We knew that we were caught, but I also knew that my face had landed in something soft and wet at the bottom of the ditch, and that there was an awful, unmistakable smell. Rough hands had me by the shoulders, and I was being lifted up, dripping. 'Oh hell,' I said. 'Watch out before you touch me. I've put my face in a bloody cow-pat.'

The MPs shone their torches on us. Ngari was merely dirty, but when they saw my face they laughed until they were weak, and it saved us.

'Want to charge 'em, Bert?' one asked the other.

'Ave to take 'em back to the Guardhouse for that,' said Bert. 'Oo's goin' to clean the jeep out afterwards?'

'Gawd, not me! Where d'you live, ladies? An 'ut nearby, I 'ope?'

'Just there,' I said miserably, pointing to the sacks.

'Wotta coincidence, sacks and all. I wonder 'ow they got there. Well give me an 'and, Bert, to put the ladies over the fence, and I warn you darlings, don't let us catch you at it again. Allez Oop!'

The taxi got clean away, of course, so I didn't have Bertie's job on my conscience, not that Dick Casey would have sacked him; he was too nice a man, and he would have seen the funny side. Bertie was shaken though, and a little disenchanted by Ngari's lightening defection to Peter; we saw little more of him before we left for Burma.

Andy managed to get in touch with me every day, and either to come out to Barrackpore for a visit, or to take me somewhere for a meal. He said that he'd be stationed in Rangoon, and insisted that we keep in touch when I reached Burma, and was allocated to a Division. I liked him, but it hadn't gone beyond that. Apart from my habitual shyness with young men I was convinced that I had a new, ineradicable form of repulsion to add to all my other deficiencies.

No matter how I scrubbed, washed my hair and creamed my face, or even wasted money on a bottle of cheap scent I could still smell, and was certain that others could smell, the lingering fragrance of cow-shit.

27

Eighty-second Division

IT SEEMED IRONIC to have travelled all the way from Australia to India, secure in the belief that I was bound for the Indian Army of my family's past, and to end up with a West African Division whose presence in Burma I hadn't even suspected. I felt cheated, but it had happened with my consent, and I couldn't complain.

I was ashamed because we had arrived too late; it was like joining a new school just in time for the break-up, and we were imposters. The real WASBies had been through a war together, a harsh, exacting war, and who were we to arrive, fresh and unblooded when it was all over and say we belonged with them.

The WASBies had never been a large service. It was originally formed, when the Japs entered the war in 1942, for cypher duties in Rangoon, and it dissolved when the Japanese advance forced the British to retreat.

One of its members then was Ninian Taylor, the wife of a Burma Rifles Colonel. With thirty-two other women she survived a gruelling journey out of Burma, and it was she who persuaded Army Command in India to let her reform the service for canteen and welfare duties. There was no other welfare for the men in the field except NAAFI, and NAAFI was restricted to behind-the-lines work in large, established bases. Nin Taylor, and a number of other women who, like her, had husbands or friends fighting on the Burma front, made the WASBies into a highly flexible and mobile group which could operate as part of the fighting Divisions. They had become a proud, close-knit sisterhood; some had been killed, some Mentioned in Despatches and others had been decorated. Some of them were surprisingly old, some very young, and they included Burmese and Indian girls, as well as British. The dangers they'd shared, the grief and the losses, their illnesses which they ignored and the constant difficulties they overcame gave them something indefinable and special. I felt it was an insult to pretend to be one of them.

The three of us had been finally transported by boat across the Bay of Bengal, and handed over to our first real, live WAS(B). We were bustled off to WAS(B) Headquarters, and told that we would be sent to our separate postings the same day to replace women who had left. 'There are three postings available,' we were told, 'And it doesn't matter which of you goes where. Pick the one you want.'

Beth, predictably, picked the least interesting one, with a well-established canteen in a large town, and I never saw her again. The two other postings were with an Indian Division near Mandalay, or to set up a new canteen with a West African Division camped in the jungle north of Rangoon and waiting to be sent back to Africa. Ngari and I looked at each other, both wanting desperately to go to the Indian Division, and Ngari said, 'Look, I've simply got to go to the one near Mandalay, Peter said he'd be there. Please, Robin, it doesn't matter to you where you go, but I'll die if I'm not near Peter.' I thought, 'Hell, why don't I stand up to her,' and said, 'Okay, I'll take the West Africans.' We both departed that afternoon in different directions, Ngari in an Indian-driven jeep, and I in a 15-cwt truck beside a huge, purple-black, beaming West African who addressed me as 'Missee'.

It occurred to me, as we drove across the Burmese plain, that I hadn't the faintest idea of how to go about setting up a canteen, and that no one had told me what to use for money, nor whether there'd be any equipment to work with. The situation seemed rather too open-ended to be funny but the Burmese landscape distracted me, and I decided to leave it to fate. We drove through paddy-fields at first, yellowish green in their lattice of paddy-bunds and stretching to the horizon, broken only by the dark green clusters of trees which sheltered villages. These clusters had a secret, enclosed look, with nothing visible from the road but the horizontals and verticals of the trees, and only wavering strands of smoke rising into the still air to tell you that people lived under them.

When the road ran through one of these shaded villages it was not mysterious at all, but full of life. There were bamboo houses on either side, washing and food-stalls and pony carts, babies and dogs and chickens and ancient, wrinkled grandparents, all scattered at random across the road and apparently oblivious of our truck until it was almost on top of them. To make matters worse, whenever we entered a village the African driver accelerated furiously, and only slowed down again when we came to open country.

'Why did you go so fast through that village?' I asked angrily after the second one. I had heard screams fading behind us, but the dust was too thick to see, and I hoped that at worst it had been a pi-dog puppy.

The driver said, 'Bad, bad men stay for village, Missee. Dacoiti men, shoot gun at us, no good for go slow.'

I hadn't heard about dacoits then, the savage little bands that robbed, murdered and terrorised at random across the Burmese countryside, but I had noticed a sten-gun behind our heads on top of the seat, and wondered what it was for. A little later we came across a small band of Burmese men loping along the paddy-bunds beside the road. They were ragged and serious-looking, and they all had rifles slung across their shoulders. The African beside me went as near grey as was possible for one of his colouring, and stood on the accelerator. The truck reached its maximum speed of perhaps 35 mph, and I looked back through the window to see if we were being threatened; the men were still on the same course, and if they had noticed our passing they gave no sign, but my driver was clearly a shaken man.

The country gradually changed from paddy to bush, and started to rise. The road got steeper and rougher, and the scrubby bush changed quite suddenly into jungle, tall, dense and diverse, smelling of moss and mould, arching over us to hide the sky so that we drove through a tunnel of tangled green. The road stopped being even a track, and became two narrow concrete strips laid over the rough ground, wide enough apart to take our wheels.

The jungle-tunnel ended abruptly, after what seemed like hours, opening out to a dusty, red-earth clearing at the foot of a high cliff. There were tents in the clearing, and huts, and a number of incomprehensible notices. I realised that we'd arrived at the Headquarters of the 82nd West African Division. My door was opened from the outside, and a voice said, 'Would you be our WAS(B) Miss?'

It was my introduction to Divisional Sergeant Major Stebbing, a regular soldier of the old school, and a man who wielded infinitely more power in the Division than its General. He was stout, red-faced, and had the most magnificent waxed moustache I had ever seen, even in picture books. He held himself ramrod-straight, and at the sound of his voice, even moderately raised, the African troops trembled. He was eyeing me rather sceptically. I said, 'I'm afraid I am your WAS(B), Sergeant Major, and I'm new to it. I haven't a clue what I'm supposed to do.'

His face relaxed, and he said comfortably, 'That's all right then, Miss, we'll sort it out together. Anyway, we've 'ad a signal there's another WAS(B) coming over 'ere tomorrow for a few days to show you 'ow. Anything you want, you just ask me. I'll take you up to your camp now, on top of the dam. Oh, and by the way, this 'ere's your jeep.'

I swallowed audibly; I hadn't expected my lie about being able to drive to catch up with me so quickly. It was a dear, battered, tough little jeep, and I shuddered to think what I might do to it.

'And this 'ere's Kwami,' said SM Stebbing, saving my life for the first of many times. He pointed to a squat, grinning African standing near the jeep, dressed in nothing but a pair of shorts and beret. 'E'll be your driver. It's regulations 'ere that either you or your driver carries a weapon at all times, in case of dacoits. Dacoits is what we call the local bandits, and there's a lot of them, and they've got some very nasty 'abits, so until you gets used to the lay of the place Kwami can drive and you sit in the back with the gun. I'll show you 'ow to use that. Now, put your gear in my jeep, and I'll take you up to the camp.'

We took a steep track up the cliff and turned right across the spillway of the dam. It was a huge, oily-calm expanse of water that reflected the dark jungle all around it. There was stillness everywhere, not the stillness of calm but of unseen things watching and waiting, and the noise of the jeep seemed like an impertinence. On our other side, below the dam wall, the treetops were thick and soft as a green wool blanket, broken only by the Divisional Headquarters clearing. I knew that there must be thousands of men camped in the area, but there was no sign of them; I tried to imagine what warfare in that solid mass of vegetation might have been like.

The track turned left after the end of the spillway and stopped on the edge of the water, half a mile further on. There was a small clearing with a woven bamboo shelter and two small tents; four sacks stretched between poles half-concealed a thunderbox, and this had been prominently placed, without cover, in the middle of the clearing.

'This 'ere's your camp,' said the SM with pride. 'Took a lot of trouble with it, the men did. They're that bloody pleased, beg yer pardon, to be getting a canteen.'

Two Africans materialised out of the bamboo shelter; they had the self-satisfied air of men about to go on holiday. SM Stebbing gave them a glare which brought them quivering to attention, and said, 'These two 'ere'll look after your camp and do the cooking. They speak a bit of English, but don't take no lip from them and make them work like buggery, beg yer pardon. If they don't, tell me. We 'ave our own methods of discipline in this Division, wot these men understand.'

I found this to be true; I never saw a flogging, though they undoubtedly happened, but several times I saw Africans tied to trees at night, their arms shackled behind the tree trunk, outside the Sergeant's Mess. They would be left there until morning to cool off after an illegal beer-drink or some other crime. I came to understand that the Africans much preferred such punishments to those laid down in King's Rules and Regulations, designed for white men and quite incomprehensible to the African mind.

SM Stebbing continued, 'There's some other things I'd better tell you, Miss. Don't go walking in the jungle on your own, please. There's snakes round 'ere, and a lotta other nasties, animals and the like; used to be a Game Park, this did. There was three of the African troops taken by tiger last week, but that was from the units on the perimeter, not 'ere. You'll 'ave guards on your camp at night because some of these black men aren't wot you'd call civilised; never seen a white woman some of 'em, I shouldn't wonder, and they might 'ave ideas.'

The senior WAS(B) arrived next day. She was older than me and had seen service in the most hair-raising conditions and places. She bustled round, purring because everything was so peaceful and easy, treated the SM with such casual irreverence that he bristled and went red in the face, and confused me by organising everything herself and not telling me how she'd done it. When she left three days later I had a hazy idea of what I was supposed to do, but no confidence at all in my ability to do it. An assistant WAS(B) would be sent to me, she said as she left, but she didn't know when. 'Anyway, you've got a good set-up here, I'm sure you can manage on your own.'

The days were divided into two sessions, the first starting at 8 a.m. in a 15-cwt truck stocked with toothpaste, Brylcreem, soap, biscuits and other male accessories which had been sent up from the Rangoon NAAFI on the senior WAS(B)'s orders, and these had to be distributed to the African units, camped in the jungle over a wide area. I had a British Corporal to drive the truck, and SM Stebbing worked out a roster so that every unit got its fair share of visits. The senior WAS(B) had ordered stock based on the requirements of relatively sophisticated Indian troops, and she would have been surprised at the African reaction to her choice of goods

Dispensing things from the back of the 15-cwt was hard work. As soon as the truck stopped the men would swarm out of the bush, shoving and screaming and pulling at my legs which were on a level with their faces, in a frenzy to get attention. It was impossible to understand what they wanted but experience soon taught me that there were only three things in demand: toothpaste, Brylcreem and biscuits. As soon as they had these in their hands they would sit down under a nearby tree, spread their Brylcreem or toothpaste on the biscuits, and eat them with the rapt enjoyment of gourmets at a five-star restaurant. It was necessary to restock with these three items at frequent intervals.

Daytime duty, Mobile Canteen duty, ended sometime in the afternoon, then one restocked the truck's shelves, had a quick wash or a swim in the pool below the dam wall, and got the night canteen ready for the British NCOs. All the officers and NCOs in the Division were British, and while the officers had their own comfortable Mess tents, and the Sergeants and Sergeant-Majors, being craftier, had an even more comfortable one, the NCOs below that rank had nothing, until our canteen started. As a result their standards weren't high, and they were wonderfully grateful for what seemed to me very little.

There was no official alcohol for Corporals and Lance Corporals, but they smuggled in their own and mixed it with the soft drinks, and no one said a word. The food was a monotonous diet of fried bread, fried eggs and potato chips, the eggs and potatoes bought from the local villagers, and they had tables and chairs of a sort, and a gramophone and packs of cards. The young men had been dying of boredom and long-stale dirty jokes in their tents, and they thought it was wonderful.

SM Stebbing and his friend, who was also a Sergeant Major, appointed themselves as my official guardians. Instead of spending the whole evening in their own Mess they set up a table and chairs just outside the canteen tent. They put a lantern on the table, and a bottle of whisky, and sat in a cloud of mosquitos until I was finished, drinking Scotch laced with a dash of tea, and talking. They had been friends for years, and what they still had to talk about was a mystery, but they never drew breath.

Every half-hour or so one of them would reach into the canteen tent, pull me out, and make me drink a slug of tea-and-scotch; with a working day which lasted from 8 a.m. to 10 p.m. in the Burmese heat I was grateful for it. When the Canteen closed they would take me with them to the Sergeant's Mess and feed me more whisky, talking all the time to each other above my head. When Stebbing decided that the bar should close he would clap his hands and two African orderlies would enter the Mess carrying a stretcher which they laid on the ground behind him. Stiff as a tree-trunk he'd fall back on it and lie full length with his eyes closed, the two orderlies would carry him to his tent and his Sergeant Major being slightly his junior, would drive me back to my camp. They were wonderful, self-appointed nannies, but not at all what Pa had led me to expect.

28

Burma

I HAD TO LEARN, SOMEHOW, to drive my jeep, before anyone found out that I couldn't drive. I watched what Kwami did every day from the back seat, and went over it in my mind at night. We hadn't had a car at home for years, not since Mama lost the sight of one eye, because Pa hated the cars anyway and used her semi-sight as an excuse. I was car-illiterate, but in the end I gritted my teeth, and one day when we were in the middle of nowhere I said, 'Kwami, you sit for back seat, hold gun. Missee drive.'

Kwami rolled his eyes a bit, but he didn't dare say no. He climbed into the back with the gun and I got behind the wheel, praying. I got the thing started and we proceeded for the first half-mile in frog-hops, wavering from side to side of the track. By the time we were travelling reasonably straight and level I realised that we were approaching Divisional HQ, that we'd have to pass it in full public view, climb the steep hill to the dam spillway and cross its narrow rim if we were to get to my camp. I wasn't sure which gear I'd have to use in order to climb the hill, so I decided to put my foot full down and rush it.

We blazed past Divisional HQ with my foot flat to the boards, past all the notices saying Max. Speed 5 MPH, and I heard shouts of protest. The brave little jeep made it to the top, its engine snarling and hiccuping, and I managed the right hand turn onto the spillway. By then I had panicked, and my foot stayed hard down. I'd been aware of shrill African lamentations from the back seat for some time, and as we reached the end of the spillway and turned left Kwami hurled himself from the jeep, hitting the ground in a cloud of dust. I wanted to stop, principally to see if he was all right, but also because the track ended a little further on at the edge of the lake. The method of actually stopping the jeep had gone from me, and the only alternative seemed to be a watery grave. A merciful God inspired me to turn off the ignition.

Kwami materialised beside the jeep unhurt, but his face was grey instead of its usual burnished black and his eyes showed more white than was decent. I was glad, for once, that we had so few words of common language. Then SM Stebbing roared up in his own jeep, having seen my record-breaking dash through Divisional HQ. He walked round me several times, as I sat pale and paralysed; his moustache was vibrating, and he said to Kwami, 'Get off down to Parade Ground, double quick! Imshi!'

'Sah!' said Kwami, and vanished.

'Why didn't you tell me you couldn't bloody well drive?' asked Stebbing.

'Sorry, Sar-Major,' I said miserably. 'I had to sign a thing to say I could drive to get over here, and I lied.'

'Well, you're a silly little bitch, beg yer pardon, you might 'ave killed yerself. Don't you never go through my 'Eadquarters like that again or I'll 'ave yer, so 'elp me I will. Now, get into my jeep 'ere and I'll teach yer to drive.'

In quiet times, and without a word to anyone else, he made a driver of me. Kwami refused to get in the jeep with me again, so he gave me a new African co-driver as well.

My assistant arrived; she was small, she looked like something out of the chorus-line of South Pacific, and her name was Terry. She said she was half Chinese and half Phillipino, and that she and her mother had been interned in Hong Kong when the Japanese war started. Terry had managed to escape from the internment camp, and with three men she had walked out of China, across the Himalayas and into India, a journey of such epic proportions that it was hard to believe, looking at her, that it was possible. It was true enough, confirmed and documented, but Terry hardly ever mentioned it. Her whole soul was concentrated on the one ambition which had sustained her through all the miles of snow and hunger and hardship; she wanted an English husband.

The morning after she arrived I took her off in the Mobile Canteen to show her the ropes. It was a hot, muggy day, one of Burma's specials, when you had to take salt tablets just to stay on your feet and your clothes stuck to you, smelling like stale dish-rags. When we finished duty I said to Terry, 'There's a pool in the rocks down at the foot of the dam that the British NCO's swim in, and we're allowed to use it. D'you feel like a swim?'

'I sure do!'

'Okay, put on your bathers and pull your dress over the top of them, you can take it off down at the pool. It'll be full of NCOs but at least we can cool off.'

Terry always favoured a direct approach. We drove down to the pool, and it was full of young men, splashing and fooling about. They eyed the new WAS(B) with interest. I said to her, 'Go behind that bush there and take your dress off, it'll be quite safe,' and I took my own dress off. There was a yell from the pool as if someone had kicked a goal at a Grand Final, and a maelstrom of white water as the swimmers thrashed towards our bank. I looked for Terry and stifled a shout of horror. She had taken her dress off but she hadn't a stitch on underneath it and was standing naked, hands on hips, smiling provocatively at the rapturous NCOs.

Terry was sunny-natured, she worked well and I liked her; I decided that what she did with her spare time was her own affair. I was a Sergeant by then, and technically speaking I was responsible for her, but I knew my limitations. The NCOs thought she was the Almighty's blessing after a hard war.

After only a couple of months with the Division I became engaged to Andy. He was stationed in Rangoon, found out where I'd been posted, and arrived at Divisional HQ one day unannounced. I came back from Mobile Canteen duty and found him sitting in our bamboo shelter, drinking our drink with SM Stebbing who had shown him the way to our camp and was quite obviously vetting him. He came to see me quite often after that, or I'd hitch a ride to Rangoon on Sundays to have a meal with him. On one of these trips he proposed to me, and I said yes. I knew perfectly well that I wasn't in love with him and marriage seemed too far in the future to be taken seriously, but I was aware that an official attachment, such as a fiancee, would make my life a lot easier.

Inevitably I was having man-trouble; it would have happened to any single female in that time and place but I lacked Terry's light-hearted approach to it. My mother's principles were still firmly ingrained, and I took it all far too seriously. The Africans were not problem, and if the younger officers had been interested I'd probably have enjoyed it, but it was the middle-aged, married ones who should have known better. They'd have a few drinks too many at their mess, then drive up to our camp in the small hours feeling randy and deprived, and wander into my tent opening their fly buttons, convinced they were about to do me a favour.

I slept with my .38 revolver beside me. Stebbing had given it to me saying that it was regulations for me to carry it at all times, and although I was incapable of hitting anything with it I could wave it about very menacingly. I thought of Pa's almost religious belief that all British officers were perfect gentlemen, and wondered what he'd make of the present crop. If I'd told him about them he'd have accused me of lying, and probably smacked my head for being sacrilegious.

Guiltily I knew that I was using Andy, but I felt that it cut both ways. I was certain that he was no more in love with me than I with him; he was reacting normally to years of war deprived of female company, besides which with women in short supply a fiancee was a feather in his cap. He was only twenty-two, not much older than me, and there was plenty of time in the future for either of us to back off if we wanted to. The question of pre-marital sex never crossed my mind in the beginning, neither that he might demand it, nor that in return for my use of him as a safety device he had every right to it. I accepted a small sapphire and diamond ring as proof of my betrothed status, and flashed it ostentatiously under the nose of any man who seemed ambitious.

Andy was an ordinary, pleasant young middle-class Englishman, an only child, educated at a minor Public School and raised in a prosperous suburb of Brighton, Sussex. His upbringing had been narrow and his mind followed suit; he thought me quite peculiar in many ways; he excused it because I was Australian and therefore bound to be odd, yet he never wanted to know anything about Australia or my family. Once I was in England and married to him, I gathered, Australia would cease to exist. He would finish his accountancy course after his discharge, and when he was earning a certain figure we'd get married. There would be a house in the suburbs, and I'd be expected to follow the same daily routine as his mother, library, bridge and gardening. His father, he told me, owned chemist shops in London and commuted by train every day, arriving home late to grumble at his wife and to eat a specially prepared dinner on his own. It sounded alien and awful, and not at all what my parents had led me to expect from life in the Promised Land.

Letters to and from Australia were a rarity, travelling slowly by sea, and subject to delays at either end. I wrote and told my parents that I was engaged, and the little I knew about Andy and his family. Months later I got an enthusiastic letter from Mama, taking it for granted that I'd chosen a mate from the right social and financial bracket.

'We always hoped that you'd marry a young man in a Good Regiment,' she wrote. 'You say his father owns chemists shops in London. I expect that means that he owns Boots, in which case he's a millionaire.' Poor Mama; in no way could Andy's obscure Signals Unit staffed by very temporary soldiers be classed as a Good Regiment, nor could his father's three chemist shops in Hammersmith be compared to Boots.

Mama's world had resisted all but the most superficial change and in it she still lived secure, shielded by the holy myth known as 'your father's standards' which were, in fact, an invention of her own. They were admirable in theory, and unsustainable in the real world. When Andy put it to me, in the strongest possible terms, that he wasn't prepared to wait forever before taking me to bed I gave in. My virginity had become a bore and a burden to me anyway, and he was welcome to it.

The term 'taking me to bed' is misleading because we had no access to anything so comfortable. When I went to see him in Rangoon I dossed down at WAS(B) Headquarters in a room full of other women, and Andy shared a tent with another officer in his unit. My introduction to sex took place in the back of a jeep in a dark, mosquito-infested, jungly Rangoon cul-de-sac.

It was unfortunate that Andy's claims to extensive sexual experience were fictitious because I knew nothing myself, and we were both terrified I might get pregnant. It was uncomfortable and degrading, and I was completely mystified; sex was glorified in song and story, and by a whole lot of women that I knew, so surely there had to be more to it than this. Andy said that it was all my fault and I was humbly certain that he was right. After all Mama's warnings about my Down There I couldn't imagine that anyone could possibly get pleasure from it, and the idea that I might get pleasure from it myself had never crossed my mind. Apparently, I decided, it was the woman's duty to pretend to like it and to let the man enjoy himself, however unfair that seemed. Ignorant and confused, I resigned myself to a lifetime of pretending.

29

Rangoon

14TH ARMY WAS GOING HOME, the Indian troops back to their towns and villages, the Africans, most of whom would never know what country they'd been fighting in, back to Africa, The homesick British temporary soldiers would go back to a country they'd hardly recognise when they got there, the exhausted, battered British Isles.

Then there were the ex-POWs. I met some of the men who had survived the Burma Railway, and they were just bone and sinew held together by ruined skin, and although they tried to drink and laugh their deep-sunk eyes stayed blank and haunted . I remembered what Jenny had said to me about badly damaged men, and wondered how many of them would survive their homecoming.

SM Stebbing told me that the Division would be moving down to Transit Camp in Rangoon, and soon afterwards Nin Taylor, the WAS(B) Commandant arrived. She was visiting all the WAS(B) Units, asking each girl what she wanted to do with her future. There were plenty of choices; they could opt for service in Japan, in Java or with the Control Commission in Germany, or they could take immediate discharge and free transport to any part of the world they wished.

'I suppose you'll want to stay on in Rangoon,' said Nin to me, 'Seeing you've got engaged. I'll put you on the Headquarters staff, to help ship the other girls out. Gay Tucker and Dosan Penty are the other two there, and we've been allocated a compound in Golden Valley. You can get on a troopship back to England when everyone else has been sent off.'

It was sad to leave the camp on the edge of the lake. There were discomforts that one cursed all the time, like sitting on the thunderbox with one's head and shoulders above the sacking, in full view of the Africans and anyone else who happened along, but one got used to it. There were columns of man-eating ants, there were snakes, there was constant prickly heat and dehydration. There were sudden storms, with wind and rain and thunder that frequently reduced the camp into sodden canvas buried in a sea of red mud, but things dried out and tents were easy to put up again. No one cared how they looked, clothes had to be worn long after they were torn and stained, there was no make-up to be had, and we used no mirrors.

It was the lake itself, and the jungle that I hated to leave. I could see fish rising, making silver circles on the still surface, and I fished for them, but the only thing I caught was a turtle who bit me to the bone when I tried to free it. I'd walked in the jungle a lot, in spite of Stebbings' warnings about nasties. I only went in daytime, when most of the nasties slept, and there were unexpected open glades, full of sunlight, and a feeling of being watched by hidden things which wished you well. I would miss the Africans. Most of all, I'd miss Sergeant Major Stebbing. On the other hand I knew Rangoon to be frenetic, undisciplined and discharge-crazy, and it was bound to be fun.

Just before we left I saw Ngari again. I hadn't heard from her since the day we were given our postings, so I was astonished when she burst into my tent at about three o'clock one morning. She was dusty, and only half-coherent; I got her a stiff drink, yelled at the Africans to find her a camp cot, and tried to make her tell me what had happened.

'How did you get here?'

'In a jeep, it's on the track out there. I stole it.'

'I see, you stole it. Who from, and why?'

'It's just an Army jeep, I don't know. I've got to get to India to meet Peter. I'll be gone in the morning before anyone finds out I've been here.'

'Ngari, don't be a bloody idiot! I'm damned if I'm going to lie about you being here, and they'll catch up with you for sure. What's it all about?'

Peter, it seemed, had been stationed near her at Mandalay, and their love affair had raged like a bushfire. Then Peter got his discharge quite suddenly, and had been sent back to India where his wife was waiting for him. He'd sent a telegram to Ngari a couple of days earlier to say that he'd told his wife about her, ended his marriage, and that she was to meet him in Calcutta as soon as possible so they could go away together.

'But Ngari, it's crazy doing it like this! Go to Nin Taylor and tell her the whole thing, she'll give you a discharge. There'll be hell to pay if you bolt off now with a stolen jeep.'

'I don't care! I'm not waiting round for all the red tape! Anyway, I think I'm pregnant.'

She was gone by daylight. The next time I saw her was in England, in 1951, and by then she was a widow with a small son. Peter had got a divorce, and they had travelled to Australia together with their baby. They went north to Papua; Ngari was Bougainville-raised, she knew the area and she spoke pidgin They bought a barge and sailed it round the Papuan coast, picking up war-surplus equipment and selling it. They might have become rich if Peter hadn't gone below decks one evening to start the engine, lit a match to see by, and blown himself up. Ngari and the baby were thrown over the side by the explosion, and rescued, but Peter was dead.

When I arrived in Rangoon I found that our Golden Valley compound was a war-scarred relic of British-Colonial senior-management accommodation, built as a status symbol for some commercial executive. There were two houses, and a line of servants' quarters between them and the road. Before the war the houses must have been luxurious, light and airy and well designed; since the passage of the Japanese Imperial Army they were lighter and airier than ever, but far less comfortable.

Their roofs were a system of rafters between gaping holes, and this was probably caused by the Allied bombing, but before they left the Japanese had deliberately wrecked the place, together with almost every other house and service facility in Rangoon. All the doors had been torn off their hinges and smashed, every window broken, electric wiring had been torn out and the power points were just holes in the wall. There was no electricity anyway because the Power Station had been destroyed, and the disadvantage of broken water-pipes was minimised by the fact that there was no longer any water supply.

For all that there was something rather grand about living between walls after months in a tent. There was even the remains of a cracked asphalt tennis court between the two houses, and a garden which, like all Rangoon gardens, had returned to the jungle so thoroughly that it was coming in through the windows and up between the floor boards. Strange spiders and lizards disputed possession with us; everything, including ourselves, grew a rich, green mould, and smelled accordingly.

Gay Tucker and Dosan Penty had moved in by the time I arrived. Gay, the senior member, was a Major, the ex-wife of a Burma Rifles Colonel who had run off with a nurse, and she was taking it very hard. She was slim and fair, with one of those thin, handsome English faces one sees in the hunting-field, riding fearlessly at mammoth fences. She had been Mentioned in Despatches earlier in the war. Dosan was a Lieutenant: she had been Mentioned in Despatches too, and awarded the MBE. She was a Parsee, and also an economist, later to become Chief Economist at Barclay's Bank in Bombay, and she was beautiful as an old Moghul painting, fragile, gazelle-eyed, and incapable of making a movement that wasn't miraculously graceful. I was overawed by these two legendary women, quite willing to be their doormat and dogsbody, instead of which they made me their friend, and we remained friends for years.

Some of the Burmese WASBies came and went, staying for a few nights or a few hours, but always lightening and brightening the house like candle-flames. There was Ma Than We and Thin Thin Than and half-a-dozen others, but it was mostly the first two who taught me about Burmese folk-lore and wove Burmese magic. They told me wonderful, ancient things, sitting in the star-lighted dark round a broken, weed-green swimming pool, with a hedge of gardenias behind us and frogs singing so that the night throbbed with scent and sound.

The Burmese girls were Baptists, and had taught at the Baptist school in Rangoon before the war. They looked terribly frail in their white cotton blouses and their khaki-cotton lungyis wrapped round pipe-stem hips, and they always tucked bunches of orchids or jasmine into their smooth, black chignons of hair. The Baptist school was in the Indian quarter of Rangoon, and while I was in camp there had been a brief but deadly racial war between the Indians and the Burmese, with no quarter given on either side. The Burmese girls had risked their lives every night, wriggling on their stomachs through the gardens of the Indian quarter to take food to the school which was under siege, the staff and children barricaded inside.

Rangoon was chaotic. It overflowed with troops of every nationality, all on a perilous high because they were alive and going home. In addition there was a huge camp of Japanese prisoners-of-war who were waiting to be shipped back to Japan, and this was surrounded by a barbed wire fence which would have been laughed at by any self-respecting sheep. The camp was administered by a staff of junior British officers who threw continuous drunken parties, and couldn't have cared less if their charges had disappeared into thin air, set up business in Rangoon or committed hara kiri The Japanese had lost none of their arrogance, and because of the way they themselves treated POWs they were dumbfounded by the softness and stupidity of the British, who let them do more or less as they liked. Burma's three day Water Festival was normally a time of good fellowship, but in 1946 it turned out to be quite the opposite, and some anonymous military lunatic made the mistake of arming the Japanese, and using them to help discipline the anti-British locals.

By tradition the Water Festival was a harmless, messy affair in which Burmese men, women and children hurled coloured water at each other and had fun. At the end of the war Burma, like India, had become bitterly nationalistic; the Japanese oppressors might have gone but they had simply been replaced by the oppressors of old, and the Burmese had had enough of foreigners. The Water Festival was too good a chance to miss, so instead of throwing their buckets of dyed water only at each other they filled the buckets with bricks and sharp stones as well as water, and threw the contents at every Britisher they saw. Some quite serious wounds were inflicted, but it was still inexcusable to turn the Japanese loose on them.

The first day of the Festival was bad enough, but there was still a measure of tolerance on either side. On the second day things turned nasty, and any European, in a jeep or on foot, was a target and not only, as I discovered, for bricks. I had to stop my jeep at a corner on the way to my office and saw a Burmese, his lungyi raised, peeing vigorously into a tin can. He finished peeing, and before I could drive on he stepped forward and emptied the can over my head.

Later that day, having scrubbed my hair and tried to compose my temper, I got back into the jeep and set off again for the office. Even in a few hours the atmosphere had changed; there were few British troops on the streets, and they were all conspicuously armed. The only visible Burmese were groups of men, no longer cheerful but standing about holding their buckets and looking sullen. It wasn't until I was on the open road near the University that I saw half-a-dozen women and children throwing water at each other and laughing.

I was about a hundred yards away from them when an open truck rocketted past me at high speed. The back was full of armed Japanese, shouting and beating on the cab roof with their rifle butts. As they passed me they deliberately swerved off the road straight through the group of women and children, then back onto the road again, and vanished into the distance leaving a scatter of twitching, mangled bodies in the grass.

I drove straight on, to find some MPs, or anybody who could help. There was nothing much I could have done for the victims on my own, and any Burmese finding me alone with the mess would justifiably have knifed me. It wasn't an isolated incident, and on the third day of the Festival there was a general curfew with the Japanese disarmed and guarded, for once, in their camp.

Besides the Nationalists, who were serious militants, there were the Dacoits who were merely rogues and vagabonds, with no motive other than personal gain. Between the two hostile factions life outside the controlled town limits was uncertain, and a number of men who had survived the war died tragically before they could be shipped home. A favourite trick was to string a wire across the road, at neck-height for a man sitting in a jeep. Because of the all-pervading dust or mud it was necessary to drive with the windscreen down, otherwise it was impossible to see, and because often there were Burmese with rifles concealed in trees it was necessary to drive fast. The wires acted like cheese knives, neatly decapitating the jeeps' occupants before they knew what had hit them

From our WAS(B) compound in Golden Valley we could see the dome of the Shwe Dagon Pagoda, and through the trees the even more perfect Suli Pagoda, curved and spired, and covered with gold leaf. We were woken in the mornings by the deep, reverberating sound of the temple gongs, and there were always pensive, saffron-wrapped Buddhist monks passing by, gentle and absorbed, or lines of butterfly-light girls carrying offerings of fruit and flowers. Wrecked though it was, the air in Golden Valley was still gold at sunset or sunrise, and the stylised girls and the monks and pagodas gave it a patina of peace.

In the evenings Andy and I usually went to the Officer's Club, a rambling red-brick building which had been a British Club before the war. There was a band and a dance floor, and a large dining-room which produced passable food. The only thing that stopped it from being too crowded to get on the dance floor was the shortage of women, since besides a few WAC(I)s and nurses the

WASBies were the only European women in Rangoon. Some men came to the Club on their own, but most of them drank themselves into lonely oblivion at their Mess.

Andy and I were no better off in terms of privacy than we had been when I was with the Division, and coming down to Rangoon for an occasional night. Our Golden Valley houses were hopeless, always full of girls in transit, and besides that the absence of doors made even a private conversation difficult. My own room was on the ground floor of the second, smaller house so that I could keep an eye on the transit contingent, and they had to pass through it to get upstairs. As well as the WASBies a constant assortment of animal life wandered in and out through the hole where the door had once been, pi-dogs and cats, scrawny game-fowl, and even the dreamy-eyed white Hindu cattle would visit for a while, and I gave up trying to hunt them away. Andy, who had never had animals, said it was disgusting, and muttered about fleas and rabies. There were no hotels in Rangoon, of course, and the only women who had a hope of civilised love-making were the nurses, hospitals being full of beds; an alarming number of nurses became pregnant.

The line of servant's quarters in the front of our compound housed our guard unit, whose duty it was to protect us against the badmash element of Nationalists, dacoits and ordinary thieves. The Indian troops were being sent home quite quickly, but the Africans were having trouble mustering transport back to Africa, and it was they who were allocated to us, to keep them out of mischief, I suspect, as much as anything else. A platoon of enormous, coal-black men moved into the servant's quarters, and proved themselves to be entrepreneurs by immediately setting up a flourishing brothel staffed by willing Burmese girls. We let them get away with it, as long as they didn't make too much noise.

We had been to the Club, Andy and I, and Andy had drunk enough to become importunate. He stopped the jeep on the way home, as usual at a spot which he said would be solitary and romantic, but which, as usual, was swarming with mosquitos and close to a Burmese household which kept pigs. The mosquitos were ferocious, the smell appalling and once more it was a failure; once more I blamed myself. Andy lost his temper with me, and I found myself being driven home at top speed, in frosty silence. He didn't bother to go up the drive but bundled me out at the gate in front of the guard-house-cum-brothel and I stumped sadly up to my ground floor room, chased a few chickens out of my camp cot, and sat on it to ponder why I was so useless.

I knew then that my relationship with Andy was an exercise in futility. I knew I should break it off, but I had too little confidence in myself and the future to destroy the only lifeline in sight. Also I could hear the echo of Mama's voice, 'If you're not a virgin.......', and I half-believed that I'd burnt my matrimonial boats once and for all.

30

England

OUR LAST MONTHS IN RANGOON were monsoon months; the rain bucketted through the gaps in the roof, turned the roads into mud-slides and produced green mould, lush as summer grass, on everything we moved, lived or slept in. We reeked of jungle, and had ceased to notice it.

There were illnesses and a robbery, an earthquake, the constant background music of thunder, and a growing sense of isolation as Rangoon emptied itself of troops and became Burmese again. The WASBies had all left, except for us and the Burmese WASBies who had gone back to their teaching. Dosan and Gay and I were at a loose end, fighting prickly heat and boredom and drinking too much. Andy's unit, to my relief, had been posted to Singapore, and I was to take the first available transport to England and wait for him there.

Troopships direct to England from Rangoon had so far been reserved for male troops, and women had been forced to make a detour through India and leave from Calcutta or Bombay. Finally we were told that a ship with accommodation for women would be sailing in September, and that we could join it. Dosan was longing to see England, and had elected to take her discharge there; we had become close friends, and it seemed to both of us that facing the unknown together would be better than doing it alone. I blithely assured her that as all my relations were old India hands they'd be delighted to meet her, and that they'd look after us both. I sent a cable to Mama telling her when we were due to sail, and asking for the addresses of my aunts and uncles and cousins.

The day we sailed was one of steaming, rod-straight rain, so heavy that one could only see through it for a few feet. We were told to take on board only what we could fit into an Army bedding-roll, and remains of my worldly possessions fitted into one quite comfortably. The few civilian clothes I'd brought from Australia had either disintegrated or become so mouldy that I'd thrown them out, and I had only my jungle-green drill uniform and a thick, hairy male battle-dress to my name. No one had asked me to hand in my .38 revolver and ammunition, so vaguely thinking that I could hand it in at the other end of the trip I packed it in my bedding-roll.

The troopship, an old converted passenger liner, was anchored in the river and we were taken out to it in an open lighter, ourselves and our bedding-rolls sodden with rain. We could see mould sprouting on the luggage, feel it between our toes, and our prickly heat, encouraged by the humidity, tormented us all. Any hope that the female accommodation on board might be comfortable lasted only until we saw it: we were led down almost to the lowest deck, and shown into a cabin which would have been barely adequate for four people. It had been stripped of every fitting, and now held 16 bunks in tiers, so close above each other that the only way in was to slide, horizontal, and it was impossible, once in a bunk, to sit up. There wasn't so much as a hook to hang clothes on, and as it was below the waterline there were no portholes.

Furious, Gay turned to the sailor who'd shown us to the cabin. She said, 'I want to see an officer! We can't travel in this pig-sty all the way to England.'

The sailor looked uncomfortable, but he said, 'Sorry Ma'am, that's all there is for the ladies. There's another cabin alongside, same as this, and your bathroom's through there.'

Gay poked her head into the bathroom. 'How many's this for?' she asked. 'There's only one shower and one lavatory.'

'Thirty-two, Ma'am,' said the sailor. 'Now, if you'll excuse me . . .'

The voyage was not only purgatory, it was insanitary. There were permanent, urgent queues outside the one bathroom, and it stank. It was bad enough for the pregnant women, most of them nurses and unmarried, who combined morning sickness with sea-sickness and despair, but it was undoubted hell for a young mother who was packed in with us with two tiny children. She spent her time white-faced and exhausted, juggling her infants on the edge of her bunk and bravely trying to hush their incessant wailing.

Most of us dragged our mattresses up on deck every night and slept there until the crew hosed down the decks at daybreak. A lot of the troops did the same, and there were people to talk to if one couldn't sleep, or one could lean on the rail under the brilliant, star-crowded sky, and watch the phosphorus skipping along the crest of the ship's bow-wave and wake. We berthed at two ports but no one was allowed ashore, and the trip took more than three weeks.

Letters from home had been almost non-existent during the time I was in Burma, and I had almost forgotten about home. There was no air mail and letters from Australia travelled by sea to India, then through laborious Army channels to the designated Division and eventually, if one was lucky, to the addressee in his Unit. The WAS(B)s, once the war was over, became a phantom in the minds of the Army postal authorities. Once we had left our Divisions we had ceased to exist, and if letters arrived it was by accident. We seldom wrote nor expected to get them. Once in a while a letter would come from Mama with the bare bones of her own doings, and Pa's; they were almost entirely about Betty and Norman and the two boys. I head nothing from Betty herself, and I seldom wrote to her.

Life must have seemed wonderful to Betty at that time, and the future unlimited. She had the beginnings of her family, two small boys, both fair-haired and healthy, Norman, friends she'd made in the district, and a cottage she was gradually turning into the kind of home she wanted. When I thought about her then I could see her, settling with her lovely feathers fluffed out round her like a contented bird on her nest. She must have learned to handle Norman's parents by that time, or at least to keep them at a distance, and she'd have been planning for her next child. 'Please God let it be a girl this time, then more boys if you like, but one girl, please?' It would have been warm in her cottage, and there'd have been a smell of cakes baking and nappies drying, and outside her two corgies would be trying to catch the Campbell peacocks by the tail feathers. It enraged Norman's parents, but nobody could cure them, and the poor peacocks had both neuroses and tattered tails. Mama said that Betty and the boys came to Melbourne quite often, for doctors and dentists, and that she and Pa sometimes went to stay with them. I could tell that they were her consolation and her absorbing passion now, and I was glad she had them.

Mail, taken on board in Rangoon, was distributed to us the day after we sailed, and there was a letter from Mama in reply to my cable telling her I was going to England. I read it once and then, in stunned disbelief, read it again. 'We're so glad you're going Home,' she wrote. 'Andy's parents will look after you, of course, and I'm not going to send you any of the family's addresses. They've all had a hard time during the war, and I'm not going to have you being a nuisance to them.'

I was genuinely shocked. I'd taken it for granted that I could go either to the Christies or to Aunt Sheila, whom I knew and loved. Pa's sisters had been part of the fabric of my life, mine as my sisters were, or my parents, and I was horrified to realise that they might look on me as a nuisance.

There were other considerations: I'd told Dosan that my relations would welcome us, and she was counting on them too. As for Andy's parents, I'd never heard from them directly. Andy had read me rather lukewarm comments on our engagement from their letters to him, and he had given me a small, blurred photo of them, so that I knew roughly what size and shape they were. As usual I had no money. My pay in Burma had been nine pounds sterling a month, and that had gone nowhere at all during the last few months when we had been idle, and having to buy our own food. I was unqualified for any civilian job; I was determined to get work of some sort, but I'd been hoping for a family bed until I could find something. I felt a complete fool, presumptuous and stupid because I'd taken my relations for granted, and worse than that because I'd let Dosan down as well.

We docked at Tilbury early one morning in a thin, cold, English drizzle. The ship was suddenly very official and organised, and orders flowed in a deafening, unintelligible stream through the Tanoy system. We were to pack our belongings, leave them on our bunks for inspection and assemble on deck. The troops would be disembarked in stated order under their officers and taken to Transit Camps, while oddments like us would be processed individually by the Authorities before being allowed ashore. Damp and bored we huddled under inadequate shelter, and watched the troops marching down the gangplank.

'Robin listen!' said Dosan suddenly. 'That's you they're calling on the Tanoy.'

'Sergeant Walker to the Guardroom,' said the disembodied voice. 'Sergeant Walker to the Guardroom, on the Double!'

'What on earth is that all about?' I said. 'Maybe there's another Sergeant Walker,' I made my way to the Guardroom.

Three officers, very pale and elegant compared to the Mepacrin-yellow, jungly men I was used to, were sitting behind a table. They looked at me in a singularly unwelcoming manner.

'Sergeant Walker reporting, Sir,' said I, saluting.

'You're Sergeant Walker? What are you a Sergeant in?'

'The WASBies, Sir.'

'Oh God, yes. There are three of those on board, I believe, whatever they may be. Well, how d'you explain the fact that you're carrying firearms?'

'Firearms, Sir?' I remembered the .38 and the inspection of our bedding-rolls. 'Oh, that. It was issued to me in Burma, Sir, when I joined 82nd West African Division. They must have forgotten about it when they went back to Africa so I brought it with me.'

'Don't you know it's a serious offence to be in possession of firearms, particularly on board ship? Don't you read the Regulations? I see that they found ammunition in your luggage as well. You were going to take it ashore, weren't you?'

'No Sir, I was going to hand it in as soon as I could.'

'You've had the whole trip to do that. How do I know that you weren't going to sell it to someone on shore? If people got away with that half the criminals in Britain'd be armed with His Majesty's weapons! Penalty for this offence is six months gaol Without the Option, Sergeant, and as far as I'm concerned you're under arrest until further notice. We'll consider what to do with you when we've got the time to think about it. Corporal!'

An immaculate, six-foot tall MP appeared through the door. The officer said, 'This man – woman, I mean, is under arrest. I want her on deck under guard until I give you further orders. Dismiss! Next!'

Gay and Dosan were still on deck, where I'd left them; when I reappeared flanked by two large MPs they looked at me as though I'd grown an extra head. Gay advanced on the Corporal and said, 'There must be some mistake, Corporal! This is one of my WASBies, so why is she under guard?'

'Under arrest, Ma'am, that's all I know. I've got orders to guard her.'

'Firearms,' I said miserably. 'They found that rotten .38 in my bedding-roll.'

'God!' said Gay, in disgust. 'How could you be so bloody stupid!'

'I just forgot about it.'

'That's enough!' said the Corporal. 'No talking. Quick march!'

They marched me up and down the deck for a while, grew bored and paused by the rail. I stared down at the wharf, wondering how things could possibly be worse than they were. I got an immediate answer.

The wharf was deserted by now, except for a civilian couple, middle-aged and respectable, and I watched them abstractedly. They seemed to be trying to attract someone's attention on deck, waving and shouting things I couldn't hear. I looked to see who they were waving to, and there was no one. An awful thought came to me and I pulled Andy's photo of his parents out of my pocket, looked from it to them and said, 'Oh my God! They're all I needed.'

'What's that?' said the Corporal. 'D'you know them two down there?'

'I've never met them but I think they're my future in-laws.'

He frowned and shook his head. He said, 'All right then, two minutes on the dock, and don't you tell nobody I let you. Quick march!'

Andy's parents watched me step off the gangplank, took in the presence of the MPs, my crumpled, men's issue battle-dress and unkempt appearance, and a look of frozen horror spread over their faces. I said, 'How d'you do, I'm Robin, Andy's fiancee, and it's terribly kind of you to come to meet me. I'm afraid I can't spend much time with you, I'm under arrest.'

Later on I found out that they 'd gone to great trouble and pulled strings to be there, for the docks were still out of bounds to civilians. I have no idea what kind of future daughter-in-law they were expecting or hoping for, but she was obviously light-years removed from what confronted them, and they went into shock. Andy's father, who had a heavy, unsmiling, blue-jowled face, put his arm round his wife's shoulders, a rare gesture of affection from him, and said, 'Never mind, dear, never mind. Come on home.' They left without another word to me, and I watched their bowed, despairing backs retreating into the distance.

'Your future in-laws, are they?' said the Corporal thoughtfully. 'Well, I don't know, I'm sure, but good luck to you.'

Gay had to leave during the afternoon to catch a train to her home county, but Dosan waited with me. She folded herself into a small, sheltered space with the grace of a ballet dancer, and the MPs watched her, mesmerised, because they had never seen anything like her in uniform before. They brought us a meal and talked to her with grave respect, and made it clear that they thought that my arrest was ridiculous. The officers in the Guardroom had either forgotten about me, or perhaps thought they were teaching me a lesson by ignoring me. Daylight faded, the rain fell in an endless, dreary mist, and at eight o'clock Dosan decided to take action. 'I'm going to talk to them,' she said, 'Although I don't suppose they'll take much notice of an Indian woman, even if I am a Major.'

'Don't you worry, Ma'am,' said the Corporal. 'We'll all go and see them. The last train up to London goes at nine o'clock.'

The officers released me with a savage caution just in time to catch the train, and Dosan and I sat, half-drugged with tiredness, as the wet, war-damaged underbelly of London rattled past the windows. It looked monstrously unwelcoming. It was too late to change our Indian money for British currency, and between us we had not much more than a pound in negotiable small change to last us until the morning.

'Where are we going to sleep?' asked Dosan. 'We haven't enough for a hotel.'

'Let's get a taxi and ask the driver. London taxi drivers are supposed to know everything. We'd better tell him not to take us too far, or we won't be able to pay.'

We found a taxi outside the station with an elderly driver, a warm wrinkled Cockney, friendly as a buttered crumpet; we told him what had happened to us and he tut-tutted over his shoulder. He drove us through streets so dazzlingly lit that they seemed unreal after Rangoon with its dim, smoking kerosene lamps, and he stopped at a house in a street behind the Cumberland Hotel. 'The landlady 'ere's a friend of mine,' he said. 'It's no palace, mind, but I'll 'ave a word with 'er and she'll see you right. There's no charge for the ride, it's on me.'

That night we slept head-to-toe in the same bed, in deference to Dosan's Parsee sensibilities. She came from a wealthy family, and I doubt that she had ever shared a bed before, but we were only offered a single room. When I woke I thought, 'The hell with Mama and being a nuisance,' asked the landlady for a telephone book and rang Directory Enquiries. I knew that Aunt Do and her husband Barch Christie had a house near a place called Eversley, and in a surprisingly short time I found them.

Do Christie answered the phone, and when I told her who and where I was she responded with cries of wonder and delight. Dosan and I were to catch a train at eleven o'clock, and they would meet us at the other end. Why hadn't I let her know I was coming? Why hadn't Geoff or Aileen written to tell her? Anyway, now we were here we were to come and stay for as long as we liked, both of us, and she couldn't wait to see us. She was as warm as the summer sun, and the fragments of the world came together again like the pieces of a jigsaw puzzle.

The Christies were playwrights then, with two plays currently running in the West End of London. Barch, a Major-General, had been invalided out of the Army with TB, after commanding the artillery in Malta. He and Do both hated his sister-in-law, Agatha Christie, and declared that if she could make money out of writing so could they. Though Agatha was incalculably more successful than they were, at that time they were enjoying a certain eminence. Their house was full of fascinating people, and they swamped us with love and kindness and laughter while complaining that we, and everything we owned, still smelled overpoweringly of jungle.

We crossed over to Northern Ireland by ferry to stay with Pa's other sister, Sheila Landale, who was living at Craigavad, near Belfast, and once again we were treated as though we were some kind of blessing rather than as two inconvenient, jungly waifs. Sheila had saved up precious petrol coupons for us, and insisted that we take her car and drive ourselves down the then primitive West coast, 'To see Ireland properly and have a holiday.'

It was an extraordinary drive. The Partition of India was on the horizon, and Dosan, proudly Indian and filled with foreboding about the future of her country, chose the wilds of Ireland to reject Western dress and revert to the sari. She also wore a large selection of Indian jewellery, bangles and necklaces which she had brought with her unknown to me. She would have looked lovely and exotic enough anywhere, but her effect on the villagers down the windswept Donegal coast was sensational.

When we got back to Craigavad there was a letter from Andy. He was back from Singapore, with his parents in Brighton waiting to be discharged, and would I please join him there as soon as possible. The letter jolted me like the bell at the end of a school break. I knew I should rush headlong to my betrothed, but I could only think of him in the context of Rangoon and half-drunk nights at the Officers Club; I couldn't imagine him fitting in with my new-found relations, or with Ireland, at all. Besides, the look on his parents' faces when they saw me at Tilbury was still fresh in my mind, and I dreaded meeting them again.

On the other hand engagements were taken seriously in those days; by my parents standards I was committed, and I knew I had to go. I thought of Mama, and all her old warnings came flooding back. Andy had deflowered me, after all, and no other Decent Man would ever Marry Me. Aunt Sheila said of course I must go, but my room would be ready for me any time I wanted to come back. Dosan, frantic with anxiety about Partition and the safety of her family, wanted to return to London so that she could get a quick passage back to India if things there got worse.

I dragged my feet as much as possible on my way to Brighton, staying with the Christies for a couple of nights, and arranging to visit Claire and Herbert in London before I took the last, irrevocable train south to Brighton and Andy. On my second night with Aunt Do I had a truly dreadful nightmare. I was somewhere dark, a thick, tangible dark, and a voice I seemed to know was screaming for its mother, 'Mama, Mama, Mama...' again and again. Someone shook me, and it was Do beside my bed saying, 'Wake up, darling, you're screaming. You must have been having a bad dream.'

There was cold sweat running off me, and I was shaking and gasping. I asked, 'What was I screaming about? I'm so sorry, Aunt Do, I never do this sort of thing.'

'You were screaming for your mother, it sounded awful. Now, come and have a cup of tea with me and go back to sleep. It's over.' I could still hear the voice calling out, 'Mama,' but as though it was someone else's voice, not mine, and it somehow linked itself with the sound of my mother's screams when she heard of Jenny's death.

Next day I presented myself at Claire and Herbert's flat in Knightsbridge; it was the first time I'd seen them since I was a small child. Claire greeted me effusively, but I could see that my appearance made her wince. She herself was immaculate, down to the tips of her carefully enamelled fingernails. Herbert muttered something that might have been a greeting and looked straight through me with his pale, tortoise eyes, wishing I'd go away. I'd barely been there half-an-hour when the front door bell rang. Claire went to answer it, and I heard her say, 'Yes, she's here, do come in.' Then, a moment later, 'Oh no! How frightful! Will you tell her or shall I?'

My cousin Tony, Do's daughter, came into the sitting-room. She seemed close to tears. She said, 'Thank God I've found you, I wasn't sure you'd be here. A cable came just after you'd left Eversley, and Mother phoned me. I'm so terribly sorry, Betty's dead.'

Je ne vois plus le ciel bleu...

And that was the end of The Girls

EPILOGUE

THIS IS THE EPILOGUE to a story I set out to write about my sisters, The Girls, but I seem to have written mostly about myself. I found when I started that the chasms of age and absence had robbed me of so much of their short lives that I wonder now if I really knew them. I do know though, that to me and to others they were courage and comfort, love and daring and beauty in their time, and it wasn't fitting that I should be their survivor. And I know too that in spite of having so little time together there was some link beyond explanation between us.

Mama wrote and told me how Betty died. She tried to have another baby, of course, and things went wrong. Norman drove desperately over corrugated dirt roads to get her to hospital, thirty miles from Warranooke, and she died there calling for Mama at the exact time I was having my nightmare in Eversley. And besides that, there was Jenny's telegram that I never opened. Irish families, and the breath of ghosts…

After Betty's death I tried for two years, by every means possible, to get back to Australia, but I had a British passport. The authorities said I must be classed as a migrant, and sent me to the wrong end of the migrant queue. I was consumed with grief and anxiety for my parents, and with guilt at being so far away and unable to help, and with worse guilt because I was the one who was left. Andy and I parted with minimal regret on either side, and in retrospect my time in England seemed like a long sentence served in a cold, dark cellar.

When I arrived in Melbourne I didn't know what to expect, whether Mama might have reverted to her semi-comatose misery of the months after Jenny's death, or if Pa, who adored Betty, might have become a sad old man. To my surprise, when they met me they seemed quite normal, even cheerful. They were still living in the same house in South Yarra and their routine was unchanged, chops, peas and potatoes at seven and bed at nine-thirty sharp. Mama's life centred round visits to Warranooke to help poor Norman and the two small boys; Pa still devoted most of his time to the Queensland properties and lunched at the Australian Club. There was still a cat, and the same cocker spaniel. In many ways, I thought, things were a lot more normal than when I'd left home nearly four years earlier.

Three weeks after I came home I understood just how little things had changed. I was in the kitchen, and Mama was cooking the chops. I knew that she'd been wanting to ask me something because she'd been darting round details of my life in Burma and England like a minnow, and then backing off. She must finally have plucked up enough courage because she turned from the stove to face me, a saucepan of peas in one hand, a pot of potatoes in the other.

'Tell me, Robin,' she said, pale with the effort of putting it into words. 'Have you ever been to bed with a man?'

In the split second when I should have said, 'No, Mama,' to keep her happy, or 'Only one, but I was engaged to him, and I knocked back a lot of others,' I was so astonished at my mother actually asking such a thing that I just said, 'Yes, I have.'

She went white then, and both saucepans fell to the floor with a crash as she said, in a voice of utter despair, 'You know, don't you, that *no decent man will ever marry you!'*